A General Rhetoric

A General Rhetoric

by Group μ

J. Dubois, F. Edeline,
J.-M. Klinkenberg,
P. Minguet, F. Pire, H. Trinon

Center for Poetic Studies
University of Liège

Translated by Paul B. Burrell
and Edgar M. Slotkin

The Johns Hopkins University Press

Baltimore and London

This book has been brought to publication with the generous
assistance of the Andrew W. Mellon Foundation.

Originally published as *Rhétorique générale*, copyright © 1970 Librairie Larousse.

The Johns Hopkins University Press, Baltimore, Maryland 21218
The Johns Hopkins Press Ltd., London

Library of Congress Cataloging in Publication Data
Main entry under title:

A General rhetoric.

  Translation of Rhétorique générale.
  Includes bibliographical references and index.
  1. Rhetoric.   I. Dubois, Jacques, docteur en
philosophie et lettres.
PN189.R513   808   80-24495
ISBN 0-8018-2326-9

Text ist etwas, was mit der
Sprache, also aus Sprache gemacht
wird, sie aber zugleich verändert,
vermehrt, vervollkomnet, stört
oder reduziert.

Max Bense, *Texttheorie*

Contents

Translators' Preface

Literary studies in the United States have recently begun to move in the direction of a more conscious application of rhetorical procedures. Until recently in this country, the word *rhetoric* denoted chiefly the teaching of composition, usually in the context of a college Freshman English course. This restriction of meaning represented a sad decline from the time when rhetoric was a respected and important discipline. When was the last time that a holder of Harvard's Boylston Professorship of Rhetoric made a contribution to rhetoric per se? However, some Americans have continued the tradition. Kenneth Burke and more recently Wayne Booth represent approaches to philosophy, literary criticism, and poetics that are explicitly rhetorical. For the most part, however, the increasing rehabilitation of rhetoric in this country is inspired from Europe.

Belgium especially seems to nourish rhetoric. Within the discourse of French-language studies in philosophy and literary theory, two schools of specifically rhetoric-oriented research have arisen there: the "New Rhetoric" of Chaim Perelman at Brussels[1] and the neo-rhetoric being developed by the Center for Poetic Studies at the University of Liège, a collection of scholars who call themselves Group μ. It is the work of the more recent Liège School that we feel deserves a wider audience and that we present here in English for the first time. In the context of the history of rhetoric, it is perhaps worthwhile to recall that the family of Pierre Ramus came from Liège.

There is not, however, anything Ramistic about this book, unless we assume that it will have a revolutionary effect upon the discipline. The work of Group μ falls rather squarely within the world of continental structuralism, drawing heavily on the linguistics of de Saussure, Hjelmslev, Benveniste, Jakobson, Greimas, and others as well as upon the extensions of this research into literary theory by Barthes, Todorov, and Genette. This book is not for beginners, for it assumes a certain familiarity with the concepts behind what we are calling structuralism in its broadest senses.

We could not begin with the sort of explanation that would fill in for the unenlightened reader all of the concepts employed here. The literature upon

1. See the works referred to in the Introduction, n. 4 and 25.

which the authors draw directly is cited in the notes, and we have cited translations where they have been available. There are also studies in English that provide a general background to French-language scholarship in this area.[2] What we can do, indeed *must* do, is to mention in this preface a few of the basic terms employed in this study if only to explain how we have translated them and, perhaps, why.

This volume is a translation of the second French edition of *Rhétorique générale* (Paris, 1976), to which has been added a later article, "Miroirs rhétoriques: sept ans de réflexion," from the journal *Poétique,* vol. 29 (1977), pp. 1–19. The article is an apologia/response to various criticisms leveled against the book.[3] In it the authors back away somewhat from their title, which they claim is metonymic. Not all of rhetoric is treated here. The book is mostly a study of rhetorical tropes and figures, what classical rhetoric called *elocutio*. It attempts to set forth the basic principles by which all figures of language and thought are derived and can be described. Moreover, the principles adduced here can be and are applied to an entire range of verbal phenomena, from the phoneme to the extended discourse.[4] This project is in itself a major undertaking. We do not think that it is too much to claim that this study represents the first time that the complex variety of figures has been systematically and coherently derived; moreover, the method adopted here brings *elocutio* into the range of modern linguistics.

There is some reason to defend the authors from their own renunciation of the title of this book. While not a "complete rhetoric," the study goes very far in pointing the way to further research toward such a rhetoric, a search they themselves are undertaking.[5] One result of their accomplishment has been to

2. Jonathan Culler, *Structuralist Poetics* (Ithaca: Cornell University Press, 1975), besides providing a survey of issues and ideas in general, discusses *Rhétorique générale* on pp. 180–81. Terence Hawkes, *Structuralism and Semiotics* (Berkeley and Los Angeles: University of California Press, 1977); and Robert Scholes, *Structuralism in Literature* (New Haven: Yale University Press, 1974), also provide useful background. Perhaps the most immediately useful book that provides a context for Group μ's work is Oswald Ducrot and Tzvetan Todorov, *Encyclopedic Dictionary of the Sciences of Language,* trans. Catherine Porter (Baltimore: Johns Hopkins University Press, 1979).

3. Except for a review by Seymour Chatman in *Foundations of Language* 8 (1972): 436–46, the normal reviewing mechanism of English-language journals has virtually ignored *Rhétorique générale*. However, the view of metaphor that this book proposes has been subjected to a critique in Samuel R. Levin, *The Semantics of Metaphor* (Baltimore: Johns Hopkins University Press, 1977), pp. 99–103.

4. Group μ is clearly interested in extending their work to visual phenomena as well. See "La Chafetiére est sur la table: Eléments pour une rhétorique de l'image," *Communications et langages* 29 (1976): 37–49; *Revue d'esthétique* 3/4 (1978), the special issue devoted to collage and edited by Group μ; and "Iconique et plastique," ibid. 1/2 (1979): 173–92, and other articles in this "Rhétoriques, sémiotiques" issue also edited by Group μ. These references do not exhaust their publications in this direction.

5. Besides the works on visual arts mentioned in note 4, above, the most important extensions of *Rhétorique générale* are "Rhétoriques particulières," *Communications* 16 (1970): 70–124; and most recently *Rhétorique de la poésie* (Brussels: Editions Complexe, 1977).

reclaim stylistics for rhetoricians, or, rather, to reintegrate stylistics with linguistics on the one hand and literary theory and criticism on the other. Group μ is interested chiefly in literature, although *Rhétorique générale* is not a work of literary criticism in any way; but if their rhetoric is really a *general* one, as it attempts to be, the principles and methods they employ should be applicable to the entire range of human discourse. The effect of this sort of reintegration must be to reconstitute rhetoric as a major discipline. On this level alone the book deserves a wider audience.

Another implication of a *general* rhetoric is that it should extend beyond the specific culture within which it was produced. Group μ occasionally has drawn upon English or German examples to illustrate their figures, but by and large the book draws upon French-language examples. In this translation we have tried within certain limitations to substitute English-language examples for the French, to turn the study into, if not a discourse on English and American literatures, at least one that draws its support more from the English language than from the French. Our limitations in this endeavor have been twofold: (1) time: it seems more important to get the work out than to find an English example for absolutely everything; and (2) the nature of French literature: it is undeniably true that French authors have shown a greater propensity for certain sorts of literature than have English-language authors. Surrealism, for instance, is far more of a Gallic phenomenon than an Anglo-American one. French-language culture enjoys exploring the logical varieties of literary experience more than English-language culture seems to. Therefore, some of the more unusual examples of verbal figures (or visual ones in the case of film) have no immediate counterpart (as yet) in English; at least, we despaired of finding them. On the other hand, where the original draws very heavily on modern poetry, we have felt free to range more widely over the centuries for illustrations. Some may consider this change a misrepresentation; Group μ was concerned to demonstrate the relevance of their figural system to modern poetics. We feel that this aspect of the book is still well-represented and that this translation extends the relevant generality of the study.

We must also point out that on a few occasions we have had to alter the text to conform to the English-language examples. All such alterations are noted. None are silent, and most of the time we have included the original in a footnote with a translation. The major exceptions to this procedure occur in chapter VII, where the natures of French and English pronouns were too different to require simple substitution. Here some rewriting was necessary. Our additions, however, were made, not to suppress the French text, but to add the dimension of English examples in order to make the chapter relevant to both languages.

While on the subject of additions, we must point out that this translation was thoroughly reviewed by Group μ, in particular Francis Edeline, for whose careful reading we are very grateful. Moreover, the authors decided at one point to rewrite a section with which they were not satisfied in chapter IV. To a certain extent, therefore, this translation may be considered a new edition.

A few words need to be said about the technical terminology employed in this work and our translations of it. While most of what we say here is common knowledge to anyone with a smattering of linguistics, some readers without such a smattering will be interested in this book.

Group μ frequently refers to de Saussure's distinction between *langue* and *parole*, complicated for English speakers by references to *langage*. *Langage* is language in the broadest sense and could be used to define the subject of linguistics. *Langue* is any particular individual's language—the set of competence rules that allows him to produce *parole*, speech. We have translated both *langage* and *langue* as "language," and where the context does not make the word clear, we have indicated the French word employed in parentheses.

The other major Saussurian distinction used here is that between *significant* and *signifié*, which, following standard practice, we have translated as "signifier" and "signified." These are the two components of the linguistic *sign* (what we commonly think of as the *word*). The "signifier" refers, roughly speaking, to the sounds of a word; the "signified," even more roughly speaking, refers to the concept that the word is intended to convey. These two components of the sign are separable only for purposes of analysis. As we use language, the one does not exist without the other.

Group μ distinguishes frequently between *signification* and *sens*, which we have translated as "signification" and "meaning," respectively. Actually, Group μ is not consistent in their use of these two terms, both of which have taken on a variety of technical senses.[6] In general, "signification," when distinguished from "meaning" here, refers to the relationship between the signifier and signified and is commonly represented by the Ogden-Richards triangle employed by the authors in their Introduction. "Meaning," on the other hand, has a less technical, more everyday sense of the total effect of a sign or string of signs.

A very hard decision for us was the translation of the French *écart*, a word with no precise English equivalent. We have decided upon "deviation" as the least of various evils, despite the authors' rejection of the word in the Introduction. (Actually, they reject the French *déviation*, but it comes to the same thing.) The difference between *écart* and *déviation* in French is the difference between "not being average" and "not being normal" in English. When we

6. See especially John Lyons, *Semantics*, 2 vols. (Cambridge: At the University Press, 1977), vol. 1, pp. 96–99.

say that something is not average, we are not usually making a value judgment; not being average may be good or bad. However, when we claim that something is not normal, we most often intend a negative value judgment. When Group μ refers to figures as *écarts*, they obviously do not wish to characterize them as either good or bad; if anything, figures are positive, since they are the substance of literary discourse. English does not provide us with an equivalent with which we could be happy, and we have thus translated this word as "deviation." The reader must make every effort, when reading about a deviation from a norm or from "degree zero" (another term employed for its neutral value), to resist the negative connotations of *deviation*.

Other terms such as *récit, discours,* and *histoire* we have discussed in notes where they first appear. Still others posed no problems in translation; the reader can consult the works mentioned in the notes for further enlightenment. However, a word needs to be said about the terminology employed for the figures discussed. French has a somewhat more standardized tradition for figures than has ever been developed in English, and many figures have French names where English has indiscriminately employed Greek, Latin, or (in the Renaissance) English. For consistency's sake, for the various figures, we have generally employed the leading term used by Richard A. Lanham in his *A Handlist of Rhetorical Terms* (Berkeley and Los Angeles: University of California Press, 1969). The result is that the names of figures appear somewhat more "classical" here than in the original.

There is another point to be made about the use of terms for tropes and figures. It is easy to be seduced by them, to imagine that when a term like *synecdoche* appears the authors are discussing what Quintilian or Aristotle discussed. Such is not necessarily the case. This study derives figures from a set of general principles. Since these figures often are similar to or the same as figures noted by others in the past, as is only natural, traditional names have been applied to them. Synecdoche is a good case in point, since there have been a good number of vague, confusing, or misleading characterizations of this figure. It has been often confused with metonymy. Group μ derives a figure that, since it covers some (though not all) of the instances that in the past were called synecdoche, *they* call synecdoche. They might have called it *C,* I and II (see the General Table of Metaboles following chapter I). We suspect that the reason they chose to utilize classical or traditional terminology here was, at least in part, to demonstrate the range of their operational derivations of figures. However, what has been too often overlooked in assessing this study is that the system of operations is what is most important, not just the analysis of any one figure. Almost all the discussion of *Rhétorique générale* has been in terms of the theory of metaphor presented; and, as the authors complain in the Afterword, the real scope of the effort they have attempted has been overlooked. There may be other ways of characterizing metaphor than that presented below. How many of them, however, can characterize metaphor while at the same time characterizing the entire field of tropes and figures? This book is a general field theory of *elocutio,* and it seems to us that criticisms or alternatives must take place within a comparable theory. One can put the whale into the category of fish, since it inhabits the ocean, but a coherent taxonomy, a general theory of zoology, will label it a mammal.

We must acknowledge a few authors and a number of colleagues who have contributed to this translation. For examples we often resorted to Lanham's book cited above; to Geoffrey N. Leech, *A Linguistic Guide to English Poetry* (London: Longman, 1969); and to Barbara Kirshenblatt-Gimblett, ed., *Speech Play* (Philadelphia: University of Pennsylvania Press, 1976). Our greatest debt is to Group μ, who patiently answered our many questions, in particular our chief correspondent, Philippe Minguet, and our "reader," Francis Edeline. Their encouragement and interest made the translation possible, and we only hope that we have nowhere misrepresented their work. We thank the journal *Poétique* for permission to translate "Miroirs rhétoriques." Our colleagues Kornel Huvos, Lawrence Jost, Jill Rubenstein, and John Wilcox made suggestions for which we are very grateful. Our typist Marilyn Schwiers cheerfully put up with our drafts and changes of mind. Valerie Shesko helped with the diagrams. We are thankful to the University of Cincinnati Research Council, which twice granted us funds for typing and reproduction of materials, thus making the completion of this work possible without the translators' sinking into penury. Finally we wish to thank our copy editor Joanne Allen, our "well of English undefiled," for her impressive labors to help us appear coherent.

Liminary Note

The present work is the result of collective reflection. Colleagues at the University of Liège interested in problems of expression came together to study questions once again in the wind and which a discipline once illustrious and later scorned had first defined. Rhetoric as a theory of figures was rediscovered by structural linguistics. Roman Jakobson was one of the first to draw attention to the operative value of concepts already discussed by Aristotle. In homage to these two witnesses, it is quite natural that we have chosen as our symbol the first letter of the Greek word designating the most prestigious of metaboles.

Jacques Dubois, Francis Edeline,
Jean-Marie Klinkenberg, Philippe Minguet,
François Pire, and Hadelin Trinon

A General Rhetoric

Introduction
Poetics and Rhetoric

The history of ideas, like the history of nations, fluctuates—a rise here, a fall there. A dozen years ago anyone claiming that rhetoric would again become a major discipline would have been laughed at. The remark by Valéry on "the role of prime importance" that "rhetorical phenomena" play in poetry was hardly remembered.[1] We read with more or less interest some brilliant variation on "figures" done by Jean Paulhan, a distinguished and discriminating man of letters.[2] The most perceptive were not unaware that this outmoded activity was "of all the ancient disciplines the one most meriting the name of science,"[3] but even they did not seem to have any great hope of resurrecting it.

For rhetoric was certainly dead in thought if not in practice; at least this was so in France. It was true that this dying thing had been propped up for a long time, a situation in which those who had the most obvious interest in defending her were the same ones who fought hardest to bury her—that is, writers, grammarians, philosophers. As early as 1836 the *Journal d'instruction publique* was noting that "without the support of university regulations, rhetoric would today be dead in France."[4] Thanks to this official protection, the terminal class of the lycées kept a token course, the reasons for which had become more and more obscure.

Today rhetoric appears not only as a science of the future but also as a timely science within the scope of structuralism, new criticism, and semiology. Roland Barthes in 1964 noted incidentally that "rhetoric must be rethought in structural terms," and he added that "it is the object of a study already underway." Barthes's teaching at the Ecole Pratique des Hautes Etudes was devoted to an analysis of Aristotle's *Rhetoric,* and he submitted to the members of a colloquium on the sociology of literature some reflections on "rhetorical analysis."[5] At about the same time, in the review *Tel Quel,* a journal hardly suspected of being reactionary, Gérard Genette found support in a pile of dusty manuals (Lamy, Du Marsais, Crevier, Domairon, Fontanier, and so on) for his summary definition of the "space of language."[6] More recently, Tzvetan Todorov attached to his study of *Les Liaisons dangeureuses*

1

a sketch of a system of tropes and figures that accepted without hesitation words like *occupatio, expolitio, pronominatio,* and other such oddities.[7] To bless this betrothal of the ancient with the new, Kibédi Varga made the connection "Rhetoric and Structuralist Criticism."[8]

At the source of this renewal of rhetoric in France we find the unquestioned influence of the linguist Roman Jakobson and, even more specifically, of the publication by Nicolas Ruwet in 1963 of a translation of his *Essays in General Linguistics,* containing the fundamental study on *metaphor* and *metonymy.** To give an idea of the vogue this pair of tropes immediately achieved, we need simply to recall that a Marxist philosopher noted without delay their presence in the "habitat"—metaphor as the balcony in the suburbs, with its bit of lawn, image of nature, and the joy of life; as the "grand ensemble" where, by permutation, the whole is in its parts and the parts are equivalent to the whole.[9] But from urbanism to psychoanalysis is but a step. Often Victor Hugo boasted of having put to rout "frightened tropes," never suspecting that one day Dr. Lacan would diagnose a metaphor in "Booz endormi": "Sa gerbe n'était pas avare ni haineus" ("His sheaves [of wheat] were not mean or hateful"); in fact it is synecdoche.[10] In the language of the Freudian school of Paris, the formula for the metaphor is simpler:

$$f\left(\frac{S'}{S}\right) S \cong S\ (+)\ s.$$

From this we see that the "lady in the mirrors" returns to the world simply wearing new clothes.†

If, however, ancient rhetoric was less silly than stylisticians said, no one thinks seriously of bringing her back with all the old debris. We must avoid the bric-a-brac. As Genette has correctly noted, classical rhetoricians had a "mania for naming, which was one manner of expanding and of justifying themselves by multiplying the objects of their knowledge."[11] Thus we shall not follow Todorov when he tries to save *topographia* for description of a place, *chronographia* for description of time, *ethopy* for moral description, and so on. Why not, with the same justification, *cephalography* for description of a head, *podography* for description of feet, and, no doubt, *pornography,* which Sartre cultivated in his *P . . . respectueuse?* It is a fact that these endless nomenclatures have been, if not the underlying cause, at least the evident sign of rhetoric's decline. Thus we cannot be overly surprised at Charles Bally's scorn when speaking of these "technical and barbarous

*[This study will be found in Roman Jakobson and Morris Halle, *Fundamentals of Language* (The Hague: Mouton, 1956), pp. 69–96. *Trans.*]

†[For some understanding of Lacan's approach to metaphor, see the explanation by Anthony Wilden in Jacques Lacan, *The Language of the Self,* trans. Anthony Wilden (Baltimore: Johns Hopkins University Press, 1968), pp. 238–49. The "lady in the mirrors" is taken from Jean Paulhan (see above n. 2), who in turn developed it from Pascal, *Pensées,* no. 22, Brunschwicg. *Trans.*]

terms" that "are not only heavy and pedantic (*catachresis, hypallage, synecdoche, metonymy,* etc.)" but also "do not say what they mean and do not designate definite types."[12] This pioneer of a "stylistics of expression" had no doubt that a psychoanalyst was going to point out the profoundly metonymic character of human desire. We could multiply these examples of scorn for rhetoric. A certain amateur of grammar who flattered himself that he could set up a "precise inventory of means of expression" does not fail to warn us, as we begin his chapter on figures, that he has left "for the lumber-room of dusty oddities antonomasia, catachresis, epiphonema, epanorthosis, hyperbaton, hypotyposis, paronomasia, and synecdoche."[13] In this way some threw out the baby with the bath water.

From scorn to misunderstanding is but a short step. Another reputable stylistician was teaching at the Sorbonne that since the time of Balzac "the image has become the stylistic procedure *par excellence,*"[14] a banality that a Belgian poet expressed in another sententious way: "Modern poetry now walks only on the legs of the image."[15] This time we will no longer be content to throw rusty keys in the garbage: we will see that they are replaced with a master key, expressed in not one of the happiest phrases of Charles Bruneau: "The modern image absorbs a whole series of stylistic procedures, synecdoche and metonymy, for example, which are also metaphors, that is, substitutions."[16] But more seriously, it is not only a question of neglecting distinctions considered empty; it is that "modernistic" style itself would escape the distinctions of rhetoric. Still according to Bruneau, "Beginning about 1830, it is best not to talk about classical procedures using the term 'image,' which now means something quite different in its very nature." One example advanced: substitution of a proper noun for a common noun (with qualifier)—for the common noun *prostitute* Balzac substituted "Ninon of the streets." How does this process differ from the classical tropes that called Parny "the French Tibullus" or from La Fontaine's calling a cat "Attila, scourge of rats" (*scourge* serving to avoid the excessive assonance)? This is antonomasia and metaphor.

These few quotes suffice, no doubt, to indicate the complete discredit of ancient rhetoric by modern stylisticians. We need, therefore, to situate the present rethinking about rhetoric in relation to the object and method of stylistics. In fact, we would have great difficulty recognizing any homogeneous knowledge among the group of works that derive, at least in their broadest concerns, from the "science of style." There are those who would include studies on "structure, organization, characterization, order, rupture, literary genre, motifs, etc., art, the work of art, work and art, writing, literary creation, style and creation ... [here we are skipping some fifteen lines] ... aesthetics, rhetoric, oratorical aesthetics, the poetics of a work, linguistics and the poetics of an author, poetic unity, art and mind, art and emotion," and so on, and so on. No doubt we must be aware of the somewhat ironic intent of this enumeration.[17] But other lists, which seem to omit this grain of salt, do not hide their passion for inclusion: for example, to illustrate the "stylistics of themes," which would be the counterpart of the "stylistics of forms" (as an element of a literary stylistics that would not exclude extraliterary stylistics), Gérald Antoine, among others, proposed the names of R. Barthes, G. Poulet, J.-P. Richard, G. Bachelard, and J.-P. Sartre.[18] The talk of a "mad disorder" apropos of what has been called literary stylistics obviously does not keep us from attempting a theoretical ordering of this vast and crowded field.[19] Certainly we shall carefully refrain from getting into the quarrels between groups, happy if we can delimit the terrain normally subsumed under rhetoric.

We must recall here that in the past, rhetoric itself was never a very coherent discipline. We are thinking especially of the period of French classicism (the seventeenth and eighteenth centuries), when it was clear from one treatise to the next that there were more arguments, even on the object under study, than some have been willing to admit.* We would in any case falsify the historical picture of the "art of eloquence" if we reduced its object to the theory of *elocutio,* and even more if we reduced it to a simple definition of tropes and figures. In his *Rhetoric, or Rules for Eloquence* of 1730, Balthazar Gibert, "Former Rector of the University of Paris and one of the Professors of Rhetoric at the Collège Mazarin," devoted at most about 10 of the 650 pages to a commentary on tropes, failing to mention either synecdoche or metonymy.[20] Certainly, at this time in the prehistory of linguistics, we must not be surprised at some collusion between grammar, "the art of speaking"; dialectic, "the art of Discourse"; and rhetoric, "the art of speaking well." Thus the treatise of Bernard Lamy (1688) begins by explaining "The Organs of the Voice," then "the word" as a "picture of our thoughts." A bit later he treats "Substantive Nouns and Adjectives, articles, number and case of nouns." Elsewhere it is "purity of language" and "qualities of the substance of the brain" and "how we can satirize things worthy of laughter."[21]

Here again, no doubt, it is easier to be ironic than to understand. But we must remember clearly that the "science of tropes," as Fontanier said (who recommended his *Manual* to "boarding schools for young ladies where principles of belles lettres were offered"),[22] that *tropology,* which was formerly called *leporia,*[23] does not cover the whole field of rhetoric. For the ancients, as for the moderns, the declared end of rhetoric was to teach the techniques of persuasion. The ideas of *argument* and of *audience* were essential to it. Its link with dialectic in the pre-Hegelian meaning of the term was such that Aristotle began by noting their actual confusion. For the Stagirite, dialectical

*[For rhetoric in England during this period, see Wilbur Samuel Howell, *Logic and Rhetoric in England, 1500–1700* (Princeton: Princeton University Press, 1956); and idem, *Eighteenth Century British Logic and Rhetoric* (Princeton: Princeton University Press, 1971). *Trans.*]

proofs based on opinion are brought into play by rhetorical discourse, whose end is to be convincing. For various reasons, among which the Platonic problem of truth and appearances is central, rhetoricians from the beginning have had bad relations with the philosophers. Starting with Cartesian rationalism, the divorce was made final—henceforth only demonstration based on evidence could be valid in philosophy. Finally, Lalande's *Vocabulaire philosophique* would not even accept the word *rhetoric*.[24] Reason lacks competence outside experience and logical deduction, which are the only means of offering to a general audience the solution to a problem.

This impoverishment of analysis of the real workings of thought forced contemporary logicians to found a "new rhetoric," defined as the "theory of argumentation." The treatise published in 1958 by Chaim Perelman and L. Obrechts-Tyteca consists of a study of the discursive techniques "allowing us to induce or to increase the mind's adherence to the theses presented for its assent."[25] The importance and originality of the results obtained by these neo-rhetoricians are incontestable. It is clear that no one could refuse this study the title of rhetoric. We note as well that Perelman brings up especially the role of reasoning by analogy, which leads him to discuss the status of metaphor. Moreover, there is no reason why one cannot make a synthesis of these two tendencies that historically have split traditional rhetoric: the tendency to logic based on the cognitive function of language and the tendency to aesthetics, a reflection on language's poetic function. This synthesis would certainly not involve a return to the classical compromise that defined rhetoric as "the art of speaking well so as to persuade," a definition that Lamy judged redundant, since there was no teaching of an art of doing badly and since one only spoke to transmit feeling to the audience. If later manuals, such as that of Domairon (1816), finally opted for a purely literary conception, limiting rhetoric to a study of the procedures of expression ("the art of sprinkling ornaments in a prose work"),[26] this was no doubt because later rhetoricians, to the extent that they had a notion of literature, had the confused feeling that for the modern writer traffic with figures surpassed traffic with the world. Once it is common coin that art is an embellishment to be added, it will be possible to understand rhetoric, no longer as an arm of dialectics, but as a means to the poetic. For at least in principle, the orator uses metaphor only to exorcise contradiction, while the poet uses it for enchantment. But its efficacy for the one, as for the other, arises only from its *ability to please* because it creates an illusion.

However, these last of the rhetoricians hesitated before the consequences of their intuitive discovery. Enclosed in a sclerotic tradition, totally unaware of the aesthetic traditions of the German philosophers, derided by the literary world, abandoned by the early linguists, they gave up the ghost.[27] Were they replaced by stylisticians with whom we now continue the struggle? "Stylistik oder Rhetorik," said Novalis, one of the first to use the term.[28] Pierre

Guiraud, who gives us this fact, believes that "rhetoric is the ancients' stylistics."[29] But can we say that stylistics is the rhetoric of the moderns?

Aware of the rather heterogeneous character of the *corpora* of both disciplines, today's stylisticians do not seem very happy about the relationship. Henri Mitterand notes that stylistics does not have the ambition to learn to write, which was one of the goals of ancient rhetoric, and that for the literary stylist at any rate, it is not a question of "imposing on the work, at the risk of distorting it, pre-existent, *a priori* classifications." Even if the objective of the stylistician were not to study the psychological or sociocultural genesis of the work but to know "how and why a text is effective" (a question of descriptive stylistics), "the terminology of ancient rhetoric and grammatical terminology are equally inadequate" because the effect of a figure varies with its context.[30] This criticism works just as well against stylistics of language, Bally's, for instance—which Pierre Guiraud considers equally "descriptive"—as against rhetorical "tropology."[31] We consider, correctly, that all beauty is unique, that aesthetic value is the function of an original structure. If beauty, in the words of Baudelaire, is always "bizarre," only the foolishness of a "titled professor of aesthetics" could dare claim to predict its appearances. The presence of beauty can be simply noted; it is always unexpected. In other words, however descriptive (even "structural") it may be, this stylistics considers the literary work as a word outside language, as a message without code.

This position is not without weight, especially since Croce's aesthetics (which we will discuss later) has given it an implicitly professed philosophical basis. It is certainly at the antipodes from classical rhetoric, which tried to codify deviations—a practice characterizing classicism on the whole—and which codified both form and content. This is the well-known distinction between "figures of invention" and "figures of usage." Not only was the transfer of metaphoric meaning described but lists of allowed metaphors were even drawn up, lists to be added to only with care. We would be wrong, however, to believe that this distinction is without relevance. An accepted metaphor, for example, could give rise to a second-order deviation. This is the technique of "waking" sleeping metaphors: "on what has once been proven, no *shadow* of doubt *can be cast*."[32] On the other hand, it is not absurd to imagine that one might some day think once again about the ancient project of classifying "filled" figures, that is, everything joined to the idea of genre and aesthetic categories—what we will call later the *ethos* of figures. But the most approachable procedures today concern the "empty" figures, with fixed forms, not their changing substances.

Now, this study, which may well fail to explain how and why a particular text is effective, is at least in a position to explain how and why a text is a text— that is, *what the linguistic procedures characterizing literature are*. In other words, if one must admit that an image, for example, is beautiful insofar as it has never been said (in this way, in this place), it remains an image nonetheless. We postulate, therefore, that literature is first of all a singular use of language. It is, in fact, the theory of this usage that will constitute the first objective of general, and perhaps generalizable, rhetoric.

We must now indicate certain immediate and fundamental consequences of this decision to approach literature from the point of view of language. To simplify things, we shall reduce literature to poetry in the modern sense of the word, but what we say about poetry will hold for all forms of literary art insofar as these forms derive from art. We note here with Paul Valéry that poetry is literature "reduced to the essential of its active principle."* This convention of language is not without its dangers, but it will simplify the present discussion.

In defining poetry as the "art of language," in the traditional periphrase, we ought to note as well the ambiguous character of this equivalence. In English one of the modern uses of the word *art* is related to the quality of some realization and, by extension, to the group of precepts whose goal is to achieve that excellence. Thus, for the schoolmen, logic is the art of thinking; and we can also distinguish the art of love, the art of being a grandfather, and several other arts, right up to the arts of living and dying. In another sense, the "art of" refers to a class of creative activity with an aesthetic finality whose "medium" of matter is specific in its distinction from other classes. It is possible to push the first meaning of the expression "the art of language" to its furthest extent and then to see poetry with its goal of verbal expression as constituting the "proper use" of language. Such is by no means our opinion, but since the opposing theory has more than one illustrious exponent, we must give it its place. We are thinking especially of Benedetto Croce, in whose *Estetica* (1902), the concepts of art and expression, as well as expression and intuition, were courageously identified. This work made aesthetics and linguistics one. Since language for the Italian philosopher does not precede thought, language is not an instrument for communication: "It is born spontaneously with the representation it expresses."[33] Inseparable from the expressed, expression is properly aesthetic and not practical. The Crocean doctrine is opposed on several essential counts to the Saussurian doctrine, which it fought in a rear-guard action.[34]

Distinct from the Genevan master, the Neopolitan philosopher denies any meaning to the distinction between *langue* and *parole* and in any case gives no special priority to speech. The system does not precede its realization, which Saussure would admit without question, but there is not yet any system. It is simple stupidity, still according to Croce, to imagine that man speaks

*[This quotation comes from Gérard Genette, *Figures I* (Paris: Editions de Seuil, 1966), p. 253. He is paraphrasing Valéry's "Poetry and Abstract Thought" (see Paul Valéry, *The Art of Poetry*, trans. Denise Folliot [New York: Random House, 1961], pp. 52–81). *Trans.*]

according to a vocabulary and a grammar. All analyses of linguistic categories are rejected completely, in the same way as are divisions of literary works into genres or schools or even the nomenclature of figures of rhetoric. There are no ''figures,'' and if the proper is proper, there is beauty, beauty being only the determining value of the expression. (Inversely, if a figured expression is proper, it is beautiful.) Speaking strictly, there is not even any difference between the successful, or ''beautiful,'' expression and the very essence of expression—the expression existing only to the extent that it has aesthetic value. A result of this is that only the poets speak truly or, perhaps, that men speak only insofar as they are poets. There is only an empiric distinction between *Homo loquens* and *Homo poeticus*. It is simply an accident that certain men—those with richer and more complex intuition-expression—are called poets.

In so coherent a concept as Croce's, a concept in which ''philosophy of language and philosophy of art are the same thing,'' there is no problem in making verbal expressions the model of all expression—painting or music, for example—since the verbal aspect of verbal expression is in itself devoid of interest. Expression is, in fact, a quite spiritual act, a mental image completely achieved aesthetically, transcending the specificity of matter, which is itself indifferent. Everything technical is of a practical order. In the theoretical order, where art is placed, there is no particular aesthetic. To define one art is to define all of them.

It is obviously not within our scope to examine Crocean aesthetics in its tenets and particulars nor to claim to refute with a wave of the hand a doctrine that hardly lends itself to discussion. We simply need to recall the essentials of a concept that went directly to the antipodes of the place sought by the modern attempt to found a science of literature. For contemporary aesthetics has tried to bring procedures of analysis precisely to what Croce decreed beyond analysis. This is not to say that all the positions once so aggressively defended by Croce have been abandoned today. We must even note that his basic thesis, a searching study of the ideas of de Sanctis—that art is form, and nothing but form (opposing form to matter, not to content)—is more alive today than ever. By identifying art with language, Croce took exception to all linguistic concepts of art as message—concepts that reduced message to content—since for him, from the aesthetic point of view, the message was simply the message.

We are therefore justified to move boldly from Croce to Roland Barthes, from the Italian philosopher to the French neo-rhetor for whom ''literature is nothing but a language, that is, a system of signs. Its being is not in its message, but in this system.''[35] We must understand by this that what is meaningful to literature is not what carries the message but the fact of the message as system. It makes little difference to speak of literature rather than of poetry, since Croce considered *Madame Bovary* to be as much poetry as *Les Fleurs du Mal;* and the New Criticism, in attempting to catch the qualities of literature, has in mind poets just as much as novelists. We are therefore prepared to put Barthes's definition with the poet Ransom's sentence that Roman Jakobson took for his own: "Poetry is a kind of language."[36]

It is obvious that to say that poetry is language ("the art of language," in the sense of the perfection of language) is not the same as to say that poetry is a language ("the art of language," as there is an art of bronze, which is not the perfection of bronze, but an aesthetic activity whose material is bronze). For Jakobson, as for the critics and semiologists who follow in his wake, this claim for a linguistic character of poetry calls on the qualifications of linguistic science to render an account of those particular linguistic structures that are the poetic structures. We will see, however, that this linguistic approach rests finally on a recognition of the nonlinguistic character of poetry. This is the same as saying that the definition of poetry as constituting one language among many cannot be acceptable as a final definition. It is but a provisional definition, one term on the empirical plane, one step on the rational plane. Our thesis, therefore, is that the particularities of poetic language are such that they end up disqualifying poetry as language. It is, certainly, the clear statement of these particularities that reveals the nonlinguistic essence of the qualities of literature.

For the stylisticians, the interminable and often empty discussions turned around the idea that style, defined in its most general sense as the essence of the literary, could be understood as linguistic *deviation*. To hold that literary communication is in some way removed from nonliterary communication is hardly to move very far forward. It is simply to postulate that literature (or in our convention, poetry) is not non-literature (in English, it is common to call this prose). In the Crocean view, one could hold that style is simply "the element of language considered in its use for literary ends in a given work,"[37] but is this proposition not reducible to the affirmation that "style is literary language," and finally that "literature is literature"?

Since the operational value of a tautology is always among the lowest, it is no doubt better to seek the specific character of poetic discourse, and this is precisely what students of poetry have done so completely. But the term "deviation," attributed to Paul Valéry and advanced by Charles Bruneau, cannot be taken as a truly satisfying formulation any more than Charles Bally's remark according to which "the first person who called a sailing vessel a sail made a mistake."[38]

Among other equivalents proposed, often in innocence, are *abuse* (Valéry), *violation* (J. Cohen), *scandal* (R. Barthes), *anomaly* (T. Todorov), *folly* (Aragon), *deviation* (Spitzer), *subversion* (J. Peytard), *infraction* (M. Thiry)—all terms with strong moral, even political, connotations. And one must understand that some have reacted against this vocabulary that could take us back, finally, to the theory of art in vogue during the nineteenth century: as a pathological phenomenon (the poet as neurotic, El Greco with an astigmatism, and so on). It is one of the merits of Jean Cohen's fine work, *Structure du langage poétique* (Paris, 1966), that he indicates the value of reducing the deviation (*écart*), a phase of rebuilding necessarily following on the phase of destruction. To stick to a "deviation from the norm" is childish, a confusion of a figure of style with a barbarism. Once again, it is only provisionally that we accept a definition such as the following: "Poetic language is not only foreign to good usage, it is its antithesis. Its essence consists in a violation of the norms of language."[39] It is in this same way that ideologues have been able to define woman by what she lacks in comparison with man, people of color by what they lack in comparison with whites, and so on.

Certainly the ticklish point is to determine the norm from which to define this deviation, which itself is to be resolved again into a norm. Du Marsais, the eighteenth-century author of a treatise on tropes that rhetoric's present renewal has realized should be reread, already protested against Quintilian's definition of figures as being "manners of speaking that are far removed from the ordinary and natural manner," for "during one day at the central market more figures are used than during several days of academic conferences."[40] At about the same time, Vico demanded a status of priority for poetry, which Jean-Jacques Rousseau caught in the formula: "Poetry came before prose; that had to be." There is no difficulty, therefore, in admitting that herring hawkers, persons most "natural and ordinary," are authentic poets. All we need to grant is that the primitive, spontaneous, oral stage of literature preceded the existence of literature in writing and culture.

It is nonetheless true that if men did first speak in verse, this practice is certainly very restricted today. The whole question, then, is to discover to what extent the peculiarities of poetic speech, obtained by empirical observation, suffice to define the poetic fact. It is a question at this stage of obtaining the invariants of the literary use of language while preserving the historical and individual values. For the reason just given, it is not wise to take as a term of reference what is called for convenience daily, or familiar, language or the language of "the man on the street." We wish to compare poetic language rather with a theoretical model of communication, as, for example, Pius Servien did with his dichotomy: scientific language (SL language), lyric language (LL language).[41] A poetic utterance (held as such) is distinguished from scientific enunciation (reputed such) by the adherence of the meaning to the signs, by the noted impossibility to translate it, to reduce it, or to give any sort of equivalent for it. All this is well known. But what is the provenance of these properties? How is this immanence realized? Is it a question of grace or of work? of a mystery or of technique? These multiple "additional structures"[42] that the poet imposes on his discourse—do they give an account of the proper effects of the poetic work?

Among these additional structures, the constraints of meter and rhyme are the most obvious ones. But to identify versification with poetry is to go against the grain of all modern efforts to distinguish the two notions. The dictionary of the French Academy in the 1798 edition, observing that "poetry is taken for the qualities that characterize good verse," stated, for example: "These are verses, but there is no poetry in them."[43] If versification in its strict sense, however, is not able in itself to spark the poetic phenomenon, it does not follow that the specific procedures of the poetic usage of language—of which versification is simply one example—do not constitute the necessary determinants of the lyric effect. In other words, it is proper to generalize the notion of verse.

At a famous conference, Roman Jakobson tried to derive the basic principle of all poetic procedures.* He advanced the principle of equivalence to the rank of a constitutive procedure of the verbal sequence. While in ordinary language, with its referential function, equivalence does not rule the selection of the units of the paradigmatic reserve—syntagmatic arrangement obeying only a principle of contiguity between the chosen themes—in poetic language the law of similarity is an imposition added to the sequence. Once again, the regular repetition of equivalent *phonic units* is only the most obvious manifestation of the principle of equivalence. *Couplings,* to use the term proposed once by Levin, affect not only the phonemic chain: they meet also at the semantic level. Metaphor, giving the term its widest meaning here, is evidently one of the principal springs of the poetic mechanism. *Parallelism* in addition (Hopkins's term) relates to the rapport between the signifiers and the signified, for contrary to referential language, where the link between sound and sense is in the large majority of cases a link of codified contiguity, poetic language tends constantly to justify the signs, resolutely taking the side of Cratylus against Hermogenes. Either separately or concurrently, the effect of these assimilations, as Jakobson also has shown, draws the attention of the reader to the message itself. Since this reification of the message is always more or less present in any act of communication, Jakobson is led to distinguish the poetic function from the poetry itself, where this function predominates. The *poetic function* overlaps, at least in part, what Ombredane from a psychological viewpoint named the *ludic function.*[44] It would perhaps be preferable, in order to avoid all equivocation, to speak of the *rhetorical function.*

This reference to rhetoric allows us to make clear an important point. The notion of "additional" structure proper to poetic discourse is not satisfactory. In the final sense, it leads us right back to the ancient idea of ornament "added." Now, the systematic nature of language keeps one from deliber-

*[Thomas A. Sebeok, ed., *Style in Language* (Cambridge, Mass.: M.I.T. Press, 1960), comprises the conference proceedings. *Trans.*]

ately grafting base units on without altering profoundly the nature of the whole. As Jean Cohen, for example, has insisted, when the poet uses phonemes for nondistinctive ends, he only adds, only juxtaposes, one procedure with another. His operation could not be innocent, for it results in one of the basic conditions of the functioning of language. In the same way, if it is true that the "iconic" characters in Peirce's sense, or "symbolic" in Saussure's sense, are not as negligible as has been believed,[45] the poetic word remains and manifests a particular tendency to multiply mimetic procedures. To introduce the figure in discourse is to renounce that transparency of the sign that is a property of its arbitrariness, that is, of the indissolubility of the signifier and the signified. For the linguistic sign is so totally and purely sign only because it preserves its function of substitute, blotting itself out so much more easily because it is nothing itself except difference. If, according to Plato, the essence of resemblance is dissimilarity, then to speak in favor of the image is to renounce that fine clarity of signs that is the basis of language; it is to run the risk of an opaque discourse, opaque to the extent that it shows itself before it shows the world. No doubt significations are not entirely veiled by the rhetorical function. The idea of a sign that could signify nothing is contradictory; and however worthwhile might be the attempts to inaugurate a literature purely phonetic or visual, we must recognize that these attempts go beyond the purely poetic and overflow into the musical and plastic arts. The referential function of language, therefore, is not, and cannot be, destroyed by the poet who leaves for the reader the spare time to admire in a poem what is not specifically poetic. But since significations are no longer perceived there except at a distance and are totally suspended in the founding of signs, the language of the writer can do nothing but *create illusion*, that is, produce through itself its object. Howsoever *poetic* language may be, poetic *language* is nonreferential, or it is referential only to the extent that it is not poetic. This is the same as saying that art, as we have known for a long time and periodically forget, is itself situated beyond the distinction between false and true; whether the thing exists or not is without relevance for the writer.

The final consequence of this distortion of language is that the poetic word is disqualified as an act of communication. In fact, it communicates nothing, or rather, it communicates nothing but itself. We can also say that it communicates with itself, and this intracommunication is nothing other than the very principle of form. By inserting at each level of discourse, and between levels, the constraint of multiple correspondences, the poet closes discourse on itself. It is precisely this closure that we call the opus.

We are thus quite far from being able to consider poetic language as simply the model of language that is not an end in itself. To the extent that we give the word *verse* an exempletive or synecdochic value, we can subscribe to the striking formula of Etienne Gilson: "Verse is there to keep the poet from speaking.''[46] But we shall not claim that poetry (any more than literature as an art) constitutes a language apart, another language. There is but one language, modified by the poet, or better, transformed completely.

To define literature in this way—as a transformation of language—takes account, at the same time, of the modern feeling that art is creation and of the ancient observation that man creates nothing (poetic creation is the formal working of linguistic matter). In a certain way, every linguistic creation is an artistic creation to the extent that every dialectical construct is art.[47] In particular, the qualities of invention, freshness, and so on, that, since Romanticism, one likes to recognize in argot, slang, and children's speech (sometimes presuming too much of their creative possibilities),[48] give a certain consistency to the idea of a ''natural'' or ''brute'' poetry current in the streets or country. On the other hand, precisely these languages called natural carry a host of figured expressions, proverbs, comparisons, rhythmic formulas, and so on (residue of deliberate or spontaneous poetic creations), in short, a whole frozen rhetoric, but one capable of being brought back to life. However, it is clear that when a scholar coins a neologism to designate a new chemical compound, or when Bergson uses metaphors to grasp an intuition that he considered inexpressible, those acts of linguistic creation are not, in themselves, literary. According to modern conceptions of things, the writer does not use the figure: *it* uses *him*. This makes for a theoretical cleavage between aesthetic and nonaesthetic uses of language. In practice, rare are the pure writers in this sense. But a poet such as Mallarmé is a rather good example. Prose writers, and especially novelists, are most often rather unartistic *writers*, using rhetorical procedures to say something better, creating as a means of expression, while the artist expresses only as a means of creating.[49]

These considerations can lead us to the famous definition of style as ''a deviation as compared with a norm,'' a cream puff for all stylistics. We have already emphasized the equivocal and certainly unfortunate character of such a formula, as well as its operative potency. Once again, to say that the qualities of literature are deviations is to say nothing more than that literature is something particular. Everything that is marked is a deviation in comparison with something, even the concept of being compared to nothingness. At the highest level of generality, the imputed formula simply postulates that there are at least two aims of language: its function in literature and its other function or functions. On the whole, the notion is not much more than a banality. But its more current expression seems to have quasi-teratological connotations that it would be best to get rid of. When a Claudel states that ''great writers were not made to put themselves under the laws of grammarians, but to impose their own, and not only their will, but their caprice,''[50] he is well aware that such a statement is not meant to cause us to admire any dreadful errors that appear nor certainly to accept as style any use of anacoluthon. Paul Valéry, also, after defining the writer as "a maker of deviations," adds that it is a question of only "the deviations that enrich."[51]

If dislocating language is not enough to make one a poet, it is also not necessary at the same time to run through all the resources of rhetoric to produce good literature. In fact, a good number of writers have avoided the too obvious distortions that pleased the baroque, the affected, and mannerists of all types. But we ought to be careful here not to exaggerate anything. Voltaire considered the *qu'il mourût* ("let him die") as the "most sublime trait."* Other than seeing in this famous reply a litotes (avoidance of emphasis where the situation would call for it), it is easy to see that the absence of a figure can be a figure, that the deviation can be the meaningful and needed lack of deviation. In addition, when some decide to dismiss writers such as those whom Du Bos called "crystalline," those "whose style consisted of a *specific* use of the common resources,"[52] we have the right to ask whether the figures put out the door have not come back in by the window. What is specific could not be common. Moreover, claims to a "stripped-down" style or a neutrality of style are often illusory. When metaphors find their way into the writings of scientists, and paranomasia into the writings of psychoanalysts, we can expect that a purposely banal literary style does not for long hide its originality.

But the principal source of misunderstandings concerning this definition of *deviation* rests certainly with the polysemy of the word *norm*. Kinsey has shown that, psychologically, nothing is more normal than masturbation, which is nonetheless a clear deviation in the eyes of traditional morality. We can also hold that it is normal for each person to receive his daily bread, but statistics do not have the same criteria as social justice. It is a question of knowing whether the writer deviates from "what ought to be" or from "the habitual state, conforming to the majority of cases."[53] We would not hesitate to hold both cases acceptable. As suggested above, the procedures specific to literature are not the best means for assuring rapid communication of messages without ambiguity of content or for expressing and communicating information. But it is clear that if the nature of literature is to deviate from language thus defined, this deviation then becomes the norm for the writer, who is doing what he ought by not doing what non-literature ought to do.

To determine the frequency of the literary usage of the language, it would certainly be necessary to ask the Great Computer. Some elementary distinc-

---

*[Voltaire, "Commentaire sur Corneille," in *Oeuvres complètes,* ed. Louis Moland, vol. 31 (Paris: Garnier, 1885), p. 301, commenting on *Horace,* act 3, sc. 6, line 1021: Julie asks, "What did you want him to do against three?" To which the elder Horace replies, "To die. . . ." This famous line is discussed by Fontanier in *Les Figures du discours* (Paris: Flammarion, 1968), p. 22, and by Tzvetan Todorov in *Littérature et signification,* (Paris: Larousse, 1967) p. 100. *Trans.*]

tions, however, are necessary. With the hypothesis of a natural poetry inherent in the structure of actual languages empirically forged in the course of centuries, it is in fact quite possible (as in the citation above of Du Marsais's famous words) that the language of figures is in no way extraordinary. It would nonetheless remain true that this anonymous writer was not intending the figure for its own sake. If we next place ourselves at the level of literature as an institution with professional specifications, then it is highly probable that literature, whether good or bad, is not the most socially shared item in the world. Certainly we can all imagine a microsociety—a phalanstery of poets, for example, where all language would be beautiful, even when asking the maid to bring in the slippers. In this case, the norm of the Turk's Head or of the bar in the Algonquin Hotel would obviously not deviate from the language of the streets. If we understand that we are no longer defining style in general, but the style of a particular work or a particular writer, of a certain literary group, of an epoch, normality in the statistical sense varies according to that order. From this point of view, stylisticians have certainly accumulated a good number of particular studies and have formulated certain rules of method that will no doubt permit us one day to reconstruct the rhetorical codes fitting into one another and corresponding to these messages, classes of messages, classes of classes of messages, and so on.

Before coming back to the delicate task of a practical determination of degree zero, we must take account of two other objections sometimes raised about the idea of deviation. Are we going to denounce writers as agitators and use them in schools as examples not to follow? In fact, the tradition that considers them as guarantors of good usage, in the sense of normative grammarians, is not in error. Better than anyone else, they know their material, language, as a sculptor knows marble. When Todorov repeats that "the effects of style could not exist unless they opposed a norm, an established usage,"[54] we must add that the producer of the effect shows in the same operation both the deviation and the norm. A metaphor is perceived only if it acts simultaneously in the usual sense and in the figured sense. It is, therefore, the norm-deviation relationship, and not the deviation as such, that makes style. On the other hand, we have faulted the principle in question for being psychologically false because the reader never has as reference some degree zero, but, rather, takes the figure in immediately. Again we must distinguish among cases. That there exist naive readers, more attentive to the content of the message than to its form, to the story told by the novel than to its narrative structures, is certain. That there is an aware, or conscious, reading (which we believe is true only on the second reading), which even so is not always aware of the play between norm and deviation—who would deny this? Besides, one of the characteristics of the work of art is to suggest its particular truth as an absolute truth. There is a fascination with rhetorical processes that generally results in an awakening of the critical consciousness, necessarily comparative.

But whether it is a question of identifying facts of style (learned reading) or appreciating them (aesthetic reading), the mechanism of *reference* will come into play. The paradigmatic dimension of the discourse will become explicit, and tasting will become choosing and preferring. Finally, we must not lose sight of the comparisons that are present already at an automatic or spontaneous level.

Even if one did not admit the hypothesis we have just worked out for the modalities of reading, the theory of deviation would still be justifiable from a pragmatic point of view. At the very least, it constitutes an explicative model. Naturally, it is easy to caricature the approach of the rhetorician slaving to reconstitute proper meanings and to make up lists of the type "Say it this way—not that way," of making dictionaries such as the one Somaize made: "A Doctor, a Hypocratic bastard; A house, a necessary shelter; To get married, to take on legal love; A beautiful hand, a moving beauty"[55]; and so on. It is also certain that Saint-Pol-Roux did not "mean" *carafe* when he said "crystal breast."[56] It is even more obvious that he who makes up spoonerisms does not ask us to guess the proper word when it is precisely the improper, or dirty, word that he is aiming at, as though he wanted to throw into doubt the propriety of language. It is nonetheless true that only the transformations of the expression into another, somehow related equivalent allows us to give it a meaning. In practice, the reconstitution of degree zero, or the term *a quo,* is not always simple. To define a trope as a change of meaning is one thing; to determine with precision the proper meaning of a certain metaphoric term is something else. Nothing, however, keeps us from claiming that there are cases where this determination is impossible, especially when the message points not to two meanings but to several, giving the feeling or illusion of infinity. Such a concept, which corresponds to one of the current theories of symbolism, is in no way incompatible with the idea of deviation: the production of multiple meanings radicalizes the constituent process of the rhetorical formation.

A *general* rhetoric such as we are sketching in this work must be concerned with the analysis of these techniques of transformation by carefully distinguishing their kind and their objects. As we have observed, paleorhetoric was no doubt a nonstop distinguishing machine. In some ways, it distinguished itself to death. But it often made poor distinctions, and certain of its classifications of figures remind us of the surreal taxonomies of ancient China that Borges speaks of.

We must not, however, underestimate the scope of some schemas, certain of which are very old, even though they may have become blurred in the works of later authors. The theory of the *quadripartita ratio,* found notably in Quintilian,[57] passes the test of an effective instrument, as we shall see in chapter 1. In the same way, "figures of thought," which have been subject to mockery, can be integrated into a coherent whole.

The most important distinction consists in determining the fundamental aspects of language, with the understanding that rhetorical intent can aim at each of them. In the preceding pages we have at times neglected to specify that by "language" we mean the total linguistic phenomenon, of which *langue* in the Saussurian sense is only one factor. Here again we will begin by referring to the schema proposed by Jakobson, which is a generalization of the classical works by Ombredane, K. Bühler, Morris, and so on.[58] An *emitter* sends a *message* to a *receiver* by use of a *channel*. The message is *coded* and refers to a *context*. The different factors give birth to as many different functions, cumulative in principle but most often hierarchical according to the particular communication act. In practice it is the referential function that dominates, but the message may just as well be "centered" on the addresser (expressive function) or on the addressee (conative function). At times the emphasis is put on the code (metalinguistic function), even on the contact (phatic function). Finally, there are the messages centered on themselves, by predominance of what Jakobson calls the "poetic" function and what we prefer to call the "rhetorical" function.

Still, we shall not remain content with proposing this terminological correction to a theory so tempting in appearance. We think that the illustrious linguist has somewhat falsified the analysis of the language phenomenon by making the "message" only one factor among others of the communication act. In reality the message is nothing other than the result of five basic factors: the *addresser* and the *addressee* entering into *contact* by means of an intermediary *code* by way of a *referent*. No doubt "the message itself," as Jakobson says, can be known as a proper reality. It is, however, under this aspect that language appears on first reflection: language is sentences that are in some way substantial; "words" that may be "frozen"—put into writing, on tape, and so on. Next, we understand that these messages are addressed by one person to another, that they have a physical substance, that they have meaning by convention. This false substance is in reality a knot of relations.

The importance of this remark on the totalizing character of the message comes from its rhetorical function, which is itself transcendent in comparison with the other functions of language. The rhetorical intention, in fact, completely disturbs the functioning of the different aspects of the linguistic process. In the first place, it acts in a radical manner on the code—it is there, in fact, that the traditional theory of figures has been working for a long time and which in the broadest sense the present essay would like to systematize rigorously, that is, the procedures by which the language of the rhetor transforms the conventions of language in their three aspects: morphological, syntactical, and semantic. But the relationship of the message to the referent—whatever might be the interpretation given to "referent"—may itself be modified without the prescriptions of the code being violated. At the same time, and as Jakobson has noted, rhetorical language allows curious distortions of the actors in the process.[59]

We see that the "poetic" function—to keep his original phrase—is not of the same order as, for example, the metalinguistic function, which is the use of language to furnish information about the code or the expressive function, which communicates only the attitude of the addresser. To "call attention to the message itself," the poet-rhetorician can transform as he wishes any of the factors of language. Certain schools of modern poetry, for instance, are content with using variations in the graphic aspect of the message. The literary qualities of the novel are posed by the single fact that the "I" of the narrator is not the "I" of the writer or rather of the *author,* to use the distinction proposed by Barthes.* The projection of the principle of similarity from the paradigmatic axis onto the syntagmatic axis is, therefore, not the single criterion of the literary use of discourse. It is but one procedure among many, no doubt the most widespread one for what is properly called poetry. But if one takes in the entirety of the facts of literature, other criteria appear, all of which call for systematic transformations of the nonliterary use of language (daily, scientific, and so on).

We call a *metabole* any kind of change of whatever aspect of language, conforming to the meaning found in Littré.† As we have just noted, rhetorical analysis is chiefly interested in metaboles of the code. This study, built on what we believe to be a solid basis, will be the first and longest part of the present work. At this stage, rhetoric can already be considered "general" to the extent that the principal figures appear in an orthogonal schema, deriving from some fundamental operations.

Metaplasms, metataxes, and metasememes thus share the field of deviations of the code. Metalogisms cover the most immediately assignable facts in the field of transformations of the referential content. It is clear that as one becomes interested in larger and larger units for which semiology has formed only vague concepts, it becomes less possible to arrive at a satisfactory description of rhetorical procedures. A true rhetoric of the short story, in particular, is not foreseen. For other reasons, the present book has no hypothetical sketches on metaboles of the addresser and the addressee. It seems that these are psychological implications of those pragmatic aspects that at present defy analysis. Finally, metaboles of contact appear not to need much of our attention because their application is relatively limited.

*[See Roland Barthes, "From Work to Text," in *Image-Music-Text,* trans. Stephen Heath (Glasgow: Fontana, 1977), pp. 155–64; and "Ecrivains et écrivants," in *Essais critiques* (Paris: Seuil, 1964), pp. 147–54. *Trans.*]

†[Emile Littré, *Dictionnaire de la langue française,* 7 vols. (Paris: Pauvert, 1956), the French dictionary corresponding to the *Oxford English Dictionary. Trans.*]

There is a third degree of generalization, which is devoted to the properly semiological instance. The rhetorical "figures" resulting from the application of the four fundamental operations are not limited to the mode of linguistic communication. For a long time painters and art critics have spoken of the "plastic metaphor." Leaving aside superficial analogies, we believe that there are ways to compare the means of expression to reduce here again the fundamental operations to the same schema. In this case too, the chapter devoted to these questions has no pretentions of being more than a sketch of what subsequent research ought to achieve. By pulling together some hypotheses on forms of narration, which is a "translinguistic" category, we are simply making a first step in that direction.

It remains for us now to specify the relationships between the two terms we have coupled at the beginning of this work: "poetics" and "rhetoric." Linking these two ancient disciplines is nothing new. At the least we feel vaguely that they call for one another, since, for example, we have seen together in one volume Aristotle's *Poetics* and *Rhetoric,* or the *Dictionary of Poetics and Rhetoric.*[60] The patient compiler of the latter work felt no need to justify the yoking, but he does recall that the Academy in its second meeting in 1635 had made the promise to construct a poetics and a rhetoric (article 26 of the statutes).* Since there is little chance that this illustrious company will bring the project to a head, we may as well—following M. Morier and others— collaborate in this effort. But we must know where we are going. What is the relation of rhetoric to poetics?

In the light of what we have raised above, to wit, that the theory of figures was far from exhausting the rhetoric of the ancients—and this justifies Perelman's use of the expression "new rhetoric" to designate a theory of argumentation—rhetoric is the knowledge of the techniques of language characteristic of literature. By "poetics" we understand the thorough knowledge of the general principles of poetry, with the understanding that poetry *stricto sensu* is the paragon of literature. In this way, the problem that concerns us comes down to examining the contribution of rhetoric, not claiming to exhaust the literary object, in the establishment of an objective knowledge of this object.

Tzvetan Todorov, at the end of his short treatise *Tropes et figures,* poses the problem in these terms: "Is figured language identical to poetic language? If not, what are the links?"[61] After recalling that classical authors in general answered the first question in the negative and have neglected the second one, Todorov himself makes the opposition between figured language and literary (poetic) language, in that one tends toward opaque discourse ("to attract

*[For the statutes of the French Academy, see Charles C. Doucet, *Les Régistres de l'Academie française, 1672-1793,* 4 vols. (Paris: Firmin Didot, 1895-1906). *Trans.*]

attention to the message itself'' [Jakobson]), while the other one makes these very things present (the mimetic function of discourse). Nonetheless, these two languages struggle with a common adversary, which is the transparent, the imposing discourse, the abstract concept. Using the famous triangle of Ogden and Richards,[62] let us make the following division into three.

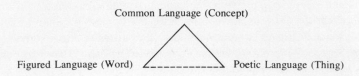

Common Language (Concept)

Figured Language (Word)   Poetic Language (Thing)

Certainly we are dealing here with pure tendencies, for every discourse implies necessarily three aspects. Literary discourse imposes its "reality" only because the referent is lacking, and the abstract meaning exists in common language only by the virtual existence of these things.

These distinctions are interesting, but, in fact, they do not reduce for us figured language to being only an unnecessary arm of literature "in its antagonism with pure meaning." As we believe we have shown adequately in the preceding pages, we can say that *there is no poetry without figures* so long as "figures" is understood in a broad enough sense; that is, every literary message includes by necessity rhyme, rhythm, assonance, proportion, intersections, oppositions, and so on. But there are also obviously *figures without poetry,* and it is on this score that the debate continues.

It is quite true that in the "language of fiction" (Blanchot) "the meaning of the words suffers from a primordial basic lack."[63] Literary language has no ostensible referent, or more correctly, the existence of a referent is not a relevant quality. The war in Vietnam was without question a hard reality, but a poem about the war is not to be judged poetic by the extent that it relates verifiable facts, that is, to the extent that it is history, document, reportage, or witness. Does this sound as if we are reducing the work to a "trifling of sonorous vapidity"? We know the poor literary results of trying to rid a work of meaning. Why is there no abstract poetry (even if one wants to call it "concrete"), while nonrepresentation is a fact of painting, not to speak of music?[64] It is certainly because the poet works with words, with composites of sound and sense. And for him, the link between the two facets of the sign is rigorous and necessary. Far from being extended into the infinite of convention, it is reduced to a point.

We are not forgetting that the Saussurian thesis of the arbitrariness of the sign can be adjusted by showing that for the speaker nothing is more necessary than the connection between the signifier and the signified. Beyond its constitutive reality, however, the sign itself is distinct from the referent. The ultimate meaning of ordinary discourse is certainly in this design of things, at once absent (the word is not the thing) and present (the word replaces the thing).

What distinguishes poetic discourse is that it does not speak of things. Poetry is totally in words (form and meaning). In the case of poetry, the Ogden-Richards triangle is no longer valid. Finding in itself its own justification, the literary message telescopes the two bottom angles of the triangle: the poetic intention is shown by this obliteration of the things by the word.

Rhetorical function has the effect of reifying language. We know that action on others (propaganda, preaching, seduction, advertising, and so on) is never without figures drawn from the arsenal of "poetic" procedures and that scientific writing also uses them to achieve economy of demonstration. To say that the writer *uses* figures is not enough: he *lives on* them. He does not adorn a statement; rather, he brings language into existence without the contingency of things. Only the figure in its most generalized sense can allow him this achievement. The "additional structures" are not therefore simply constraints, "annoyances," even "exquisite" ones, but are rather the unique way of turning language from its utilitarian role, which is the first condition for its metamorphosis into poetry. Through metaboles, literary discourse is made to close on itself. But as we have known for a long time, figures are clearly not enough to accomplish this, to achieve its creation. The most learned "wir- ·ings" do not always allow the "current" to pass.

Rhetoric as the study of formal structures moves then necessarily into transrhetoric, which is precisely what was once called second rhetoric or poetics. Its task was to explain the effect and value of those modified expressions that poets put forth, and first of all to determine what proportion of modification was compatible not only with the correct functioning of the figure but also with its acceptability by the aesthetic consciousness.[65] But must we agree with Jean Cohen, who takes up a hypothesis in vogue in English-language criticism that such a study ends up by recognizing the existence of a "code of connotaters," poetry violating the denotative meaning only so as to better obtain an emotional or affective meaning? What Cohen himself says about this "appearance of the pathetic face of the world" raises many questions.[66] We have noted earlier, and will repeat it in the third chapter (sec. 2.3.1), that we reserve for a later work a systematic study of the ethos of figures, recognizing that the psycho-aesthetic effect is not a function of purely linguistic mechanisms. A sketch of such a systematic study, however, will be found as an appendix to the first part of this work. Aestheticians in this field have at times tried analyses prying into such and such a "category." There is certainly considerable literature on the elegant, the tragic, the comic, and so on. But today, such attempts at systematization are laughable. The one we present furnishes at least a working hypothesis.

Finally, if the certain, the probable, and the possible are spread in unequal parts through the following pages, it is perhaps not in the places we think.

Part One
FUNDAMENTAL RHETORIC

Chapter I
A General Theory
of the Figures of Language

1. ANALYSIS OF DISCOURSE

1.1. The Units of Signification

Rhetoric is a set of operations made on language necessarily dependent on certain characteristics of language. We shall see that *all* rhetorical operations rest on a fundamental property of linear discourse—that discourse can be decomposed into smaller and smaller units.

A theory of linguistic levels has been developed by Benveniste.[1] We shall apply it here in a somewhat more general aspect, which will better suit our remarks. Whether this application is on the plane of signifier (phonic or graphic element) or of the signified (meaning), the chain that is manifested can be considered a hierarchy of planes where discrete units are "articulated." Several units on the same level are fitted (or "integrated," in Benveniste's terminology) into a unit of a higher order, and each of them in turn embodies units of a lower order.

Decomposition continues on each of the two planes until it reaches an atomic, or indivisible, level. On the plane of the signifier, accordingly, we shall reach the level of distinctive features, while on the plane of the signified we reach the level of semes. It is to be noted that the last state of decomposition reached is always infralinguistic: neither distinctive features nor semes have an explicit, independent existence in language. The units of signification, as they are manifested in discourse, begin at the immediately higher level (see table 1).

All the units of signification employed in this work will therefore be considered as collections of elements built upon preexisting stocks (the sounds of the English language, words from the lexicon, and so on). These stocks are hierarchical with binary oppositions, through which we are able to show them in the form of disjunctive trees (Linnaean taxonomies, vowel trees, and so on) or as graphs. Each element can be defined by its coordinates on a certain tree,

Table 1. The Levels of Articulation

Level of Articulation	Units of the Signifier (form of the expression)	Units of the Signified (form of the content)
0	Distinctive features	Semes
1 *a* *b* *c*	Graphemes Phonemes Syllables Words	Bases* Morphemes Hypolexemes Lexemes Clauses
2 *a* *b*	Syntagms Sentences	Developments†
3	"Texts" (nonformalized level)	

*Base or semic kernels.
†Sequences of clauses used for description, narration, deduction, etc.
----Since the number of articulations on the plane of the signifier is larger than what is found on the plane of the signified, we have indicated by broken lines the principal correspondence.

and every rhetorical figure will be an alteration of coordinates or a displacement on these trees. Rhetoric will thus be the set of rules of movement on the trees.

Drawing upon the fundamental distinctions proposed by Hjelmslev, we shall note also that our analysis bears only on the forms (of expression as well as content), excluding substance. When we speak of "substantial" alterations in section 3.1, it will not require an understanding of this word in the Hjelmslevian sense. On the other hand, we shall use the categories of the Danish linguist in the chapter on the figures of narration (chap. 8).

The arrows in table 1 indicate connections between the levels of articulation; for each of them there is a corresponding type of rhetorical figure. It is possible to rearrange them into three large groups with homogeneous characteristics (as in table 2).

We should note that rhetorical figures are generally concerned with contiguous or neighboring levels (for example, a phonetic spoonerism with a

Table 2. Connections between the Levels of Articulation

Group	Definition	Examples
A	Integration from level 0 to level 1	0–1*a*
B	Connections within level 1	1*a*–1*b* 1*b*–1*c* 1*a*–1*c*
C	Integration from level 1 to level 2 and connections within level 2	1*c*–2*a* 1*c*–2*b* 2*a*–2*b*

syntagm), rarely linking levels at a distance from one another (assonance or repetition of distinctive features in an entire sentence).

The connections that activate level 3 also define new types of figures, whose conditions we shall try to establish for the first time in Part Two of this volume.

The inventory of segments is of prime importance, since it allows us to define the field of the four large families that we count among rhetorical figures. This four-part scheme results from two dichotomies applied simultaneously: first a division along the line signifier/signified, and second a division according to the level of decomposed units: word/sentence.

This second set requires justification because our first analysis led to three distinct groups (A, B, C), not two. In fact, it seemed simpler to us to make the first classification keeping the usual analyzed fields of discourse, with the possibility of dividing these fields later according to more exact componential criteria (see sec. 3.3).

It appeared in analysis that this last distinction had a share of arbitrariness. On the one hand were the figures made up of words (for example, the spoonerism) that are able to include several words without becoming syntactic figures. On the other hand, we can claim, not without reason, that there are levels other than word and sentence. Hence, we find phonemic figures (alliteration, assonance), syllabic figures (*verlen*),* or figures built on entities considerably larger than the sentence (the novel *Ulysses*). The limit adopted here is strictly didactic. Anyway, it is perfectly all right to consider our table "open" at the bottom (see table 3). There is no reason why a system of figures may not go beyond the traditional bounds of linguistics.

Table 3. The Types of Metaboles

	Expression (form)	Content (meaning)
Words (and <)	Metaplasms	Metasememes
Sentences (and >)	Metataxes	Metalogisms

NOTE: Since *metabole* and *metaplasm* are already accepted, we have by analogy created three other designations on the same model.

We might even consider the system in the end as a nonrigorous hierarchy containing perhaps ten levels. This hierarchy is not rigorous in the sense that certain levels can be juggled: the word, for example, can be decomposed into syllables or directly into phonemes.

Finally, it is even permissible not to accept the orthogonal character we have attributed to the two dichotomies but rather to see the situation as a

---

*[*Verlen* is a form of backwards language in which syllables are reversed: *verlen* for *l'envers*, *urefig* for *figure*, and so on. *Trans.*]

progressive succession of fields, marking the passage from pure form to pure content:

Plastic field   Pure and arbitrary form, not signifying but distinctive.
↓

Syntactic field   Form signifying to the extent that it is function: the word does not have its full meaning until it enters "functionally" into a sentence.

Semic field   Portions of the signified arbitrarily analyzed and limited by a form.

Logical field   Content, or pure signified, not under any constraint or limitation of a linguistic kind.

1.2. Description of the Fields

1.2.1. THE FIELD OF METAPLASMS

The field of metaplasms is that of figures that act on the sound or graphic aspect of words and on units smaller than the word and which the figures decompose according to the following models:

Word = a collection of *syllables* (vowels and supporting consonants) arranged in a meaningful order and admitting of repetition.

Word = a collection of *phonemes* (or *graphemes*) arranged in a meaningful order and admitting of repetition.

Phoneme = a collection of hierarchically *distinctive features* with neither repetition nor linear order.

Grapheme = a collection of *distinctive features* (not yet definitely formalized).

1.2.2. THE FIELD OF METATAXES

The field of metataxes is the field of figures acting on the structure of the sentence. The English sentence is defined by the minimal presence of certain constituents, the syntagms. The syntagms are defined in turn by morphemes proper to them, which divide them into classes. Syntagms and morphemes occupy given positions in the sequence. Thus:

Sentence = a collection of syntagms and morphemes endowed with an order and admitting of repetition.

1.2.3. THE FIELD OF METASEMEMES

A metasememe is a figure that replaces one sememe by another; that is, it modifies the groupings of degree-zero sememes. This type of figures supposes that the

Word = a collection of *nuclear semes* without internal order and not admitting of repetition.

The seme is, in fact, an infralinguistic unit of a qualitative nature, and the word is a semantic slice, or a grouping of privileged semes in the language. There is no sense, therefore, in imagining at the interior of the word the repetition of the same seme nor the existence of an order between the semes.

But we could as easily take the view that certain words refer as mediators to an

Object = a collection of coordinated parts

and that this decomposition of the object into its parts (at the level of the referent) has its linguistic counterpart (at the level of concepts) and both can be designated by words. We shall see, moreover, that the results of these two decompositions are completely different.

1.2.4. THE FIELD OF METALOGISMS

The field of metalogisms is partly that of the former "figures of thought," which modify the logical value of the sentence and consequently are no longer under linguistic restrictions. If we are unable to repeat a seme at the interior of a word, we can certainly repeat a word in a sentence and *a fortiori* in units of a larger order. The degree zero of such figures raises, instead of criteria of linguistic correction, the notion of a "logical" order of the presentation of facts or the notion of a "logical" progression of reasoning.

Sentence = a collection of grouped semes in sememes (the words) in a certain order and admitting of repetition.

1.2.5. SUMMARY

In conclusion, in order to present a general view of the different fields defined, we can graph them on the Ogden-Richards triangle, indicating by an arrow the place where the constitutive deviation (*écart*) of each figure appears (see fig. 1):

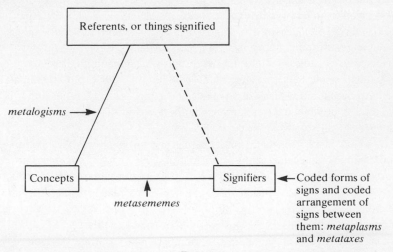

FIG. 1

2. THE OPERATING CONCEPTS

So far, we have said in a vague way that rhetorical figures "modify," "replace," "act upon." Now it is a question of specifying this terminology and defining first of all what we mean by *degree zero, deviation* or *alteration, mark, redundancy, autocorrection,* and *invariant.*

2.1. Degree Zero

2.1.1. INTUITIVE DEFINITION

While every concept of deviation calls for a norm, or degree zero, it is extremely difficult to give this norm an acceptable definition. We might be content with an intuitive definition, that is, a "naive" discourse without artifice, without connotations, in which "a hole is a hole."[2] However, difficulties arise in judging whether a certain text is or is not figured. Every speech act, every word in fact, is the act of an addresser. No speech act, no word, could be presumed innocent without great caution.

2.1.2. UNIVOCAL LIMIT

We can also conceive of degree zero as the ideal that scientific language aspires to achieve. In this view, we can see that the criterion of such a language would be *univocality.*[3] But we are well aware how such a necessity to redefine terms can plague scholars. Is this like saying that degree zero is not contained in language (*langage*) as we have it? It is precisely this position that we would like to defend.

While on the one hand words are privileged foci of the semantic universe, constructed from more or less vast collections of semes, and on the other hand our discourses are necessarily composed of words (semes are on the other side of language, we must remember), we are constantly forced to introduce into our discourses semes that are not essential to our meaning. *Absolute degree zero,* then, would be a discourse reduced to its *essential semes* (by a metalinguistic process, since these semes are not distinct lexical entities), that is, to the semes that we could not suppress without at the same time depriving our discourse of all signification.

In all our discourses the essential semes certainly appear, but enveloped in supplementary and nonessential information, *not at all redundant, but contiguous.* According to this perspective, almost all our names are synecdochic. We shall agree to call *practical degree zero* utterances containing all the essential semes along with a number of contiguous semes reduced to a minimum as functions of the possibilities of the vocabulary.

Let us take a look at another example given by Jean Paulhan. If we compare the following utterances, we recognize in each one a common degree zero that could be stated, "There you are":*

Well, now, it's you!
It's him, without a doubt.
Here's my main man!
Hush, here he is!
Good. You're back.
Salutations.
Hello there.
What, you?
Well, he got here anyway.
There you are, sweetheart.
What, you here?
Is it you or your ghost?
What are you doing here?
Ah, Old Faithful!
Is it really you, Marge?
You're finally here.
Well, hi!
My God, is it really you?
We were wondering what the hell you were doing.
You? Not really!
What brought you here?
Look what the cat dragged in!

If, in the same way, at degree zero a character in a story is to be assassinated, we are forced to choose a weapon even if the particular weapon has no influence on the development of the plot. The triads of Propp and Brémond[4] are put in general terms. They are simply the degree zero of the narrative. But when a Russian folk tale actualizes the function "marking the hero," it must choose a concrete object as a marker as well as give the precise circumstances, even though they are unessential for its production.[5]

Our definition of *degree zero* will remain a promise rather than an effective instrument so long as we fail to specify the methods for attaining it. Nonetheless, by assigning it this place outside language, we certainly recognize the endless discussions concerning it,[6] and we acknowledge the concept of degree zero as an "ideal."

2.1.3.   STATISTICS OF VOCABULARY

Certain authors have sought a way to describe the literary act employing word frequency, on the basis of frequency lists called *normales,* lists obtained by sufficiently broad enumerations. The "Vander Beke List" is an example of such a *norm,* considered as the degree zero against which deviations might

*[The list translates equivalent idiomatic French greetings. *Trans.*]

be measured.[7] We shall not comment on the interest of such a method, emphasizing only that it leads to a macroaesthetic study of style, while we are working here with a microaesthetic study.

2.1.4. SUBJECTIVE PROBABILITIES (FULFILLED EXPECTATIONS)

To avoid defining an often ungraspable norm, we can at least indicate that an empirical method for the determination of degree zero is imaginable and based on a definition like "Degree zero of a given point is what the reader expects at that point." By bringing the reader in at this stage, we bring in an argument for a thesis that will be considered in our chapter devoted to ethos and according to which effect is not contained in the figure but is produced in the reader as a response to a stimulus. The proposed method (for which a test is in preparation) is based on subjective probabilities, that is, on the reader's knowledge about

1) the code (vocabulary, grammar, syntax);
2) the general semantic universe (history, culture, science);
3) the particular semantic universe (other works by the author); and
4) the immediate past of the message (classemes "illuminated" but not yet saturated by their argument).

We can immediately guess that degree zero obtained in this way will rarely be seen in precise words but generally will be a series of constraints *on the elements* that could be used in certain situations.

The relation between the predictable/unpredictable and banal/original oppositions of information theory is clear. It opens a road for research on experimental poetics.

2.1.5. ISOTOPY

A.-J. Greimas has insisted on the idea of isotopy as the semantic norm of discourse whereby each message or text seeks to be "grasped as a meaningful whole."[8] To be actually effective, communication must avoid ambiguities and double meanings, which is most obviously done by being based on the strong redundancy of morphological categories.

The simple fact that we can conceive the literary message (or rhetorical function) as carrying an actualized degree and also a degree zero, absent but identifiable, indicates for us that it is deliberately based on non-isotopy. In certain cases (notably metaphor) rhetoric clearly breaks the lexical code at the same time that it breaks the rule of isotopy. But in other cases the code is retained and only non-isotopy indicates the figure; this is the situation of antanaclasis and antimetabole, which will be analyzed later:

The heart has its reasons which reason does not know

[Pascal]*

*[In French: "Le coeur a ses raisons que la raison ne connaît pas." *Trans.*]

The concept of isotopy allows us also to build an even more general idea of the rhetorical act. We have supposed until now that the literary message was defined by comparison with a unique model serving as a norm. The metasememe (or trope), for example, imparts a new though not powerful source of interest and pleasure with respect to a message that is always appreciated as a function of what it is not. This feature by itself would suffice to define the rhetorical function. But it is not certain that such a binary concept of the use of language would be the only possible one. Non-isotopy does not necessarily mean double isotopy. In fact, certain messages aim at a multiplicity of planes of reading in which none of them is able to claim the privilege of degree zero. *L'Assommoir* of Zola is at the same time a bar, the sign of a bar, alcohol, social evil.

This willed plurality of interpretation certainly seems to be a constant in literature, as the medieval theory of the four levels of meaning indicates, but the limiting examples have been furnished by contemporary writers, especially, in a systematic manner, by Joyce. Thus in *Finnegans Wake,* "the couple Shem-Shaun, in addition to changing names constantly, successively incarnates Cain and Abel, Napoleon and Wellington, Joyce and Wyndham Lewis, time and space, tree and stone.'"[9] We suppose that in such a case the subordinate position of the figured degree compared with degree zero is abolished, giving way to the organization of multiple and coordinated isotopies.

The existence of such phenomena does not limit the range of our undertaking. A theory of multiple meanings expects the formalization first of a theory of double meanings that can account for a large portion of the facts of literature.

2.1.6. DEGREE ZERO AND CODIFICATION

Everything that is included in the linguistic code constitutes a norm, that is, a degree zero: orthography, grammar, word meaning. We add to this the "logical" code, defined by the veracity of discourse. But it goes without saying that all sorts of more or less tacit conventions may give rise to perceptible deviations. This is what Blaise Cendrars is doing when he systematically puts on the first page of his books, under the heading "By the same author": "In preparation: 33 volumes."

2.2. Autocorrection and Redundancy

2.2.1. DEFINITIONS

We know that at all its levels language is redundant, repetitive. This uneconomical practice aims at assuring linguistic messages a certain immunity from errors of transmission. The rate of written language's entire redundancy has been measured: in modern French it would come to about 55 percent.[10] In other words, if 55 percent of the units of meaning were randomly suppressed, a message could still be understood. We call this property of the code *autocorrection of errors*. The rate of redundancy is variable according to the type of message (journalism, essay, poetry), but it is instinctively known by all users of a language.

If we now replace nonsignificant and chance alteration with significant alteration, which we have called *deviation,* we shall throw new light on rhetoric.[11] If in fact the first stage of rhetoric consists in an author's creating deviations, the second stage consists in a reader's deciphering them.[12] This deciphering is nothing other than autocorrection, and it is possible only to the exact extent that the rate of alteration does not exceed the rate of redundancy. A whole field of rhetoric operates in the redundancy zone of language, which it shrinks radically but which assigns it nonetheless an insurmountable limit without which the message is destroyed (hermeticism). It would be useful, however, to note precisely the different forms of redundancy in language and to examine the effect that different rhetorical procedures have on them. For this, we shall use the definition given by Vitold Bélévitch: "Redundance is the refusal to consider all the possible combinations as distinct."[13] In a language without redundancy, each change of a word in the code transforms it into another word of the code. Thus in a redundant language the words are often separated by considerable distance (determined by the number of elements to be changed).

2.2.2. PHONETIC OR GRAPHIC REDUNDANCY

A poorly pronounced word (or one difficult to read) may be deciphered thanks to its redundancy. This operation will not make use of the meaning of the word (what its context might suggest) nor the grammatical or syntactic rules (with the help of the syntagm of which it is a member).

Certain rhetorical deviations (metaplasms) reduce phonetic redundancy. But they cannot suppress it entirely, for degree zero could no longer be established by the reader and the message would be destroyed. For instance, in a portmanteau word some of the elements from each of the constituents must remain in order that all may be identified. In these lines from E. E. Cummings one can recognize, with difficulty to be sure, English words distorted by a Black accent:

ydoan
yunnuhstan.

2.2.3. SYNTACTIC AND GRAMMATICAL REDUNDANCY

Syntactic and grammatical redundancy is especially high in written language. It is revealed mostly by repeated marks: agreement of gender, number, agreement of verbs. In the syntagm "the tall trees," we find one graphic mark and one phonic for plural.* Metataxes partially destroy this redundancy, but they allow enough to remain for it to be deciphered. In the following verse of Ben Jonson, for instance, agreement of person is not observed, but autocorrection is achieved through punctuation:

Thou has begun well, Roe, which stand well too.†

2.2.4. SEMANTIC REDUNDANCY

Semantic redundancy is not subject to strict rules like the preceding ones (orthographic or grammatical rules). It is a result partially of logical rules and partially of the pragmatic necessity for communication, the coherence of messages. In the midst of a given passage, the concepts evoked are generally close or related. At the level of the syntagm, this need can even be a partial determinant of the meaning of words in their context. We express this property by saying that certain semes—the classemes—are iterative.[14] The object of the verb *to drink,* for example, will be a liquid in all probability; if not, there is a deviation, as in "all shame drunk." In the same way, "the black sun of melancholy" violates this rule of semantic coherence.**

Another way of expressing this is to say that after each junction or interval, there is a certain probability of meeting one or several new semes. Such a probability has never yet been quantified, but its level is clear and appreciable for every user of the language who modifies his expectations according to the genre of the message received—journalism, novel, treatise.

Our expectation is fooled in the other direction, and a deviation is perceived, when we read in Péguy:

It is the earth who gains and the earth who pleads
And who takes to trial our growing old
And who makes us beautiful and makes us plain
And who sketches out for us our exiles.
It is the earth who gains and the earth who counts
And who takes to trial our registrations
And who takes account and makes discounts
And who sketches out for us our descriptions.‡

---

*[Three graphic and two phonic marks in the French, *les grands arbres. Trans.*]

†[Epigram 98. *Rhétorique générale* cites this line of Geo Norge. "Z'encens, vous peut bien grésiller." *Trans.*]

**[In French, "toute honte bue," from Villon's "le Testament"; "le soleil noir de la mélancolie" from Nerval's "El Desdichado." *Trans.*]

‡[In French:
  C'est la terre qui gagne et la terre qui plaide
  Et qui fait le procès de nos vieillissements
  Et qui fait une belle et qui fait une laide
  Et qui fait le tracé de nos bannissements.
  C'est la terre qui gagne et la terre qui compte
  Et qui fait le procès de nos inscriptions
  Et qui fait le mémoire et qui fait le décompte
  Et qui fait le tracé de nos descriptions. *Trans.*]

2.2.5. CONVENTIONAL REDUNDANCY

A certain rate of redundancy can be artificially added to language thanks to the groups of supplementary rules to which it can be subjected. Conventions, which are syntactic only in exceptional cases, are more likely to involve the signifier: metric scheme, fixed form, rhyme schemes. But we also find conventions that clearly reduce the rate of redundancy: suppressing capital letters and punctuation.

Conventions of the same order exist in speech as well: stops, silences, intonation. Verse diction can follow caesurae and rhyme, or on the other hand it can follow the flow of the syntax.

2.2.6. INTERPENETRATIONS

Obviously, the different kinds of redundancy are spread throughout the discourse and are partially hidden. A hidden phonetic redundancy can be compensated for by a semantic redundancy, and so on. The respective percentages of the different forms have not yet been quantified, it seems. With the help of a primitive test, we have obtained the following estimations for a prose text:[15]

Morphological redundancy	22%
Syntactic and grammatical redundancy	23
Semantic redundancy	55
Total redundancy	55%

2.2.7. LEVELS OF REDUNDANCY AND MARK

We have, in sum, just defined three levels of redundancy. The first is normal; that is, it is part of degree zero. The other two, one diminished and the other augmented, are both marked in comparison with the first. The possibility of the three different states for a message $(-, 0, +)$ yields 1.6 bits of information, which are, in fact, exploited as a "parasite" code and point to general signifieds (such as literature, child language, slang, and so on).

If rhetoric is based on the double movement of creation and reduction of deviations, these deviations must meanwhile be deciphered by a reader or a hearer. They must therefore be signaled by a *mark*. This fact is less trivial than it appears. Indeed, it is quite possible to create deviations starting from a given degree zero that end up, not in decipherable figures, but at another degree zero. In such a case the reader perceives no variation of the redundancy rate. But we have just seen that every figure alters the rate of redundancy of the text, whether by increase or by reduction. Since the normal level of redundancy constitutes an implicit knowledge of every user of a language (*langue*), a positive or negative alteration of this level is a mark.

2.3. Deviation and Convention

2.3.1. DEVIATION

In the rhetorical sense, we shall understand deviation as the detected alteration of degree zero. Here immediately arise two difficulties. First, there exist voluntary alterations, aiming to make up for deficiencies of vocabulary. In situations where "the word does not exist," one must either forge a new word or shift the meaning of an old word. The operations at work on this occasion differ from operations of rhetoric properly so called in intention only. We shall agree to call rhetorical only those operations trying for poetic effect (in the Jakobsonian sense) and found especially in poetry, jokes, slang, and so on. Second, our conception of degree zero obliges us to divide deviations into two parts. The first covers the distance that separates essential semes from lexical elements; the second covers the supplementary distance, this time in linguistic terrain, between these elements and the lexemes finally chosen. Only the second part of the deviation is properly rhetorical, but on first sight it appears impossible to find the precise limit between the two. An essential seme, in fact, is generally found included in several lexemes among which occurs a negative selection (by rejection of inessential semes). For the analyst, several of these lexemes can be considered valuable in this light as practical degree zero. Without doubt it is impossible to decide at what degree of accumulation of inessential semes a deviation begins to be perceived.[16]

It is true that these difficulties concern only metasememes. Deviation is much more easily understood in the field of metaplasms and metataxes, while it has brought about a formulation of criteria of normality not perceived outside rhetorical studies (for example, "normal modern syntax does not admit symmetries that are too obvious"). In the field of metalogisms, on the other hand, degree zero is again very troublesome to define. On the formal plane, deviation is addressed to a unit of signification on whatever level and causes a decomposition of that unit according to the precise modes of section 1, above.

We stated above that we shall call rhetorical only those deviations aiming at "poetic" effects. In this way, we satisfy the empirical observation according to which every deviation perceived by a receiver is immediately attributed with a signification. Outside the *nature* of the deviation, simply the *act* of deviation is charged with meaning: specifically it means rhetoric—that is, literature, poetry, joke, and so on. It is clear, however, that different figures produce differing aesthetic effects. The nature of the deviation also plays a part, and here we have a delicate problem, but one that does not interfere with our formal analysis of figures.

2.3.2. CONVENTION

The deviation of which we have just spoken is a *local* alteration of degree zero. It presents no systematic character and is, therefore, always unexpected. It is opposed to another kind of change, this one systematic, which is convention. As its name indicates, convention ties the addresser to the addressee. It understandably creates no surprise. We can imagine it as a supplementary formal constraint, adding to grammar, syntax, orthography. As we have seen, it most often deals with meter, rhythm, rhyme, the plastic aspects of language, and extends to the whole message. Convention is a form of deviation, and as such it tries to draw our attention to the message rather than to its meaning. Therefore, it can be considered a rhetorical procedure and can be classed with figures.

2.3.3. COMPENSATION OF REDUNDANCIES

Poetry uses at the same time deviations and conventions, which one can contrast according to the criteria in table 4. This table is useful only for additive conventions. Deviations always diminish predictability, even in the case (Péguy)* where they seem paradoxically to increase redundancy.

Table 4. Deviation and Convention

Deviation	Convention
Nonsystematic	Systematic
Localized	General
Surprising	Not surprising
Lowers predictability	Increases predictability

In broad terms, therefore, poetry operates in two opposite ways on the messages it expresses. First, there is a lowering of redundancy (deviations); and second, a reinforcement of it (conventions). It is tempting to see here a play of compensations whose goal is the maintenance of the overall intelligibility of messages.

Additive conventions, whose distribution is extremely regular (as opposed to linguistic constraints, which are distributed by chance), create by this very fact fulfilled expectations and have a strong unifying function. Suppressive conventions seem to play a secondary role by creating a general ambiguity from which other figures benefit. Conventions are certainly rules, but they lack the stability of linguistic and logical rules and thus are only broken occasionally by a deviation.

Deviations, as we have seen, always lower the predictability of a message, even when they seemingly raise the redundancy (for example, epithet, repeti-

*[Above, sec. 2.2.4. *Trans.*]

tion, pleonasmus, chiasmus). Therefore, they create frustrated expectations. But the rhetoric of deviations is of such current usage in poetry that it becomes more or less systematic. Deviation is conventionalized. In this way, conditions give rise to "deviations of deviations," which we sometimes find in certain tongue-in-cheek texts (Michaux, Vian, Queneau, Nabokov, Brautigan).

We summarize these features in table 5, italicizing the most important cases.

Table 5. Deviation and Convention As Functions of Redundancy

	Redundancy	
	Raised	Lowered
Deviation	Nonexistent	*Frustrated expectation*
Convention	*Fulfilled expectation*	General ambiguity

Table 5 brings out the two following facts: (*a*) the code is imposed on the subject from outside: the deviation will be sought; and (*b*) the convention is freely chosen by the subject: deviation will be proscribed. We can guess that they reinforce the theory of style as expressive value, that is, as denial of nonindividual values.

2.4. Invariant

We have just examined the general conditions under which autocorrection (that is, spontaneous reduction of deviations) is possible. It remains to be seen concretely how this reduction is possible.

In figured discourse, we can distinguish two parts: that which has not been modified, or the *base,* and that which has undergone rhetorical deviations. On the other hand, a figured expression keeps a certain nongratuitous but systematic relationship with its degree zero. We shall later analyze this relationship in detail, but here let us say simply that it can be substantial or relational. This connecting thread we shall call the invariant, and the reduction of deviations will be able to work essentially because the invariant is based first on the nonfigured part of the discourse and next on the invariants remaining in the other part.

As we have said, the figured term is indicated by a mark. Once decoded, it is broken down into units of smaller order according to the different possible modes (see above, sec. 1). At this point it is still impossible to decide which of these smaller units is the invariant of the figure; any one of them will do. The exact invariant is finally identified (at times not without difficulty and not without ambiguity) by an evaluation of the compatibilities between reckoned invariants and the base.

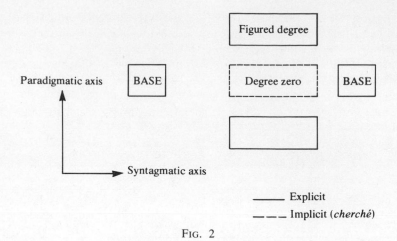

FIG. 2

On the linguistic plane, these measures correspond exactly to the measures of selection and combination, which make up, respectively, paradigms and syntagms. What we have just called base is only a particular form of syntagm. As for the invariant, it is the structure constituting a paradigm, one where both degree zero and the figured degree are found. The syntagm is actual, and the paradigm is virtual; the problem of the reduction of rhetorical deviations boils down to determining their point of intersection (see fig. 2).

A particularly interesting case is the one in which, by the operation to be described later (sec. 3.1), a unit of signification is suppressed and disappears from the message (ellipsis, silence, . . .). In this case, no invariant remains, and the base alone has to allow for, by its redundancy, a reconstitution of degree zero. But in suppressing one unit, we have suppressed it as a plastic and syntactic signifier and at the same time as a semantic and logical signified. Therefore, at times and according to what we want, figures of this type may be interpreted as forming a part of any one of our four categories:

as metaplasms they will be deletions,

as metataxes they will be ellipses,

as metasememes they will be asemias (*asémies*),

as metalogisms they will be silence and suspensions.

Many discussions on the nature of ellipsis have no other origin, and we see that it is the invariant and not the base that allows us to place a certain figure in a certain category.

2.5. Summary

In conclusion, rhetoric is a collection of *deviations* capable of *autocorrection;* that is to say, they modify the normal level of *redundancy* of language by breaking rules or by inventing new ones. The deviation created by an author is perceived by the reader thanks to a *mark* and subsequently is reduced thanks to the presence of an *invariant*. The totality of these operations, those generated from the producer as well as those grasped by the receiver, produces a specific aesthetic effect called *ethos*, which is the real object of artistic communication.

The complete description of a rhetorical figure ought, therefore, by necessity to include the description of its deviation (constituent operations of the deviation), of its mark, of its invariant, and of its ethos.

3. THE RHETORICAL OPERATIONS

Now that we have described in this way the material on which the operations work as well as their context, the operations themselves remain to be described. Until now we have grouped them under the general term "alteration," but it is clear that the term covers several types. On the general plane where we are trying to establish our structure, therefore, the operations themselves can be only quite general or very fundamental. We shall distinguish two large families: the substantial operations and the relational operations. The first alter the very substance of the units on which they work, while the second are limited to modifying the positional relations that hold between these units.[17]

3.1. The Substantial Operations

The substantial operations can be of only two sorts: those that suppress units and those that add to units. Thanks to the mechanics of decomposition described at length above, every apparent "transformation" can be reduced to suppressions of or additions to units. It is also possible to conceive of a united operation, which would be a result of a suppression and an addition.

We shall designate these respective operations by A and S, and alongside them we shall place a numerical index marking the number of units reached by the operation. The numerical value of this index will not be closely interpreted here, since this will be done later in the work. We can say simply that the more units suppressed (or added), the more the quantity of information of the message is lowered (or raised). We speak of semantic information here in the sense of Carnap and Bar-Hillel:* the precision of information is determined by the number of binary choices that one must make to receive it. In the field of metasememes, it is the level of the message's generality that is thereby raised or lowered in inverse proportion to the additions or suppressions made. The numerical index, then, marks a distance covered on a scale of generality. To conclude this question, let us finally make an empirical observation: during a

*[Y. Bar-Hillel and R. Carnap, "An Outline of a Theory of Semantic Information," in Y. Bar-Hillel, *Language and Information* (Reading, Mass.: Addison-Wesley, 1964), pp. 221–74. *Trans.*]

mixed operation AmSn we generally get $m \simeq n$ such that the quantity of information and the level of generality are more or less conserved.

The different types of general operations admit particular cases; for example, suppression may be partial or complete (in this last case, n equals the number of subunits in the unit), and addition may be simple or repetitive (if it is limited to repeating the units of degree zero signification). As for a mixed operation, it can be partial or complete but may also be negative when it suppresses one unit and replaces it by its negation.

3.2. The Relational Operations

The relational operations are simpler, since they are limited to altering the linear order of units without modifying the nature of the units themselves. We have here, in fact, *permutation*, which can be of any sort or by inversion. In the latter case, the order of the units in a spoken or written string is simply reversed.

3.3. Graphic Representation of Orthogonality

Table 6 assembles the different operations described—the only possible ones in the system—and reveals at the same time the relationships between these operations and the three groups of figures described above (sec. 1.1).

Table 6.   Compatability of the Operations and the Fields

	Group A (Infralinguistic decomposition— distinctive features)		Groups B and C (Linguistic decomposition and beyond)	
	Signifier	Signified	Signifier	Signified
Suppression				
Partial	+	+	+	+
Complete	+	+	+	+
Addition				
Simple	+	+	+	+
Repetitive*	−	−	+	+
Suppression-Addition				
Partial	+	+	+	+
Complete	+	+	+	+
Negative†	−	+	−	+
Permutation				
Of any sort*	−	−	+	+
By inversion*	−	−	+	+

NOTE: + = possible; − = impossible.
*A and B are opposed to C; that is, the infralinguistic to the "remainder."
†Signifier and signified are always opposed.

We note that the operation that would deny the existence of a phoneme, a grapheme, a syntactic structure, and so on, is without meaning. In the same way, the repetition of a seme within a lexeme is an empty concept. Permutation of semes within a lexeme also is impossible, since the subunits have a hierarchical order and not simply a linear one. For the same reason, the permutation of distinctive features is impossible within phonemes. It is doubtful that permutations are possible on the propositional plane, even though the hypothesis of a logical order allows us to imagine them. In addition, the simultaneous substitution of all the syntactic constants seems to be excluded.

Fig. 3

If we draw a linear scale beginning at zero (see fig. 3), we can segment it into a number of discrete units starting at zero and (at least in theory) going to infinity. Only the number of units (the index m or n) is to be considered, not the nature of the units. On such a graph, a unit with signification U can be represented by a point. The position of point U will correspond to the number n of subunits into which U can be decomposed. Operations A and S will then be displacements in the opposite direction on the line, as the schema shows.

The relational operations (permutations) change nothing in the number of units. They cannot be inscribed on the same axis and have to be considered as *orthogonal* (that is, conceptually independent) in comparison with the substantial operations. Completing our representation, we shall indicate them on the perpendiculars of the linear scale zero to infinity somewhat as we would the complex numbers in algebra. The theoretical number of permutations is

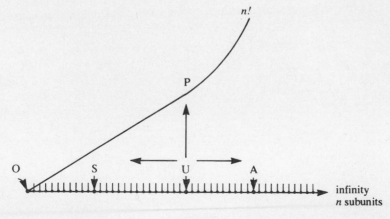

Fig. 4

limited by the number of subunits (for example, the number of letters in a word, number of words in a sentence). Its formula is exactly $n! = n\,(n\text{-}1)\,(n\text{-}2)\ldots 3.2.1$. The field of permutations P will then be limited by the curve $n!$, and we arrive at figure 4, which represents in some way a two-dimensional rhetorical space. This representation, far from useless, shows us immediately that the space is "enlarged" to the extent that n increases. The possibilities of rhetorical treatment of a unit are increasingly large in relation to the extent that it can be broken down into a larger number of subunits.

The table on the next page collects as examples a certain number of figures whose descriptions are to be found in the chapters devoted to the four large fields of metaboles (chaps. II–V).

General Table of Metaboles, or the Figures of Rhetoric

	EXPRESSION		CONTENT	
	GRAMMATICALS (Code)		LOGICALS (Referent)	
OPERATIONS	A. Metaplasms — On morphology	B. Metataxes — On syntax	C. Metasememes — On semantics	D. Metalogisms — On logic
I. SUPPRESSION 1.1. Partial	Aphaeresis, apocope, syncope, synaeresis	Crasis	Synecdoche and antonomasia (*partim*), simile, metaphor in praesentia	Litotes 1
1.2. Complete	Deletion, omission	Ellipsis, zeugma, asyndeton, parataxis	Asemia	Aposiopesis, reticentia, silence
II. ADDITION 2.1. Simple	Prosthesis, diaeresis, affixation, epenthesis,	Parenthesis, gradatio, epexegesis, enumeratio	Synecdoche and antonomasia (*partim*), archilexis	Hyperbole, hyperbolic silence
2.2. Repetitive	Reduplicatio, commoratio, rhyme, alliteration, assonance, paronomasia	Epimone, polysyndeton, meter, symmetry	*nothing*	Repetitio, pleonasmus, antithesis
III. SUPPRESSION-ADDITION 3.1. Partial	Child language, substitution of affixes, pun	Syllepsis, anacoluthon	Metaphor in absentia	Euphemism
3.2. Complete	Synonymy without morphological base, archaism, neologism, forgery, borrowing	Transfer of order, chiasmus	Metonymy	Allegory, parable, fable
3.3. Negative	*nothing*	*nothing*	Oxymoron	Irony; paradox, antiphrasis, litotes 2
IV. PERMUTATION 4.1. Of any sort	Spoonerism, anagram, metathesis	Tmesis, hyperbaton	*nothing*	Logical inversion, chronological inversion
4.2. By inversion	Palindrome, backwards talk	Inversion		

Chapter II
Metaplasms

0. GENERAL

0.1. The Phonetic Word

Metaplasm is an operation altering the phonic or graphic continuity of the message, that is, the expression-form in which phonic or graphic realization takes place. In this phonic continuity, the alteration that affects one or more phonemes is revealed only through its relationship to the whole unit or to higher units. In fact, a string of phonemes no element of which could be incorporated into a linguistic sign (sign in the Saussurian sense) would certainly constitute an alteration, but one definable only externally by a comparison with other phonic continuities whose relationship to the higher unit is clearly established. Hence, it is necessary first to define this higher unit, the word. We know that we are dealing here with a tricky question that at regular intervals disturbs the linguistic community. We are aware of the controversies engaging Vendryes, Trnka, Togeby, Martinet, Holt, Greenberg. From their works flows a whole stream that sometimes favors dropping the idea of the word; a disturbing stream, for all the other concepts built around the word/sentence axis are bound to fall. Nevertheless, we are forced to note one fact: the idea of the word is intuitively well established. Moreover, word as symbolic substance is an object that we encounter in our daily existence and, therefore, that can be described empirically. Finally, the essential point of controversy (which involves knowing whether the fundamental lexical unit is in fact constituted by the word or is to be sought at a lower level, a level analytically more elaborate) leaves intact for us the most important fact: the phonetic word exists; for "syntagmatic theory finds no difficulty in defining it as the lexicalized microsyntagm with a high degree of interior coherence among the terms."[1] Bloomfield calls it "a minimum free form."[2]

We may, then, provide a definition of *word,* and with respect for the findings of modern science, the definition will be analytic. If through a mental operation we dissociate the signified from the signifier in the act of reference, we can be content for the time being with a definition of one of these two isolated elements. On the plane of the signifier, therefore, the word will be *the discrete and given unit constituted by a decomposable collection of syllables or phonemes arranged in a meaningful order and allowing for repetition.*

Certain terms of this definition call for explanation. First, *discrete,* which takes into account the high degree of coherence of the microsyntagm. We know perfectly well that the contours of the word are at times fluid in their realization in speech, that different connections can appear between neighboring words in certain contexts and that this can obscure for some auditors the notion of the word. But here as elsewhere the pathological can clarify the normal. The delimiting guides of the lexical unit are certainly there to assure a certain coherence to each unit. The word *given* also needs clarification. If the word is part of the code, it must, in fact, be endowed with a certain stability in the speaking subject's competence. But all the products of the sound-producing apparatus do not enjoy the same stability. This is espcially the case with a number of onomatopeias that are not yet lexicalized and therefore present a relatively fluid aspect. Hence, in all these cases there will be some difficulty in speaking of rhetorical alteration. In fact, we can pose in principal that the less an organic group comprises constitutive parts (and from this moment they are less fluid), the more strongly the infraction of the system's laws is felt, and vice versa. An example that may appear somewhat silly is the onomatopoeia *boom,* a more or less faithful transcription of the noise of an explosion in the English phonological system.* We can compare it with its cousins *bam* and *baroom,* found in comic books. But these last two cannot be considered metaplasms by addition. Since onomatopeia is only weakly lexicalized, all its variants seem equally "plausible." But nonfunctional variations permitted in this way in the English language are in total number quite small, at least on the strictly phonetic plane. Therefore, it is thanks to the stability of the word that the listener can at once perceive the very existence of an eventual metabole and appreciate the deviation separating the new term from the form to which it is reducible because of the high degree of redundancy of the language.

0.2. Metaplasms and Metagraphs

Until now we have spoken of the word only as an essentially phonetic phenomenon. But the message is often perceived through another medium, writing. We must note here that orthography, a simple epiphenomenon when compared with the idiom as long as we remain on the strictly psychological or

---

*[In French *boum,* later *baoum* and *braoum.* In the original this sentence ends: "and illustrated by Charles Trenet." *Trans.*]

historical plane, plays a strong part in the image that the user has of his language.[3] The intellectual apprenticeship of the English language, in fact, emphasizes orthography, and it is often through this medium that the reader is in contact with the text. Strictly speaking, even if writing is not "a part of the language," as is stated in a work that makes some dangerously confusing proposals,[4] it is still necessary to note that the linguistic form can be manifested in graphic substance addressing itself only to the eye. One can know a language that one does not speak. Hjelmslev defended the linguistic status of the graphic substance by noting that "it is not always certain what is derived and what not" and that, anyway, "diachronic considerations are irrelevant for synchronic description."[5] These remarks lead us to make a distinction between the modes of production of the metaplasmic deviations. Metaboles, in fact, may be realized in the phonic substance (level p), where the definition of *word* given above is valid. But they can also be realized at the graphic level (level q). Now we are ready to propose a new definition of *word* to fit the matter at hand. It could be as follows: *a given discrete unit constituted by a collection of graphic signs arranged in a meaningful order and admitting of repetition*. We intend to call typographical signs *graphemes,* since they are carriers of signification. To distinguish the two fields is not, however, to oppose them, for between the two exists an area of intersection. The phenomena of transformation p that can alter the phonic constitution of the word will equally affect in the quasi totality of cases its graphic representation. In short, almost everything that is of p would be in q. We obviously mean here the *significant* transformations, and that is why we write *quasi* totality. For example, the substitution of apico-dental R for a velar r in a statement affects in no way either the content of the message or the form of expression. Nevertheless, the use of $R,$ $r,$ or ʁ is not without meaning for what it communicates—the social or geographical origin of the speaker or a parodic intent. These nonsignificant but phonostylistic variations do not appear in the written utterance ($p\bar{q}$), except in the regional pronunciations Twain may give his characters: the Dauphin says *kin* for *can,* and Tom Sawyer says *resky* for *risky*. This is why we speak of intersection (see fig. 5). If there is intersection, there are acts that embody q and not p ($\bar{p}q$). English orthography rejects, in fact, a rigorous transcription of the spoken chain; it is most often reduced to a series of *signals,* independent of the symbolized phonic substance. This characteristic, therefore, makes possible certain oper-

$\bar{p}q$: area of metagraphs

pq: metaplasms strictly speaking

$p\bar{q}$: area of phonostylistics

FIG. 5

ations on the graphic materials without which, in the operation of verbal decoding, the phonetic realization of the terms may be affected by a change. *Marseille* can be pronounced in an English way, but the relation unifying this emission with its graphic stimulus is not biunivocal, since E. E. Cummings has written *Mah-say* and we can easily imagine *Mar-say*.

We shall analyze by themselves the cases of *metagraphs,* or operations modifying the written aspect of the word without affecting its phonetic form. This paragraph is to be seen as only a simple byway in the field of meta-plasms. There should be no surprise if it is not always possible to create symmetry out of the cases of metaplastic and metagraphic tables. This is not the result of an inconsistency of rhetorical analysis but simply the anarchic graphic representation of English.[6]

0.3. The Levels

The caution we have shown defining *word* brings us to a third order of remarks. In question is the level on which one must base the fundamental lexical unit, finding the smallest meaning-bearing unit that is unable to be analyzed into further parts. We mentioned in chapter I the theory of levels and the two types of relations that units at each level could have. Certain units can have a smaller dimension than the word, others a larger one. In the spoken chain in English, as in all languages, connections of groups of elements can be made. Obviously, the series presenting the greatest coherence and clearest stability is the word. But each series can be tied more or less closely to preceding and subsequent series, and so on.

It is therefore important for us to define the successive points of view adopted in the course of this study. We shall choose three planes, of increasing complexity. We shall call the first the *infralinguistic* plane. This is the level of distinctive features that do not have any expression as such in language. From the phonetic point of view, these distinctive features are phemes (according to currently adopted terminology) or merisms (in Benveniste's terminology): voiced/unvoiced, only dental, labial; occlusive or fricative character. From the graphic point of view, these are the formal characteristics of the graphemes, which the analysts of electronic tooling companies have had to study to perfect their automatic photoreaders: straight, curved, curled, slanted, closed or open aspects. The second plane we call the elementary plane: this plane comprises the phonemes, which can be divided into morphemes and monemes (if we take a syntagmatic view), or syllables (from a purely formal view), before being regrouped into words. The third level, or *complex level,* is syntagms or regroupings of words endowed with a certain relatedness. The syntagms, in turn, may be grouped into sentences. The border between the field of metaplasms and that of metataxes is not, therefore, airtight, as we certainly suspected. Every metaplastic operation is, in our opinion, connected to this level, those operations altering the word as we have defined it having more than one lexical unit as a point of departure or as a result.[7] This tripartition, whose value on the general, theoretical plane[8] we have already seen, will permit us to classify in a rather precise manner all the possible types of metaplasms.

Another criterion, this one purely empirical, can refine this classification even further. When a group of elements is characterized by its linear extension (as is the case in levels 2 and 3), we can determine accurately the spot in this group where a substantial modification will take place. In this way suppression or addition can take place at the beginning, the end, or the middle of a word. Also in the course of our description of metaplasms and metataxes we shall have occasion to call on certain phenomena proper to versified poetry. We can consider this poetry as a type of subcode within language, a subcode imposing supplementary, formal conventions on the addresser.

Prepared in this way, we may now proceed to an abstract of the phenomena of the metaplastic order with no claim to exhaustiveness. For ease of description, in this chapter and in following ones, we shall class metaboles according to the operator in question.

1. SUPPRESSION

1.1. Suppression can exercise its effects at the infralinguistic level, as when one of the phemes is removed from the phoneme without hindrance to the production of the unit. The articulated quality of the word is thus altered. In a sentence such as "Ve haf vays of makink you talk," it is the disappearance of the bilabial feature that gives the impression of German pronunciation.[9]

Suppression at the elementary level can be more or less important and can be done at the beginning, end, or interior of the word. We obtain in each of the possibilities aphaeresis (*'pon* for *upon, 'nuf* for *enough*) and apocope (*prof, doc,* for *professor, doctor*). The *abscisio de medio* is represented by syncope (*ne'er, ma'am, bos'n*).[10]

Apocope can reach rather important proportions, as in the name of the Kafka character K or in some obscene exclamations that civilized convention used to abbreviate (s---, g-- d---, m----- f-----; the reader's imagination can complete the list).

Synaeresis, which is used as an artifice in versification, may be thought of as a suppression: *jewelry,* which formally has three syllables, may be reduced to two. There is a new arrangement of the phonetic elements according to a schema that reduces the number of groups forming syllables in a unit. The ancients also knew phenomena such as systole (the contraction of a long syllable) and synalepha (a fusion of vowels).

1.2. Every suppression, it should be remembered, may be complete. We then have the loss of the word, clear and simple, which is indicated in the sentence by a certain melodic inflection and represented typographically by a convention—three periods of suspension.[11] For example, in a citation taken from William Burroughs: "He looked at me through the tentative, ectoplasmic flesh of cure . . . thirty pounds materialized in a month when you kick . . . soft pink putty that fades at the first silent touch of junk . . ." (*Naked Lunch*). And a section of William Gass's "In the Heart of the Heart of the Country" begins

Politics

. . . for all those not in love,

Evidently we can speak of deletion only when the redundancy is sufficiently high to fill in each indicated absence. On the other hand, as we have already said, the operation of complete suppression has identical results in all four columns of the General Table of Metaboles: deletion is also ellipsis, asemia, silence. We can also claim that it is even more related to figures of content than to metaboles of form, since the type of redundancy involved is often semantic in nature.

2. ADDITION

2.1. At the infralinguistic level, the operation is again very simple. Under certain conditions (the combination of these elements obeying rather strict rules), a pheme can be added to an already existing phoneme. The result is exactly symmetrical with the result of suppression. Replacing *can* by *gan*, where the occlusive has been voiced, represents the same kind of phenomenon.

At the elementary level, addition can also take place at the beginning or end of the word. In the first case, we detail all types of prosthesis (as we encounter in *irregardless* and *yestereve* or in Joyce's "Horhot ho hray ho rhother's hest"), and of prefixation if the added element is a morpheme. In a writer's attempt to create archaic forms, we find *besought* and *howbeit,* while Rolfe writes *explete, surridiculous, perfricate, perpallid, subhilariously.* In the second case, addition creates a paragoge (*beforne*), and suffixation if the added unit is a morpheme: *birdie, girlie, fastidiose, Jesukin,* and all the verbs with *-(e)st* that were poetically perpetuated into this century. At the interior of the word, it is epenthesis (*steadyfast* or *visitating*), or infixation, as in Queneau's sentence "This is what I was thinkening while on my way to see Marcel," taken from *Odile.*

As the inverse of synaeresis, diaeresis can be considered addition, since it multiples the units within the word by changing a phonetic monosyllable into two syllables. In the following, scansion forces us to pronounce *medieval* in four syllables (the word usually has three) and *cruel* in two:

> Yet gained and grew and at a cruel pace
>
> [Wilbur]

> Miniver cursed the commonplace
>   And eyed a khaki suit with loathing;
> He missed the medieval grace
>   Of iron clothing.
>
> [E. A. Robinson]

The ancients were aware of a parallel phenomenon, ecstasis, changing a short syllable to a long. To poetry also belongs the convention of pronouncing final -*ed*'s, but it is to be found also in other contexts, particularly in quasi-biblical or quasi-epic language: "I bade farewell to my hornless goathood and struck out, a hornèd human student, for Commencement Gate" (John Barth).

At the complex level, addition gives us the chance to notice the interesting phenomenon, named by Humpty Dumpty, *portmanteau word*. This consists of the fusion of two words having a certain number of formal characteristics in common. The common element in *evolution* and *voluptuous* is *volu*. Thus a new word, *evoluption*, can be created that contains the first two words. It is certainly a case of addition, since one of the two words always remains predominant. When a solemn kiss is given by a character in his cups, and Raymond Queneau expresses it as "giving an *alcoolade*," the most important of the words is *accolade*, since it imposes on the phrase its semantic and grammatical function. The syntagmatic relations demand, moreover, the dominance of one of the words: *giving* has *accolade* as its complement and not *alcohol*. We cite a number of examples from Sir Thomas Urquhart's translation of Rabelais: *loobies* (*loon* plus *booby*), *snuttering* (*snorting* and *uttering*), *diabliculating*. A particular kind of portmanteau word has been called a "sandwich word" by Gaston Ferdière, a great specialist in this matter. In this case it is purely and simply the introduction of one unchanged word into another, such as Joyce's *comicsongbook*.[12]

2.2. We must add, finally, that addition may be repetitive. We shall not speak of *geminatio*, in which there is the repetition of the same word or group of words in the sentence, since the figure does not alter the form of the word itself. But doubling the whole word is within our province if the result is a new unit, as in the case of *bonbon*. We find this procedure in certain child languages, where all the words in the sentence are doubled. Obviously, repetitive addition may affect only a part of the word. If this unit is the phoneme, we shall get emphasis, as in "She is so sweeet!" or in this sentence: "The door went sqeeeeeeeeeeak and then I was on a dusty corridor with other doors" (Anthony Burgess). The element may be a syllable, where hypocorisms of the type *wowoman* are obtained. In France several sixteenth-century authors, especially Du Bartas, are noted for this type of creation by layering (*floflotter*), and the practice was not unknown in England (Skelton's *tytyvylles*).

These examples may seem sillilly. But it is by such additions that the most visible characteristics of universal poetry work. Rhyme is, in fact, nothing more than the regular recurrence of similar phonic units, since it can be defined as "homophony of the last stressed syllables of verse as well as of the eventually following phonemes."[13] Assonance, the homophony of the last stressed vowel of a defined verbal group (syntagm, verse), is also part of this series of procedures. The phenomenon of repetitive addition is especially clear in the case of echo rhyme:

O Who will show me those delights on high?
   Echo.   I.
Thou, Echo, thou art mortall, all men know.
   Echo.   No. . . .
Then tell me, what is that supreme delight?
   Echo.   Light. . . .

[Herbert, "Heaven"]

In this example the perception of the recurrence is reinforced by the contiguity of the phonic elements. The same is found in the case of crowned rhyme

By a grey eye's heed steered well, one crew, fall to;

[G. M. Hopkins]

or *rime emperière*

With a lover's pain to attain the plain

[Lanier]

Mary, Mary, quite contrary

which is nothing more than a particular case of internal rhyme:

Stuprate they rend each other when they kiss,
The pieces kiss again, no end to this.

[J. C. Ransom]

Hence, we obtain all types of alliteration, concatenated rhymes, anagram rhymes, and so on.

Come *sleepe*, o *sleepe*, the *ce*rtaine knot of p*ea*ce,
The *bai*ting pl*a*ce of *w*it, the *b*alme of *w*oe,
The *p*oore man's wealth, the *p*risoner's release,
The indifferent judge betweene the high and low;

[Sidney]

Note that graphic recurrence may be different from phonic recurrence. Thus in the first of the lines cited, there are three alliterating consonants, but only two initial graphemes are repeated.

Obviously, we cannot stop here. The phenomenon of homophony, taken simply from the metaplasmic point of view, is unable to account for the effectiveness of the rhetorical phenomenon. For it is clear that at the contextual level of style (see chap. VI) the effect of these repetitions depends just as much on the signified that they bring into play (grammaticality or ungrammaticality of the rhyme,[14] contrast of meaning as claimed by the theorists of paronomasia, and so on). Distortion between the phonic sequences and the semantic sequences can be better illustrated by the well-known holorhyme verses cited by Charles Cros or invented by Alphonse Allais:

> Où, dure, Eve d'efforts sa langue irrite (erreur!)
> Ou du rêve des forts alanguis rit (terreur!)*

In the example, for the entire length of similar phonic elements there are two completely distinct distributions of Saussurian signs. The signifier ends up, therefore, no longer distinctive. On the syntagmatic plane, we are stopped by the equivlance, or quasi-equivalence, of the two utterances. When these two utterances are integrated with the signifieds that they manifest, we are made aware of a dissimilarity at the higher distributional level.

Note that the conflict between grapheme and phoneme, on which we have already commented, has left traces here. Rhyme was, no doubt, made for the ear, but classical poetry wants the eye also to be satisfied. Racan's famous observations remind us of this.† Suddenly "rhyme for the eye" was born, and it can be found in Wordsworth (*call-festival*) as well as in Wilfred Owen (*groined-groaned*).

3.   SUPPRESSION-ADDITION

3.1. Modification can affect first of all certain distinctive features. This supplies examples like *grampa,* current in dialects, where the dental character of the nasalized occlusive has been replaced by a bilabial, or the phenomenon of dissimilation as well, as in *collidor* or *celebral.*

Instead of operating on a single distinctive feature, suppression-addition can concern several phemes and, therefore, several phonemes in the interior of a word. In this way we get Lewis Carroll's *burbled,* Spenser's *wimble,* and many traits of child language. If these phenomena affect all sounds presenting identical characteristics in a spoken sequence, we can get a representation of the aspirated pronunciation often attributed to Cockneys ("An' 'ere's to you,

---

*[In English we might propose something like the following:
 The sun's rays meet:
 The sons raise meat. *Trans.*]
†[Honorat de Bueil, Marquis de Racan (1589–1670), poet, disciple of Malherbe. *Trans.*]

Fuzzy-Wuzzy, with your 'ayrick 'ead of 'air'') or those amusing folk songs found everywhere where all the vowels are reduced to one only (in French the saw ''Buvons un coup, ma serpette est perdue''; in English ''How much wood would a woodchuck chuck . . .'') or those verses from an erotic poem by Papillon De Laphrise:

> I wanna wook on your gweaming eyes:
> For dey are the mirwors of chilwish Wuwerbyes,
> After I bites your bwosom my apwicot.
> Sudden I woosens your pwetty wittle titties,
> Then I tickles your wovewy wittle twat[15]

But to come back to less frivolous examples, substitution can affect a whole morpheme. Such is the case with the archaic word *fardel,* borrowed from French *fardal,* where the singular form was created from *farde* by analogy with nouns ending in *-al,* whose plural ends in *-aux;* or in the pidgin that Defoe made famous in *Robinson Crusoe:* ''O master! You give me te leave. Me shakee te hand with him. . . .'' It was also by substitution of the suffix that Sir Thomas Urquhart, translator of Rabelais, created the nouns *marsupies, unquicule,* and *inquirations.*

3.2. But we have stated that suppression-addition can be complete. In the field of metaplasms this operation gives rise to nothing less than synonymy.[16] Even if one feels that the results are trivial, complete suppression-addition as it functions is not basically different from the substitution of only one part of the word. The same type of relationship unites the synonymous pairs *to leave / to go away* and *despair / desperation.* In the second case suppression-addition is felt; in the first it is not. And yet we can explain it in the following way: all the elements of the signifier are suppressed for an identical signified and replaced by other elements. In other words, starting from the same concept, there is substitution at the level at which the concept is designated. In this way numerous lexical items lend themselves to the same semic analysis and yet are not formally identical: *to mete* and *to give,* for example, or even the series *to die, to expire,* and *to perish.*[17] These forms with identical semic content are differentiated, however, on the level of connotation, which semic analysis as it is usually practiced does not take into consideration.[18] Therefore, it seems that to each seme characterizing the lexical item another series of marks is added, marks used to distinguish the different levels of usage or the tone that separates certain words; thus the verbs *to conceal* and *to secrete* may be analyzed in the same way, but they are differentiated by a mark proper to the first and missing in the second.[19] But the semic kernel remains the same. We see, then, that synonymy is certainly a case of suppression-addition. The more or less homogeneous kernel is retained, but the plastic signifying elements are replaced, the substitution accompanied by displacements at the level of connotation.

The metaplasmic status of synonymy A (without a morphological base) is not as clear as morphological synonymy (B). In the case of suffix substitution, the invariant can be obtained just by using the signifier. Such is always the case when deviation is manifested through the lower levels (distinctive features, phonemes, even affixes). It is always achieved in a perceived unit relationship vs. a conceived unit relationship; for example, in *chaze* for *chase*, the perceived phoneme is /z/, the conceived phoneme /s/. Even if the deviation's reduction crosses several levels (including the semantic), it always takes place in an elementary relationship at the level of the signifiers. In synonymy A the invariant is, on the contrary, perceived through the signified. This is not easily imagined if one believes that in the phonemena taking place at the lower levels we go from the phonemes to the complete units that integrate them. At this more complex level we achieve the deviation between the emitted signifier and the conceived signifier, and then by a move backwards we join the deviation of the whole to the part, of the word to the phoneme. Apparently, the process is the same for any metaplasm where there is complete suppression-addition, where synonomy without a morphological base is only a particular case. But the integrating whole that permits the deviation's reduction is obviously to be found at a higher level—at that of the syntagm or the sentence. Hence, the reduction is almost always a semantic one. All these considerations demonstrate why there is a temptation to describe synonymy in terms of metasememes; that is, to replace *to think* by *to reason* does have, in fact, certain analogues with the process that is basic to metaphor and metonymy. But it is nevertheless true that synonymy may be completely understood through its signifying aspect in spite of the complexity caused by the level at which it is achieved. We shall, moreover, return to this question briefly in chapter IV, section 0.2.

In his work on synonomy Bernard Pottier demonstrates that a language's words can be characterized and classed through the relationships of inclusion and exclusion at the level of semes.[20] There are four possible relationships: (1) reciprocal exclusion, that is, having no seme in common (for example, *ship* and *mercury*); (2) intersection, where a certain affinity already exists (*ship* and *train* have in common the semes /means of transport/); (3) inclusion, that is, "partial synonymy" (for example, *boat* and *ship*); and (4) identity. This last case, theoretically possible, involves perfect synonymy, which is never realized. Obviously we share this perspective. Synonymy is certainly a case of inclusion. We shall close these remarks by stating that the included term is the unmarked term, usable in all circumstances, and that the marked term is the including term. The difference, more or less important, between the two terms resides in the inessential semes of connotation.

Some particular cases of stylistic synonymy are the archaism and neologism. The pairs *to mete* / *to give*, *beat* / *rub*, and *station* / *place* each have an unmarked referential term and a term marked as archaic.[21] One term will then be called archaic if it can be seen in the ''current''/''old'' opposition with another, synonymous, unmarked term. The verb *to mete* belongs to a chronological layer A of the language; *to give* to a higher layer B. The concept indicated by *mete* at time A has not undergone modification in time B. Only the relationships of designation have changed. In other words, there has been substitution of signifiers for the same signified. From that moment, the appearance to the word from layer A to designate the concept *to give* in a verbal act taking place at time B will have the effect of a distortion. But this depends more on the verbal material employed than on the simple presence of a figure. We shall discuss this point further.

Mutantis mutandis, the mechanism is identical for neologism,[22] where a relationship of synonymy is perceived at the same time that the character drops relationships that the invented word has with the state of the language.[23]

The neologism may be total, which gives us a coining. Lewis Carroll's ''Jabberwocky'' is the most famous extended example in English verse:

'Twas brillig, and the slithy toves
 Did gyre and gimble in the wabe;
 All mimsy were the borogoves, . . .

Note that the phenomenon of coining, which may extend to the entire sentence, leads us outside the linguistic frame when it is a sequence of different sounds to which, although no doubt they have been chosen from the spoken language, it is impossible to attach the slightest meaning. The redundancies of the discourse would no longer be enough to preserve communication. Such is not the case with ''Jabberwocky,'' since the regular syntactic structure and the portmanteau nature of some of the neologisms provide an approximate meaning. It is also not the case in certain artistic pieces where verbs, nouns, and pronouns can be distinguished, but it is certainly true for various gibberish pieces, the most famous of which were examined by Etienne Souriau in his *Sur l'esthétique des mots et des langages forgés*.[24] If we need convincing, a glance at the first lines of Lanternish, which Rabelais puts in Panurge's mouth, should suffice: ''Prust frest strinst sorgdmand strochdt drhds pag. . . .''

We can distinguish two kinds of complete neologisms. The first substitutes for the base term another unit already existing in the code. The second creates from scratch. The first type is often found in the works of Jean Tardieu, collected under the title *Un mot pour un autre*, but the classic English example is Mrs. Malaprop in *The Rivals*:

I would by no means wish a daughter of mine to be a progeny of learning. . . . I would never let her meddle with Greek, or Hebrew, or Algebra, or Simony, or Fluxions, or Paradoxes, or such inflammatory branches of learning, . . . but . . . I would send her, at nine years old, to a boarding-school, in order to learn a little ingenuity and artifice. Then, Sir, she should have a supercilious knowledge in accounts. . . .

In this type of metaplasm the author substitutes words, not as a function of their common semes, but as a function of their common qualities and certain common phonemes. The deviation is located at the level of lexical units, but it starts from phonic similarities and dissimilarities between emitted and conceived signifiers (as in paronomasia). In principle, the signified as such is not indicated, while by the very force of the emitted signifier the play /emitted signified/-/conceived signified/ for the moment upsets the decoding process. If, for example, "you still have the frying pan" can only mean "the word to laugh," it is nonetheless true that the relative propriety of *pan* and *frying* is clear. The second type of coining, frequent in the works of Michaux, Lewis Carroll, and Joyce, is more complex. Starting from the line of emission, in fact, several integrations are possible at the level of conceived signifiers and, from there, of signifieds. Francois van Laere, speaking of *Finnegans Wake,* proposed calling the most obvious figure of the book "hypogram," a term used by Saussure to designate the phenomena of anagram and apophony.[25] Take the sentence: "Walalhoo, Walalhoo, Walalhoo, mourn is plain." In addition to the verse by Victor Hugo, obvious at a glance,* one can alternate between "Walhalla, Walhalla, Walhalla, mourning is done" and ". . . the moon is full." Several readings, therefore, are possible, and they can be complementary or exclusive, according to the contexts or the decoders.

It should be remembered, finally, that the use of foreign terms also ought to be considered a metabole by complete suppression-addition. Obviously, these borrowings may well have different structures and functions:

I have rented an *atelier*

But all feel that *primo,* you should have your
family doctor tell her the facts of life. . . .

[Nabokov]

But nowe *debetis scire*
And groundly *audire,*
In your *convenire,*
Of this premenyre. . . .

[Skelton]

Before leaving the field of addition-suppression, let us again remark that substitution at the complex level may be effected from a word to a complex expression presenting neighboring articulatory peculiarities, or vice versa. This is play on words, for which we prefer the more precise "quasi-homonymic substitution." Here we can draw on folk speech play, especially certain children's genres: "As I walked down to the wayrail station, I met a bark and it dogged at me. I pulled a hedge out of a stake and necked its knock out."[26] It is hard to resist the pleasure of citing one of Brian O'Nolan's

---

*[Perhaps not all that obvious to the English reader. The reference is to the first line of "L'Expiation" (The atonement): "Waterloo! Waterloo! Waterloo! morne plaine!" (that is, "dismal plain!"). *Trans.*]

creations, published under the pseudonym of Myles na gCopaleen: of a dismal fund-raising carnival, he wrote, "A fête worse than debt."[27]

At first sight, the distinction between the phenomena of homophonic order originating, respectively, in repetitive additions and in addition-suppressions appears gratuitous. In fact, in all of the cases of repetitive addition (rhymes, paronomasia, and so on), the homophonic elements entertain by necessity syntagmatic relationships (for example: "all that cries, flies, sighs"); in addition-suppression, the initial term's manifestation is not required for there to be a figure. Hence we could define puns as paronomasia *in absentia* by taking account of the fact that through the similarity of signifiers it is the disparity of the signifieds that creates the metabole (for example, *The Tiger's Revenge,* by Claude Bawls). The perfect pun would involve total homonymy. In "Many a blonde dyes by her own hand," there is no longer phonetic opposition between *dyes* and *dies,* and we are on the ground of metagraphs.

4. PERMUTATION

4.1. There is no difficulty finding numerous metatheses among the morphological slips that good usage prohibits. Everyone has heard slips like *uncomftorble, hynoptism, pisgetti,* or the terrible *mitsake.* The anagram is only a further variety of permutation: François Rabelais wrote first under the anagram Alcofribas Nasier. This next example demonstrates that permutation can play with a number of words to the famous question *Quid est veritas?* ("What is Truth?") we get the answer *Est vir qui adest* ("The man who is here"). A certain modern painter has expressed his passion in his own name, since *Salvador Dali* can become *Avida dollars* or *va laid, d'or las* ("go ugly, bored of gold").[28] Instead of operating on simple phonemes, permutation can affect entire syllables, even in those cases where the syllables belong to distinct words, as in the case of the spoonerism, several volumes of which have been published by Jean-Jacques Pauvert.[29] Here is a whole poem largely constructed on phonetic and syllabic permutations:

Alerte de Laerte	Alert Laertes
Ophelie	of Ophelia's
est folie	folly and
et faux lys;	lily falsity;
aime-la	let's love her
Hamlet	Hamlet

[Michel Leiris]

4.2. But we know that permutation can occur through inversion. When two permuted units are elementary units, we get the palindrome, which is scarcely more than a social game.[30] The best-known examples of it are

"Madam, I'm Adam" and "Able was I ere I saw Elba," or parallelisms such as "Roma-amor." If the units are syllables, we get the game of mottos such as "Harold old Hair." Here the anagram is authentic, meaning that there is a real displacement of phonic elements, the groups [ŌLD] and [HĀR] permuting. In the other examples cited (anagrams for the eye), there is in particular a displacement of graphic elements with which the phonemes correspond, a displacement done in such a way so as to preserve a coherent signification for the phonetic sequence.[31] Therefore, we move here to the plane of metagraphs.

5. PARTICULAR QUESTIONS

5.1. Metaplasms and Literature

All these examples carry us into the field of verbal teratology. The reader wishing to find for himself numerous examples of the figures briefly examined here can check the venerable collection *Amusements philologiques* by Peignot or the indispensable work of Alfred Liede.[32] Let us lay to rest two harmful misunderstandings. The first concerns the literary status of metaplasms. We might be criticized for having borrowed a large number of our examples from what is generally called infra- or para-literature. Critics have already censured Jakobson for putting "I like Ike" on the same footing as the sonnets of Keats, for example. Our answer to this charge is that we are trying to take into account manifestations of rhetoric's function in its entire context, and to do this we ought, for the moment, to put aside every consideration of aesthetic order and, *a fortiori,* every value judgment.

The second misunderstanding is more serious, for it could be used to undermine the very foundations of this study. The illustrations we have supplied—and we have wanted to use striking ones—could lead to the belief that the generalized rhetoric we propose in this work claims to disparage the analysis of literary acts by the detection and dissection of flagrant abnormalities—a collection of "clinical cases," as one of the masters of stylistics would have said.[33] We ourselves, however, have pointed out the evils of a notion of deviation conceived of as a pathological phenomenon.[34] Paul Valéry, writing that style was a willed fault, did not then know what perilous ways he was going to open for certain stylisticians. Conscious of this danger, we are careful to note that it is the field here under examination that is responsible for this *trompe l'oeil* perspective. In the totality of the phenomena of literature, metaplastic manipulations, especially the relational ones,[35] are relatively rare, while the other metaboles—metasememes and metalogisms in particular—are very common.[36] This claim will be convincingly established in the course of the following pages. In any case, we do not have to be concerned here with the rarity or frequency of the phenomena we discuss.

5.2. Argot

Argot, which Marouzeau defined as "a special language with a parasite vocabulary used by members of a group or a social category concerned with distinguishing itself from the mass of speaking subjects,"[37] has frequent recourse to procedures altering the common language. Among these procedures a large proportion are metaplastic. We move rapidly over the case of truncation, whether made at the end, as in *cop, pug, prelim,* or initially, as in *bus, coon.* These are excellent examples of suppression. Let us pass just as quickly over the parasitic suffixations, which characterize *situationwise, bunkum, hornswoggle,* or *happymaking.* In some cases we can observe suppression-addition of the suffix (or at least of the end of the word): *momzer, splendiferous, triggerman.* More interesting to us are the procedures of metaplastic coding: there is the secret language called Arague, where the parasitic syllable *-arag-* is introduced into the body of the word. Other codes are more elaborate, like backwards language, or *verlen,* a perfect case of inversion by syllables (*partridge* becomes *ridgepart; peau de balle* becomes *balpeau,* which is complicated by suppression; and so on).* This process has corresponding ones in various languages: the *bahase balih* of Borneo women, the English *backslang* where the order of letters is reversed. Among all these types of coding, no doubt the most complex one is called in French *loucherbem:* for each word it calls for a simple permutation and a double addition. *Boucher,* the paradigm word, becomes *oucherb* by permutation, *loucherb* by initial addition, and *loucherbem* by parasitic suffixation. This process is similar to the one used by the Haiphong sampan population. Alfredo Niceforo, in his *Génie d'argot,* points out that they use a triple metaplastic alternation. They begin by suppressing the initial part of the word, proceed to an addition by repetition of the remaining sounds, and preface each of the repetitions by a *b* or an *s.*[38]

5.3. Metagraphs

Metagraphs or metaplasms that exist only on the graphic plane are relatively infrequent. Let us point out immediately that it is difficult to find purely visual permutations, although it is easier in English than in French—*meter* versus *metre,* for instance. Graphic addition is hardly more current. No one has contributed more metagraphs to English literature than has Cummings, in whose work we find *ssky, cccome, f-oo-l.* In the following passage from

---

*[For some discussion of the word games described here as well as others, see Joel Sherzer, "Play Languages: Implications for (Socio) Linguistics," in *Speech Play,* ed. Barbara Kirshenblatt-Gimblett (Philadelphia: University of Pennsylvania Press, 1976). pp. 19–36. *Trans.*]

Eliot's "East Coker," metagraphs by addition are used to achieve the impression of archaism:

> The association of man and woman
> In daunsinge, signifying matrimonie—
> A dignified and commodious sacrament,
> Two and two, necessarye coniunction. . . .*

In French, diacritical signs are easily added: from Céline's pen, next to *boûquins* we find *âmours*, which approximates the *hamour* of Flaubert.

It is also possible to conceive of addition by nongraphemic signs, as in *Hotel**** or *Croe$u$*, but here we are leaving the linguistic field proper. These are other elements coming into play: support and other diverse semiological substances.[39] When we read *Croe$u$*, we call on two substances: the conceived grapheme is certainly *s*, but another system is superimposed on it. These phenomena are less empty than they seem at first glance, for the text itself is also an *object*, and reading is not a purely linguistic operation.[40] The person who takes cognizance of a text may be impressed not only by the arrangement of the words but also by the form and color of the type, the grain of the paper, the shape on the pages.[41] Art is sometimes served by these features.[42] We have but to remember calligrams, which gain status from their use by Rabelais, Lewis Carroll, and Apollinaire.[43] Graphic suppression is equally rare: suppression of signs such as mute *h* or the *u* that unfailingly follows the letter *q* are conceivable, as well as the graphic apocopes regularly found in poetry (*nothin, th', 'em* for them). Obviously the most important phenomenon is suppression-addition, which makes the complex English orthography possible. Shaw's *ghoti* for *fish* is well known, and we encounter Dos Passos's *champeen*, Cummings's *cright, tratesmen,* and *missians,* as well as the sequence from Balzac, "une femme, une *femme,* la PHAMME." Moreover, place must be made for the archaizing metagraph: Spenser's poetry abounds in *shoote, blisse, hardie, brest, yvory, temperaunce, feend, glitterand.* These are phenomena similar to the substitutions that allow for puns that find their principal spring in homophony. But metagraphic phenomena do not interest us at the first level, since they come from the chance way that one can find graphics in any particular language and are not characteristics proper to the linguistic tool.

---

*[Since the lines are "borrowed" from Sir Thomas Elyot's *The Governour*, the archaism is somewhat more than an impression. *Trans.*]

Chapter III
Metataxes

0. GENERAL

Acting on the form of sentences, metataxes focus attention on syntax. One must then refer to the grammatical norm to attempt a definition of their degree zero. We state at the outset that our attitude toward syntax will depend on methodologies of distributional linguistics. According to these methodologies, grammar describes the possible combinations of the constituents of the sentence and defines them according to the combinations they can form. Syntax includes, then, the essentially structural relationships between morphemes. This means that grammatical description obviates a good number of logical criteria or semantic traits inherited from a long tradition. From this perspective, and using only one example taken from a contribution by René Lagane,[1] the subject of the sentence will cease to be considered as the term designating either the being or the object that accomplishes or undergoes the action, or even the being or object serving as the point of departure for the thought. We identify the subject as ''the substantive term indispensable for the realization of this utterance (the minimum utterance) by association with another term endowed with different morphological characteristics (the 'verb')''; to be precise, the subject precedes the verb, and by opposition with the object, it confers on this verb its marks of person, number, and, eventually, gender. Meaningful in this description are the distinctive formal features, such as combination, position, or mark.

It remains nonetheless difficult to eliminate all semantic value from the field of grammar. When syntacticians oppose the categories of active and passive or singular and plural, they are forced to bring content into the analysis, though they are now freed from having to give it the primordial role. In a more general way, syntax continues to occupy a shifting area between morphology, logic, and semantics. Thus, when Jakobson reveals an iconic or diagrammatic aspect of the phenomena of syntax, he brings us back to a logic of the sentence structure.[2] He shows that in most languages the order of words responds in different ways to the logic of the content: the succession of verbs corresponds to the chronology of the actions (*Veni, vidi, vici*), the priority of subject over object indicates the "hero" of the message, and so on. This is why, in defining metataxes according to distributional criteria, we will not forget that quite often they operate in a fashion concomitant with content and expression.

How is the syntactical degree zero to be defined? We cannot enter here into the maze of grammarians' discussions about the syntagm, the sentence, and their norms. It is rather a question of sketching a simple model acceptable to the majority and able to be used effectively as a point of reference.

The undertaking remains hazardous nonetheless and runs up against difficulties, the first of which arises from the fact that the concept of sentence is uncertain: there are as many definitions of the sentence as there are grammarians. The other major obstacle arises from the idea of norm in syntax. If one can say, operationally, that words have given forms—by means of which every alteration reveals itself evidentially as metaplasm—we form sentences and combinations of words starting only from virtual schemes, whose plasticity is at times quite broad. In many cases the speaker with a constant sum of information elements has recourse to different constructions of the sentence, no one of which may be obviously more normal than others. Preference is seen, then, as a "choice between . . . possibilities of the semantic stress's distribution among the different components of the sentence."[3] Our answer is that grammar, by prescription and description, establishes rules of formation and that consequently this freedom is quite relative. But this is only displacing the difficulty. What grammar in fact codifies in a certain number of cases are constructions convertible into a number of equivalents. At first sight, these "equivalents" are no more "normal" than the first ones: active voice changed into passive voice, substantive group plus adjective changed into an abstract substantive plus substantive. To resolve the problem there remains but one solution: aside from the fact that they are not the whole of English grammar, the competing forms may be classified (within the general system or within systems of particular usage) according to the frequency of use. The most common forms will also be the most normal and will more nearly approach degree zero. Such could be the theoretical solution. In practice, it will be still simpler to note that parallel constructions are often of such general usage, so common (active and passive, for example), that, from the point of view of rhetorical deviation, they have lost any force and hence their interest. We shall leave them to the grammarians, except for particular cases or uses.

In English, the degree zero of syntax may operationally be reduced to the description that is called "the minimal successful sentence." This is defined by the presence of two syntagms, the one nominal and the other verbal, by the relative order of these syntagms, and by the complementarity of their marks. In turn, these two syntagms have a minimal composition: the presence of a substantive and its determinant for the first; a verb (with the time, person, and number marked) eventually followed by another syntagm for the second.[4] From this schematization of the English sentence may be abstracted four major distinctive features, those most susceptible of rhetorical alterations:

1) The coherence of the sentence and the syntagms, that is, the presence of their minimal constituents
2) The function of the morphemes in classes (substantive, article, verb, adverb) that are defined first by the ability of the elements to fit certain positions in certain syntagms
3) The complementary marks that link the morphemes and syntagms and which are the representative signs of at least four large categories: gender, number, person, and tense
4) The relative order of syntagms in the sentence and of morphemes within the syntagm, including the linear distribution of the text.

Each of these points merits a brief commentary. Concerning the coherence of the sentence, it is natural that its definition first be minimal. But we could also think of defining a higher limit for it, for from the point of view of our operations, without a recognized maximum there is no longer perceptible addition. How is this idea to be introduced into grammatical theory? For a moment, it will perhaps be useful to borrow from certain linguists the distinction they make between competence and performance. The competence I have in a language teaches me that however well formed the sentence may be, its expansion is not limited. On the other hand, my experience in performance teaches me that a sentence in which, for example, several relative clauses are fitted together in a complex schema risks falling apart, either in being spoken or in being received. Here again, if thresholds of frequency were well established, we could be in a position to appreciate objectively facts of deviation. Until then, nonetheless, there is no doubt that these thresholds do exist.

As for classes, we simply note that they are situated at the place where syntax meets lexis. According to the usage of dictionaries, the definition of the word includes a mention of the class to which the word belongs. And, in fact, we shall see later that the metataxis obtained by substitution of class has something in common with metaphor, which belongs to the field of metasememes.

The complementary and categorical marks would have a certain tendency to lean toward metaplasm in their alterations. They possess, in fact, a tightly morphological character. When the mark appears, the word simply finds a segment added (affixation) or one of its segments changed (the index may be reduced to quite a small thing, like the *s* for plural). In fact, only alterations operate on the redundancy of the marks and consist of disturbances of agreement of syntagms. The most direct alterations hardly rise above the phonetic level (*two fishes*); others operate on more mediate and less constraining relationships between marked elements, allowing us to find the true syntactic plane.

From the rhetorical as well as the grammatical point of view, the order of words is the prime aspect of syntax. A poet such as Mallarmé, who loosens the ordinary sentence and remakes it in a hundred different ways, gives an accurate idea of the unknown possibilities offered by the distribution of the syntagms and their elements. Among these variations, all do not have the same importance. Even before reaching the rhetorical level, it is best to make a distinction, in company with the grammarians, between an intellectual order and an affective order of words: this is, for example, the difference in French between *un homme pauvre* ("a poor man") and *un pauvre homme* ("a wretched man"). Moreover, the syntagms that are assigned a fixed place in the sentence are not on an equal footing with other, more mobile elements. We know that English usage rigorously determines the position of certain syntactical constituents. The place of noun determinants is in general quite fixed, and other than for limited exceptions, the verb appears after the nominal-subject syntagm. Nonconformity to these rules results in flagrant transgressions. On the other hand, deviations become difficult to understand as soon as they affect elements with mobility. Consider, for instance, the circumstantial nominal-case syntagms and the detached adjectives, whose position is in large measure free from constraint. Consider even the place of adverbs and epithets. What difference are we to see, speaking syntactically, between "a tour unforgettable of Italy," "an unforgettable tour of Italy," and "a tour of Italy unforgettable"? But to see this more clearly, let us start with a complete sentence and its transformations:

    a) Furious, the man upsets the chair.

    b) The man, furious, upsets the chair.

    c) The man upsets, furious, the chair.

    d) The man upsets the chair, furious.

Analyzing this example, the best thing to do is to establish degress of normality or of alteration. It will be said that the first construction is perceived as more common and logical than the others, while constructions *c* and *d*, which put a distance between the substantive and its adjective, seem to deviate more from a certain norm. Here we find ourselves in that slippery zone of language where the freedom of the most ordinary speaker is exercised, where in one sense each realization constitutes a deviation by comparison with a more schematic or more abstract model.

Another problem is to discover by what operation these modifications of the relative order of syntagms and morphemes arise. Let us say immediately that we tend to link them as a group to permutation. To change an order is to displace it. Is it necessarily permuted? We must remember that the order in question is relative and that if the place of one segment is modified, the place of at least one other segment is caught in the mechanism of alteration. We can look again, for example, at the statements above and agree that the first of them represents the norm. There are four syntagms and, consequently, four positions. If I shift *furious* to position 2, then *man* moves to position 1; this is elementary permutation. If *furious* is shifted to position 4, two other syntagms change position, making for a more complex permutation. Thus the operation reveals its total meaning only when one is attentive to the displacement of the mobile element in relation to all the other elements in the sentence. This, however, does not preclude the possibility of certain doubtful cases. As we shall see later, hyperbaton also is derived from addition as well as permutation. This point will be discussed in the proper place, but here it allows us to make another point about the mechanism of permutation. In the same way as we understood substitution, we can see it as a mixed operation, using suppression and addition. An element is suppressed in one position and added in another. And, reciprocally, at least one other element is suppressed in its position and added in another. But all this is happening within a given context—a simple exchange made on the syntagmatic axis—while substitution calls into play elements outside the given base. By its mixed character, therefore, permutation is understood as an operation rich in resources. By maneuvering the positions, it appears to be the syntagmatic operation *par excellence*.

A last point: as was seen in the preceding chapter, there exist deviations founded on a convention and working within a system. Meter offers the perfect example of this: as a group of rules, it forms a code superimposed on the code of usual expression. One might think of including this systematized deviation in metataxis. Certainly it is first necessary to distinguish between the action of meter on the breakdown of the sentence and its phonic features, stresses and rhyme. Meter is to be considered here only as a mode of distribution of syntagms. Analyzing the sentence according to stress models, English meter either emphasizes and reinforces ordinary syntax or comes into conflict with it and distorts it. It is also to be noted, however, that classical versification allows for syntactical alterations such as inversions, ellipses, and so on, as ways of adapting the ordinary sentence to a metric scheme, making these alterations, therefore, figures of figures.

Considered as a total system, meter arises from a unique operation: addition. In fact, to a "text" whose fragmentation in sentences and syntagms is translated by intonation and pauses or by spaces and punctuation, versification adds the structure of verses, which is defined by a more substantial—because stressed—and more regular distribution. When there is the tendency, as in classical English poetry, for the verse to confirm and accentuate the sentence structure, so that in essence the limits of the sentence and of the iambic pentameters coincide, meter is not only an addition but even a repetition:

> But most by Numbers judge a poet's song,
> And smooth or rough with them is right or wrong;
> In the bright Muse though thousand charms conspire,
> Her voice is all these tuneful Fools admire. . . .
>
> [Pope]

Verse is presented, then, as a total phenomenon of metatactic addition. We could, however, reverse the perspective. We could start from the point according to which meter, working basically on feet and not on morphemes, belongs to a presyntactic level. Then it would be agreed that in poetry it is syntax that is made to conform to meter, and not the contrary. This would allow an easier evaluation in terms of deviations from the syntax that disturb the harmony of the parallelism between verse and sentence—enjambment, for example. We can, in fact, succeed in doing this by keeping our first point of view. Since meter is posed as an additive deviation of the whole, we are in a good position to inventory the particular deviations or alterations within the system. From this point of view, enjambment is understood as a partial suppression of the metric form (to which we shall return later). In the same way, substitution and permutation could disturb this norm at the second degree, which the rules of versification define.

Although not codified, the harmony of the sentence is assimilable with versification and can be counted as metataxis by addition. If anyone is surprised at seeing the effects of harmony called alterations, we note that common discourse is hardly concerned with creating regularity or equilibrium. It is only through a second try and by departing from standard usage that common discourse tries to put words in a well-ordered way. Harmony is, then, seeking a goal foreign to simple, effective communication and aiming to focus attention on the message by granting privilege to the expression. For this reason, the processes of harmony are without doubt figures. The most elementary of these is symmetry:

What murdered Wentworth and what exiled Hyde,
By kings protected and to kings allied?

[Samuel Johnson]

My daughter! with thy name this song begun—
My daughter! with thy name thus much shall end!

[Byron]

Symmetry is the repetition, in a way that is to be perceived, of a certain syntactic sequence. Therefore, it adds structure to whatever structure the ordinary sentence had.[5] It can also be simply something like a balancing of parts of the sentence. Squared period was the name given to periodic sentences where protasis and apodosis each had two members of nearly equal length. From this procedure to the introduction of measure in prose is hardly a step, and there can be found in the works of prose writers sentences in which the feet can be scanned as iambic pentameters or derivatives. But, as soon as the harmony of the sentence is established as a norm or habit, new deviations may be formed, here again by comparison with the first figure.

1. SUPPRESSION

Since we have given as norms a minimal sentence and minimal syntagms as defined by the presence of certain syntagms and certain morphemes, it goes without saying that every break in the coherence of these groups will be the equivalent of a suppression and will constitute a figure.

1.1. It would seem that partial suppression is rarely found in syntax so long as one keeps to the smallest units. The most obvious traits correspond to a kind of *crasis*, in which is found usually a substantive and/or its adjective contracted to form a single element: *miniskirt, wash-o-matic* (for *automatic washer*). The process arises from grammatical affixation and from lexicalization, but it first derives from a phonic suppression. Along with this, we cite the case so frequent today in journalistic, technical, and advertising language of running two nouns together by an abridgement that at the same time shortens both thought and syntax. *Mini-golf,* which is well known today, was first called miniature golf, which in turn was originally an abbreviation of "golf in miniature." Here is a similar abridgment used parodistically:

Who owns these questionable brains? *Death*
All this messy blood? *Death*
These minimum efficiency eyes? *Death*
[T. Hughes, "Examination at the Womb Door"]

In fact, the resulting syntactic reduction is less meaningful than semantic suppression. In a slogan like Operation Milk Bottles, while the logical norm calls for a formulation such as "operation for collecting milk bottles," the syntactical order could be satisfied by a correction such as "operation for milk bottles." This is why we speak of partial suppression. But if one does, in fact, wish to consider that the nouns *milk bottles* and *minimum-efficiency,* as they are used above, tend to become adjectives, the initial suppression is emphasized by substitution of the class, a more radical operation.

1.2. Complete suppression is *ellipsis*. Aposiopesis, ordinarily related to it, is the failure to finish the sentence, so that part of its meaning is lost. This is a figure more of content than of expression, even if the syntax is affected, and which will be discussed in the chapter on metalogisms. In what is properly called ellipsis, on the other hand, the information remains complete in spite of the incomplete form. Is it proper to speak of something "understood," as in the tradition of grammarians and rhetoricians? The different modes of ellipsis will allow us to propose a more refined explanation according to which, in a general way, the normal elements that are omitted remain in mediated form, in one way or another, in the context.

The following sentences represent, successively, ellipses of the subject, the determinant of the noun (definite article), the verb, and the verb phrase (nominal-object syntagm):

> Am strong myself compared to yonder crabs
>
>   [Browning]
>
> No mouth had, no nor mind, expressed
> What heart heard of, ghost guessed
>
>   [Hopkins]
>
> And he to England shall along with you
>
>   [Shakespeare]
>
> I replied to the yells of him who clamored. I re-echoed—
> I aided—I surpassed them in volume and in strength.
>
>   [Poe]

The absence of *I* in the first sentence and of *the* in the second is allowable because of the redundant, that is, strongly predictable, character of these forms. Thus, the marks of person and number that *I* expresses are already found in *am; heart* is recognized as a definite noun even without the article, and the logic of the text carries the rest. On the other hand, the words used by Shakespeare and Poe are words with distinct and complete meaning that the writers have chosen to use economically. And yet their predictability is scarcely weaker, and their absence is no less justified: the omitted terms have already been used (in the same sentence in the Poe; in the same passage in the Shakespeare). When ellipsis is used, parallelism of the construction allows completion of the sense. The ellipses in the Poe are revealed by the absence of the pronoun-object syntagm after the transitive verb. The complete and normal expression is easily established because the verbs *re-echoed* and *aided* pick up *yells* of the previous sentence and the later *them*. The suppression worked by Shakespeare is known as *zeugma,* a figure that R. LeBidois defined in his column in *Le Monde* (August 1964) as "a construction that consists in not repeating in one member of the sentence a word or group of words expressed in an identical or analogous form in an immediately neighboring clause without which the incomplete clause would be unintelligible." Other examples of this type of ellipsis follow:

> One leaf she lays down, a floor of granite; then a thousand ages, and a bed of slate; a thousand ages, and a measure of coal; a thousand ages, and a layer of marl and mud; vegetable forms appear; her first misshapen animals, zoöphyte, trilobium. . . .
>
>   [Emerson]
>
> She stained her honour, and her new brocade
>
>   [Pope]

The case of the nominal sentence, the sentence without verb, is worth special treatment. No word has undergone ellipsis, but since the verbal syntagm is missing, the "minimal sentence" is not respected. It may be that the verb has in some way been changed into a noun, has shifted to a noun its meaning and part of its function. Thus, in the first of the following examples it could be said that the noun *races* has taken the place of the verb *run,* a verb present in the preceding sentence. In the last example, on the other hand, there is simply suppression of the verbal function:

The children run, the pigeons fly off. Races, white flashes, minor rout. [Sartre]

Funny sight of them together, their bellies out. Molly and Mrs. Moisel. [Joyce]

I have made myself rules: no touching, nothing overt. Only the spoken tones of joy and desire. [Hawkes]

Gas looming through fog in divers places in the streets, much as the sun may, from the spongey fields, be seen to loom by husbandman and ploughboy. [Dickens]

The suppression of connecting words is a deviation felt in different ways. The most obvious figure, known as *asyndeton* or *articulo,* designates the suppression of marks of coordination. It is quite clear at the end of a series or when a plural determinant is linked with two substantives simply posed:

Faynt, wearie, sore, embroyled, grieved, brent
With heat, toyle, wounds, armes, smart, and inward fire.

[Spenser]

You will enter the world where death by fear and explosion
Is waited; longed for by many; by all dreamed.

[Rukeyser]

The sentence from Sartre above could also have included an *and* in the place of the comma. If, however, one considers the meaning, a causal or sequential link would have been more expected. The ellipsis of this linkage is an example of *parataxis,* a figure that is evident only to the extent that one tends to finalize occasionally the connections between signifiers. I can see the logical connection between the two independent clauses perfectly, but I prefer to see it expressed clearly by a conjunction or an adverb. We obviously know that the relative order of clauses and certain punctuation marks already indicate logical or temporal relationships, but it is, then, a case of weak signs that show even more clearly any absence indicating parataxis:

They're incredibly soft. They're real cloth. They're Soft Cloths. [Advertisement in *Redbook*]

Close to asyndeton and parataxis is the suppression of punctuation. One can debate at length the usefulness of certain commas, but to totally eliminate punctuation, as so many poets and prose writers since Apollinaire have done, has certainly become a figure. Jean Cohen has spoken elegantly[6] about the second verse of "Le Pont Mirabeau," a syntagm-verse that because of its lack of punctuation may be attached meaningfully either to the preceding or to the following phrase. The suppression of commas and periods may muddy syntax to the point of creating semantic uncertainty, but this is not always the case. In the following lines of James Joyce the disappearance of punctuation weakens the lines of articulation of the message, but in spite of the use of a sort of adjectival style (using participles rather than verbs), the normal distribution of syntagms maintains the desired clarity of the sentence structures:

> . . . whenever he was there meaning him of course glauming me over and when I said I washed up and down as far as possible asking me did you wash possible the women are always egging on to that putting it on thick when hes there they know by his sly eye blinking a bit putting on the indifferent when they come out with something. . . .
> [*Ulysses*]

After the attack on punctuation, certain poets—spatialists among others—took off against the ususal linear shape of verse, preferring a freer, more inventive topology. This was a radical form of suppression one merit of which was to reveal that the normal syntax of a sentence in a text is also defined by the linear topology. Pierre Garnier uses a mosaic form to sketch a new system of relations between words:

<pre>
                            Praise of God
                            MAHOMET
                SUN   POPLAR
RIMBAUD   GOD   BEETHOVEN
                WHEEL   STAR
                            JESUS
</pre>

Returning to poetry faithful to versification, we can say something about the suppression operating on metrical number. Enjambment partially denies meter. When the sentence of one verse impinges on the following verse, there is a break in the parallelism expected between verse measure and syntactic form. Enjambment is, therefore, a return to a sort of prosaic language by suppression of "form":

> The question everywhere was why should Paul
> Object to being asked a civil question—
> A man you could say almost anything to
> Short of a fighting word. You have the answers.
>
> [Frost]

While considering the harmony of the sentence, we find a similar suppression in "The eternal silence of these infinite spaces scares me" (Pascal). The mechanism of deviation is quite clear: the sentence first establishes itself in terms of number and symmetry, since the nominal-subject syntagm comprises two groups of six syllables each formed with the same sequence (determinant

+ epithet + noun); then with the two-syllable verbal syntagm there is a break. The sentence is "cut short" and loses its balance.

2. ADDITION

The minimal complete sentence that has been represented in schematic fashion constitutes also the maximum sentence. While it is both permitted and common to multiply the principal elements, adding all sorts of secondary syntagms and morphemes, we can still consider deviational additions (1) the act of according primacy to secondary elements (the primacy felt principally by their relatively greater length); (2) the act of increasing the relations, and reducing the contacts, between the principal elements; and (3) the act of adding any particular structure to the normal structure with the view of bringing attention to the message. When Marcel Proust modifies a noun with a string of three or four adjectives, he is already sinning against the normally constituted model. When Max Beerbohm keeps putting off the principal clause, he is honing his parody on the "elasticity" of English syntax:

> In the heart of insular Cosmos, remote by some scores of leagues of Hodgetrod arable or pastoral, not more than a snuff-pinch for gaping tourist nostrils accustomed to inhalation of prairie winds, but enough for perspective from those marginal sands, trident-scraped, we are to fancy, by a helmeted Dame Abstract familiarly profiled on discs of current bronze—price of a loaf for humbler maws disdainful of Gallic side-dishes for the titillation of choicer palates—*stands Clashthought Park,* a house of some pretension, mentioned at Runnymede, with the spreading exception of wings given to it in later times by Daedalean masters not to be baulked of billiards or traps for Terpsichore, and owned for unbroken generations by a healthy line of procreant Clashthoughts, to the undoing of collateral branches eager for the birth of a female.

2.1. Simple addition, at least, presents a case where there is an infraction not relative to the grammatical code—the added elements are what could be called closed syntagms. A fine example of this is seen in the use of intransitive verbs, those not ordinarily followed by an object syntagm but which may at times have one used figuratively (in certain cases with pleonastic value):

> Build then the ship of death, for you must take
> the longest journey, to oblivion.
> And die the death, the long and painful death
> that lies between the old self and the new.

> [D. H. Lawrence]

But generally, simple addition results from two typical procedures, digression or development. In the case of digression, the central line of the text or sentence is broken because it is overcharged with annexed elements, which are threaded into the parts or may even change the original direction. This is *interpositio* or *parenthesis:*

> But a critic having written that in Vermeer's *View of Delft* (on loan from the Museum at The Hague for a Dutch exposition), a painting which he adored and believed he knew quite well, a small patch of yellow wall (which he didn't remember) was so well painted that it was, when looked at in particular like a precious piece of Chinese art with a beauty sufficient to itself, Bergotte ate a few potatoes, left and went to the exposition. [Proust][7]

Elsewhere it is *gradatio* or *climax:*

> For your brother and my sister no sooner met but they looked; no sooner looked but they loved; no sooner loved but they sighed; no sooner sighed but they asked one another the reason; no sooner they knew the reason than they sought the remedy; and in these degrees have they made a pair of stairs to marriage. [*As You Like It,* act 5, sc. 2, lines 36–42]

Expletion also corresponds to this development. The syntagm can be surrounded with expletives to make it stand out:

> That night, that year
> Of now done darkness I wretch lay wrestling with (my God) my God.
>   [G. M. Hopkins]

One can also open up the syntagm by multiplying aspects of attributes of one of its lexemes. This is *enumeratio* or *accumulatio,* by its nature synecdochic:

> All things counter, original, spare, strange;
> Whatever is fickle, freckled (who knows how?)
> With swift, slow; sweet, sour; adazzle, dim. . . .
>   [Hopkins]

It must also be noted that rhetoricians of the past saw certain kinds of appositions as figures of development. Fontanier speaks of them as ''construction through exuberance.''[8]

2.2. To make something out of repetitive addition is perhaps to be understood as considering every word repetition as metataxis. We must distinguish clearly here between the semantic and syntactic because repeating a word is adding a meaning. We can nonetheless take as a specifically formal procedure the *epimone* of a verb or noun when the goal is to introduce determinants in order to make its meaning more precise. This is another form of expletion, where the repeated term has first of all a supporting value:

> Or if thy mistress some rich anger show,
>   Imprison her soft hand, and let her rave,
>   And feed deep, deep upon her peerless eyes.
>   [Keats]

In the same way, a figure such as *polysyndeton,* which emphasizes and gives special value to the syntactic relation by repeating marks of coordination, is certainly metataxis by addition:

Then the camel men cursing and grumbling
And running away, and wanting their liquor and women,
And the night fires going out, and the lack of shelters,
And the cities hostile and the towns unfriendly
And the villages dirty and charging high prices

[T. S. Eliot]

In Eliot's lines the coordinating function of *and* is doubly strong because of its anaphoric value, as the parallel series of participles clearly shows. Polysyndeton, in fact, is responsible for the harmony of the sentence and the metrical scheme of the verse. This is not by chance, since, as we have seen, harmony and metrics are systematic groups of practices and rules, two vast syntactic figures that proceed by addition and repetition.

We have already shown in what way symmetry and the classical heroic couplet constitute metataxis. We shall simply add here that it is not rare in poetry for accentual measure and parallel syntactic sequences to go hand in hand to form a strong formal redundancy. In Dryden's *All for Love,* for example, the two procedures tie relationships in a tight mimeticism. On the one hand, the median caesura corresponds to the end of a sentence or of a phrase, or even of the reply; the second hemistich is a perfect reflection grammatically of the first:

CLEOPATRA: I knew him well.
Ah, no, I know him not; I knew him once,
But now 'tis past.
IRAS: Let it be past with you;
Forget him, madam.

At its extreme, as we see by the second sample, "perfect" syntactic addition could be confused with the simple repetition of a syntagm or a whole sentence.

3. SUPPRESSION-ADDITION

This double or mixed operation will be able to take effect beginning with classes and categories such as we have defined above. An element of one class is substituted for one of another class, and the mark of one category is replaced by another, inadequate mark taken from the same category.

3.1. *Syllepsis* includes any rhetorical omission relating to the rules of agreement between morphemes and syntagms, whether it is agreement of gender, number, person, or tense. The substitution achieved here is only partial in that it is not between categories but simply from one mark to the other inside a category, Strictly speaking, however, the operation is double only in certain cases. Thus, present tense and singular number considered as unmarked cases are modified only by addition of a mark, and they modify only by suppression of a mark.

Because of the imperative character of the grammatical rules of agreement, alterations are rarely evident. As Henri Morier notes,[9] the verse of Racine "[this fearful place]/From which your sex and your impiety banishes you" appears to us today as simply incorrect. Few syllepses of this type are to be found in modern authors, with the exception of surrealist writers with a mind for play. In John Berryman's *Dream Songs*, however, this kind of syllepsis serves to distinguish voice:

> Nothin very bad happen to me lately.
> How you explain that?...
> —You is from hunger, Mr. Bones,
> I offers you this handkerchief....

Syllepsis rarely occurs in cases where the terms are so clearly tied as subject/verb or noun/epithet; it is more frequent in the relationship between somewhat separated, autonomous elements. Usually it disturbs the agreement between two verbs or the agreement of a pronoun with the noun for which it is substituted. Person, number, and gender can be modified by this change from noun to pronoun:

> Morning, one awakes, and a whole family
> Embraces you, a mother, a sister, a daughter.
>
> [Hugo]*

> i try if you are a gentleman not to sense something un poco putrido
> when we contemplate her uneyes safely ensconsed in thick glass
>
> [Cummings]

> Here my sweete sonnes and daughters all my blisse,
> Yonder mine owne deere husband is.
>
> [Puttenham]

The problem of substitution of person, as in our first example, calls for particular comment. We should say first that within the system of personal pronouns just about all exchanges are permissible, as literature and affective language show. Not many of them, however, derive strictly from syntax. If Hugo can, within the same sentence, create equivalence between the second and third persons (*you* and *one*), it is because he can exploit the well-known plasticity of one (*on*), a pronoun able to take on the value of any other

---

*[In the original: "Le matin, on s'éveille, et toute une famille / Voux embrasse, une mére, une soeur, une fille!" *Trans.*]

pronoun (to the extent that French grammar allows this unmarked pronoun to be masculine, feminine, singular, or plural). But most often the transpositions of persons escape the notice of grammarians because the deviation refers to a reality outside of or prior to the text. In the following examples, we can see a third and first person successively take the place of a second person, a first, and a third: in the formula, "Madame is served"; when De Gaulle speaks of himself—or Caesar writes of himself—as "he"; and when Homais says of the poisoning of Emma Bovary, "We first had a feeling of siccity in the pharynx," how can we establish a norm for speech? By our awareness of a referent because we know the voice of De Gaulle and we know that Homais has not poisoned himself. Note, however, that the psychological maneuvering that employs one personal pronoun for another may have consequences even at the grammatical level. This is the case when in the same text two different pronouns refer to the same signified. Here we see a syntactic dimension reappear, as in the passage from Cummings above or in that from Flaubert below, where we find *I* and *you* neighbors, *he* for beings, *that* (*ça*) for things:

> She stays home to mend socks. And how bored one is! How wonderful to be able to live in a city, dance the polka every night! Poor little woman! One [*ça*] yearns for love as a carp on a kitchen table yearns for water.

The sequence of tenses offers a rich field of exploitation to suppression-addition. Syllepsis can remain limited in scope:

> From the other side of the corridor, looking through a window covered completely by a material woven from drops of rain, you guess from that reflection of aluminum that what is approaching, passes by and disappears was an oil tanker. [Butor]

Syllepsis may also occur as a series of verbs having a sustained character. Think of the appearance of the historical present, or even of indirect, free discourse, for several lines in a text. Remarkable in the next example is that the figure is created by making a sequence of tenses at the wrong time. In fact, in free, indirect style, the verbs of the surrounding story are in the third person past tense, while the sentences keep the form of direct style:

> I am a rather elderly man. The nature of my avocations, for the last thirty years, has brought me into more than ordinary contact with what would seem an interesting and somewhat singular set of men, of whom, as yet, nothing, that I know of, has ever been written—I mean, the law-copyists, or scriveners. I have known very many of them, professionally and privately, and, if I pleased, could relate divers histories. . . . Bartleby was one of those beings of whom nothing is ascertainable. . . . [Melville]

Syllepsis may also be the product of a break in the structure, then called *anacoluthon*. For the noun-subject syntagm that the first elements of the sentence implied (participial phrase, adjectives in apposition) is substituted, for example, another with different agreement:

> Rather proclaim it, Westmoreland, through my host,
> That he which hath no stomach to this fight,
> Let him depart.
>
> [*Henry V*, act 4, sc. 3, lines 34–36]
>
> . . . they which brought me in my Master's hate,
> I live to look upon their tragedy.
>
> [*Richard III*, act 3, sc. 2, lines 55–59]

Prose as free as Céline's brings anacoluthon to a rupture and more radical substitution. In the following sentence, the final *shaken* is attached only to an absent and hypothetical *us:*

> Everything in the immense building and the building itself shook, from top to toe, possessed by the quake; it was coming from the windows and floor and the iron work, shocks, shaken from top to bottom.

3.2. Complete suppression-addition has come to mean the replacement of an element belonging to one class by an element borrowed from another class and the creation in this way of an incongruous relationship between the constituents of the syntagm or of the sentence. Common language accepts the phenomenon of transfer from one class to another, since it lexicalizes commonly as nouns, for example, verbs, adjectives, locutions (under their original form or under a derived form). In this case, the first verbal or adjectival value has a tendency to disappear, except when the poet chooses to bring it back to life as in the hybrid construction: "Thou has bound bones and veins in me, fastened me flesh" (Hopkins).

It would certainly be correct to call the figure under discussion a "syntactical metaphor." As in metaphor, there is substitution based on a certain similarity. It is true that the formal resemblance that we find here is not as clear as the semantic resemblance of comparisons. We observe, nonetheless, that syntactical substitution operates more easily by creating a less brutal deviation, working from neighboring or assimilated classes rather than from distant or opposed classes. A few examples will show this quite well. In the same way as a substantive, the infinitive and clause hold nominal value. Thus we can easily substitute or coordinate one with the other:

> On the long shore, lit by the moon
> To show them properly alone,
> Two lovers suddenly embraced
>
> [Nemerov]

> He noticed for the first time some small figures painted in blue, that the sand was rose, and finally the most precious matter of the small patch of yellow wall. [Proust][10]

To exchange or combine in the same way substantive and adverb or substantive and adjective is already a further mark, but it also relies on a certain relationship:

A grief ago

[Dylan Thomas]

She jabs her wedge head in a cup

[Robert Lowell]

The hurt that troubles a whore's eyes
And lovely as a panther

[Apollinaire]

The hot of him is purest in the heart

[Wallace Stevens]

In this last example, the substitution depends on a figure of permutation to be discussed later, the shifting of the epithet behind the substantive it determines. The actual transformation of the group adjective + noun often gives rise to a deviation of the adjective into an abstract noun: "Renée disappeared into the vague whiteness of her gown" (Goncourt).

The most marked deviation seems to be that represented by the figures that bring into conflict the two basic classes of the minimal sentence, the substantive and the verb. Those who try to utilize this figure risk dissolving the act of communication, at least on the denotative plane:

he sang his didn't he danced his did.

[Cummings]

More perhaps than in poetry, it would be interesting to study these syntactical transfers in the most spontaneous and familiar oral language. We would perceive that when we fail to find immediately the word or expression needed, it is not rare to "jump" quickly from one class to another for those substitutes that will carry the signification *grosso modo,* with no concern for grammatical coherence. This time, differing from poetic figures, priority is given to the signified at the expense of the signifier. Queneau, as was proper, was interested in these oral bifurcations and made from them a literary school. He uses at times a shortening that can catch in a word-sentence a complete verbal syntagm. Other times he uses periphrasis, which moves a simple determiner into a clause. E. E. Cummings operates in his prose in the same way:

O sir this is a Watch; not just a watch: why, this Watch is "incroyable" and "suisse" and "guarantie" and it costs—not a mere $50—only 3½ Turkish lire. & what should the face of Watch of supremely of perfect of wondrous of just-like-that be labelled but
"TOSCA."

Note also P. G. Wodehouse's "*Mens sana in*-ah-*corpore,* in fact, *Sano,* yes!"

We come back now to those additions in the sentence that are metrical and rhythmical. In both cases, the fundamental figure can enter into any combination with a suppression. Thus, in a periodic sentence it can happen that the order in the first part may be changed symmetrically in the later development. We obtain *chiasmus* in this way. Chiasmus is the traditional name for a crossed symmetry that emphasizes both meaning and grammar. We prefer to give here examples that show syntactical types of crossings:

What's Hecuba to him or he to Hecuba

[Shakespeare]

Charles felt himself growing weaker at this continual repetition of prayers and torches, beneath these oppressive odors of wax and cassock. [Flaubert]*

In the second example, in addition to the shift of the substantive-adjective group from one place to the other, there is also the opposition of a singular noun determined by two plurals and a plural noun determined by two singular nouns.

A completely different picture is the phenomenon of poetry without punctuation. While the heroic couplet in the hands of Dryden, Pope, and Johnson reinforced syntactic structures, verse freed from puncutation leads to the obliteration of grammatical links and groupings. When not simply artifice, suppression of periods and commas gives the word and syllable a kind of autonomy. Their position is defined at will by the establishment of the verse line. As a double figure, verse without punctuation is no longer satisfied with adding its measure to sentence formation; it takes the lead and substitutes for it. In the stanza from Dylan Thomas that follows, note how the connection between lines 1 and 2 and lines 4 and 5 is more by association than by logic, at least in the first reading:

Like the park birds he came early
Like the water he sat down
And Mister they called hey Mister
The truant boys from the town
Running when he had heard them clearly
On out of sound

4. PERMUTATION

Permutation as a relational operation modifies the order of the syntagms in the sentence and of morphemes in the syntagm. In spite of the constraints it is under in English—in some ways by reason of these constraints—this order

*[In the original: "Charles se sentait défaillir à cette continuelle répétition de prières et de flambeaux, sous ces odeurs affadissantes de cire et de soutane." Since *affadissantes* naturally follows the French noun, the chiasmus as explained in the following remarks cannot be fully rendered into English. *Trans.*]

itself is the chosen field of metataxis, for it lends itself easily, and often effectively, to numerous figures. There can be no thought of outlining here all the possibilities of deviation. We shall point out only certain clearly marked and directed combinations. We note first that certain idiomatic permutations are part of the norm, such as inversion of the subject for an interrogative sentence (and after some adverbial expression such as *so*) or the positioning of some adjectives.

To get a better hold on the variety of possible operations, it might be useful to try first for a theoretical sifting. Take a simple sentence close to the minimal scheme we represented by the sequence $A + B + C + D$. In addition to its basic form, it allows for twenty-three permutations. In practice, however, certain of these permutations are never found except in "mad rhetoric" because of their completely ungrammatical forms. We can, therefore, exclude at the beginning deviations that would rob the sentence of all coherence. In the same way, ambiguous sequences will be very infrequent and thus of little interest. To bring the different aberrant cases under a single heading, we can say that the construction *subject + object + verb + adjective* is hardly able to be done. Other combinations remain that can be grouped around some known and well-marked structures. Thus we find three groups and three orientations:

1) Two elements can be separated from the sequence to allow the insertion of one or more others.
2) Several elements of the sequence can be extracted and moved to either the beginning or the end.
3) The order can be inverted by shifting two or more elements.

Two of these processes or even all three can be carried out together in the permutation of the same sequence. It is also true that a permutation may be explained as well by one process as by another (certain inversions can be explained as insertions).

4.1. Insertion is no doubt the most elementary form of any permutation. The minimal sentence increased by an element undergoes an addition; at the same time, it undergoes a displacement of its primary constituents. The most characteristic figure of insertion seems to be *tmesis*. We keep this name for less restricted uses than classical rhetoric allowed—that is, using it for all the cases where two morphemes or syntagms that grammatical usage ties strictly together are separated by the insertion of additional elements. Thus, the insertion between subject pronoun and verb, verb and preposition, preposition and its object, two coordinate subjects, and so on:

The untuned and jarring sense O wind up
Of this child-changéd father!

[Shakespeare]

Lay your sleeping head, my love,
Human on my faithless arm

[Auden]

On the divan are piled (at night her bed)
Stockings, slippers, camisoles, and stays

[Eliot]

See his wing—lilylocks—laced

[Hopkins]

The first example offers us one of those doubtful cases mentioned above. Do we have an insertion of "O" or a displacement of "untuned and jarring senses" to the beginning of the sentence? In the second hypothesis, a new doubt appears: true permutation or addition? In fact, it is legitimate to see in Shakespeare's sentence *hyperbaton*, a figure that consists in shifting one of the fixed constituents outside the normal frame of the sentence. When it is a question of hyperbaton of one of the two coordinated subject syntagms, the deviation is certainly better defined by speaking of displacement rather than of delayed addition, because justifying addition would suppose also zeugma of the verb implied by the second subject:

Some other power
As great might have aspired, and me, though mean,
Drawn to his part.

[Milton]

The arms of morning are beautiful, and the sea

[Saint-John Perse]

See Pan with flocks, with fruits Ramona crowned

[Pope]

The anterior position of the object corresponds to the rear position of the subject. Displaced in this way, the nomimal-syntagm object remains nonetheless most often represented in the sequence by a pronoun or other substitute:

Still, citizen sparrow, this vulture which you call
Unnatural, let him but lumber again to air
Over the rotten office

[Richard Wilbur]

The light, love,
the light we felt then,
grayly, was it, that
came in, on us, not
merely my hands or yours

[Robert Creeley]

The mind, that ocean where each kind
Does straight its own resemblance find;
Yet it creates, transcending these,
Far other worlds and other seas.

[Marvell]

Hyperbaton less frequently brings together two nominal syntagms, subject and object. It is certainly because of the typicality of its use in oral expression that certain authors use this strongly affirmed process of permutation, although parody can be another motive:

Before born babe bliss had.

[Joyce]

He didn't suspect that each time he walked by her store
she watched him, the store-keeper the soldier Bru.

[Queneau]

4.2. Inversion is the complete reversal of the interior order of a fragment of a sentence or even the interior of a complete sentence. Usually, however, the disturbance is not great, for it plays with only two terms, subject and verb, noun and adjective, and so on. Between these two terms, however, there is more than simply an exchange of positions; there is a hint of exchange of functions. The inverted syntagms and morphemes have, in fact, lost one of their distinctive traits, position. In addition, there is a slight shift through which they have more or less taken on the attributes of the position they now hold. Since in general, for example, the "hero" or the "theme" of a sentence is announced first, a verb placed first will borrow the function of the subject and a bit of its value:

Starts again always in Henry's ears
the little cough somewhere, an odour, a chime.

[Berryman]

A very common figure, the inversion of the subject-verb order, is frequently based on the presence of secondary syntagms at the head of the sentence (circumstantials, for instance):

Notable enough too, here as elsewhere, wilt thou find the potency of Names....

[Carlyle]

Thus inevitably does the universe wear our color, and every object fall successively into the subject itself.

[Emerson]

The inversion of the nominally expanded verb order is a Latinism that at times in English poetry of the past has been made into a rule and which helps give the sentence the flexible organization that meter calls for:

(Faire Soule) in this blacke Age so shin'd thou bright,
And made all Eyes with Wonder thee beholde,
Till uglie *Death* depriving us of Líght,
In his grimme mistie Armes thee did enfolde.
Who more shall vaunt true Beautie heere to see?

[Wm. Drummond]

The sequence *object* + *verb* + *subject* represents, by comparison with the minimal and normal sentence, a complete permutation $(C + B + A)$ and perfect inversion. When the permutation is performed, there must be a pronoun with a clear antecedent to avoid the ambiguity that the simple exchange of subject and object could give rise to. But if, as in the first of the following examples, the verb has a predicate adjective, there is no risk of misunderstanding, and the subject is grasped simply by its form:

> Cold are the crabs that crawl on yonder hills
>
> [Lear]
>
> Magnifying and applying come I
>
> [Whitman]
>
> To whom replied King Arthur, faint and pale·
>
> [Tennyson]

If inversion is achieved primarily by a shift in the order of the three principal constituents of the sentence, there is really no problem in extending this characteristic to similar operations on pairs such as verb/adverb or adjective/noun. Thus, to the extent that certain adjectives have a fixed place in ordinary usage, the changing of this position will be considered an inversion:

> Breathing bloom of a chastity in mansex fine
>
> [Hopkins]
>
> Now gently rail on Henry Pussycat
>
> [Berryman]

The same permutation is complicated by a substitution when the adjective is also shifted into a substantive in its ordinary form or in the form of an abstract noun: "the dull of time," "the faint white of her peignoir." This is only a supplementary example of the consciously complex character of syntactic permutations and, more generally, of metataxes.

In written texts, permutations of segments of the sentence have a value for the eye. They attract the eye to the text as spatial order and not simply as temporal or causal order. Among the last examples given, certain ones make us think of verbal architecture. But the figures of permutation are not the only ones under consideration. Symmetry and chiasmus, repetition and meter, enumeration and parenthesis—all the processes that depend on the order of words—aim at making a space for language, making language be *seen*. It is from this angle that the most formal, not to say the most formalist, metataxes are grasped. At the end of the road they open up the "topographical" experiments of Pound and Cummings, of William Carlos Williams and the Concrete poets.

In conclusion, we contend that the syntactic system of English does permit deviations and creates figures at all levels. Each of the principal distinctive traits seems to concentrate the action of a particular operator. It appears most likely, however, that the majority of the inventoried figures are to be found in other systems also. And we certainly ought to think not only of other languages but also of what is called today the grammar of the short story, the syntax of the film. Our contemporary awareness of the importance of the syntagmatic axis, common to all kinds of discourse, can take account of the wide range of application of certain metataxes, from ellipsis to inversion, from syllepsis to gradatio.

5. APPLICATION: METATAXES IN NEWSPAPER HEADINGS

The analysis just completed invites us to study the syntax in a particular corpus. Such a study would permit at the same time a control of the validity of our inventory and a characterization of the corpus under examination according to the figures in this work. We find it useful to sketch out an examination of this kind, using a nonliterary but quite specific and directed field: press headlines. In these headlines the English sentence frequently undergoes a particular treatment whose process is clearly discernible. What particular forms of deviation will be used? Will unexpected figures appear?

The sample used will be modest and has no statistical value. We use the first forty titles we came across that showed syntactic deviation.* Headline sentences were chosen, therefore, that were not normal or finished but werĕ certainly sentences (formulae such as *Fishing* or *General Eisenhower* were eliminated). Samples were chosen from daily and weekly American publications.†

The manner of the diffusion of news, like the page layout of a newspaper, has an influence on the linguistic matters we are studying; and we must, therefore, take them into account. The syntax of a headline often reflects the "telegraphic style" of dispatches. For the journalist, it means keeping the first freshness of the news and its force, and condensing all the information into a few words quickly assimilated by the eye and the mind. Hence the abbreviated sentence is common: "Rock Star Hurt," "Dubček Booted." Also to be noted is that the typography of the headlines differs in general from the text type face. The newspaper page is a mosaic, in which the word set off by the title is to have the value of an image. The sentence will be in large type, sometimes in several type faces. It will take the width of the column or of the

---

*[It was obviously impossible for the translators to proceed along these lines. Instead, we attempted where possible to find English-language headlines that reproduce the metataxes for which the French-language headlines served as examples. We found Roberta Kevelson's *The Inverted Pyramid: An Introduction to a Semiotics of Media Language*, Studies in Semiotics (Lisse: Peter de Riddler Press, 1977), useful in this search. Needless to say, the statistics cited below in the text refer to Group μ's French-language sample. *Trans.*]

†["French or Belgian publications during 1968 and 1969" in the original. *Trans.*]

spread. In short, the substance and the graphic layout already compromise the regular syntactic line.

The telegraphic style and the iconic arrangement give headlines two typical alterations: suppression on the one hand and permutation on the other. The sample used tells us, in fact, that these two operations dominate, and it is soon observed that the art of writing headlines concentrates on the two figures ellipsis and hyperbaton. We shall see the frequency and the form that these two basic metataxes take.

5.1. Ellipsis is strongly represented—twenty-seven of the forty "sentences" have no verb. There are twenty-six noun phrases, and this case of an adjectival phrase: "Beautiful for Homecoming" (*Marie-Claire*). Following are headlines where the absence of the verb is easily excused:

Olivia Newton-John: Not Really the 'Girl Next Door' [*New York Times*]

Photographer Mitchell: talented eye, gentle hand [*Cincinnati Post*]

1979 economy: not great—but not bad [*Cincinnati Post*]

Three verbs—*is, has,* and *is predicted to be,* respectively—could translate the perceived relationship between the two syntagms in each sentence. In each case, we find a colon in place of the verb. This punctuation is found in half the samples and certainly appears to be the best index of originality in the syntax studied. Ordinarily a modest punctuation mark, it acquires here the value of a morpheme. It indicates and supplies an absence (ellipsis), but it works as an indicator as well (hyperbaton). It could also be shown that both these roles are not distinct and are complementary rather than contradictory. Moreover, the absence that this sign shows and fills can be more obvious than the simple lack of a verb. In both the following cases, the expression moves toward a true shortening of the narrative:

President Firm For Our Demands: / Will Center With Bernstorff [*New York Times*]

'Dickie' Callei Slain, / Dumped in Grave [*Providence Journal*]

Behind these shortened sentences are found parataxes and suppression of conjunctive elements between sentences. In the same way, the prepositional link between substantives will often be altered to produce these crases with a particularly English flavor:*

Starring Vacation Pieces [*Femmes d'aujourd'hui*]

Today operation "curtains lowered" throughout the country [*Le Figaro*]

---

*[To a French reader, obviously. It did not seem advisable to replace these examples with English-language examples, since it would involve considerable disruption in the discussion. The originals read, "En vedette les ouvrages vacances" and "Aujourd'hui opération 'rideaux baissés' dans tout le pays." *Trans.*]

We can now complete what we said about this deviation in section 1.1. Crasis turns the second substantive into an appositive that does not determine, does not explain, but designates by convention or allusion, as does a baptismal name or a maker's label in clothes. One must be an addicted reader of fashion writing to grasp the meaning and scope of "vacation pieces," and one must have been following the latest happenings and know their symbolism to grasp "operation 'curtains lowered,' " a very allusive formula.

The last ellipsis, not the least, the one announcing the merger of two shops, is as follows:

Soon: B. M. + Inno [*Meuse*]

The metaplasmic suppression echoes the syntactic abbreviation. There is a kind of threshold where the sentence is reduced to a skeleton whose articulations are made from symbolic graphisms, very rudimentary but perfectly fixed (: and +).

5.2. In addition to abridging and eliding, the syntax of headlines likes to detach a shock word, putting it out front, isolating it by the layout of the page or by a colon. At times the foreground is used as a promised title before the actual theme of the article is given. One thinks of the street vendor and his "suspense" pitch:

Manfashion: see how pros put it together [*Cincinnati Post*]

At other times the theme itself is starred, but a theme that only rarely corresponds to the grammatical subject of the sentence; hence the hyperbatons that focus a sequence of different complements:

4 Unmarried Women: No Stereotypes, These [*Cincinnati Enquirer*]

Brown vs. Smith: Seasoned Pros Clash in Rematch [*Cincinnati Enquirer*]

New land rush: airlines poised for deregulation [*Cincinnati Post*]

In the case of questions, a true inversion can be obtained:

Barnard Hughes—Born to Play 'Da'? [*New York Times*]

Slender waist, yes, but how? [*Marie-Claire*]

Note also that the nominal-subject syntagm can itself be found detached and out front by a similar process, so that the narrative and the grammatical subjects are the same. Then it is a question of a kind of expletion using a colon and a pronoun with antecedent, a figure deriving more correctly from addition than from permutation. Even so, in the second of the following examples, the emphasis on the subject has involved also a displacement of a circumstantial:

Earthworms in your burger: Big Lie spreads [*Cincinnati Post*]

Problem with CETA funding: it, too, shall pass [*Cincinnati Post*]

5.3. One is tempted to think of addition as contrary to the spirit of economy and speed of telegraphic style. Not so. The initial shortening can, in fact, jam into a single sentence what ordinarily would require two or more sequences. In the following example we see the use of additional parentheses, frequent in journal headlines:

Lierse (tired) beaten by Standard in Second half (0–2) [*Le Peuple*]

On the other hand, we shall see that however laconic and summary the headline is, this is compensated for in some ways by harmonious additions, usually with symmetrical structure:

Clean Up Fast, Then Have Fun [*Cincinnati Enquirer*]

Be Naughty / Get Spanked [*Boston Herald Adviser*]

5.4. Headlines, therefore, try to achieve brevity of expression and a mass of information. Their typical attraction is this brusque, dense convergence. But in a number of cases it is possible to find not just addition and suppression combined but also suppression-addition; that is, substitution.

The figure in question is difficult to define. A branch of the ellipses we have spoken of, it could be classed with them. The verb, as we have seen, has little chance in headline deviation. But after a certain point its absence is no longer noticed, because with the repetition of headlines, there is created a shift in the formation and reading of the sentence. In fact, a secondary constituent, the preposition, tends to take over the place and fill the role of the absent verb. From this point, it can be found in a central position between two nominal syntagms, which it unites. A kind of rudimentary speech is thus built, one to which the public is accustomed and which gives formulas of the type: "this for that," "this against that," "this in that," "this according to that," "this with that." Prepositions, substantives, and their determiners form, then, the unique substance of the sentence. Compared with the verb for which it is substituted, the preposition represents semantically and syntactically a rather clumsy cheville but one with the advantage of indicating in an intense and economical way the rules governing the relation between the two elements. One could well envision the day when these prepositions could be replaced by mathematical symbols $(=, 0, +, -)$.

Women in Jazz, Past and Present [*New York Times*]

Illustrator for an Age With Idealistic Images of Life [*New York Times*]

Public For Free Press Despite Court Verdicts [*Cincinnati Enquirer*]

Mysterious Explosions Up Security [*The State*, Columbia, S.C.]

Newspaper headlines are, as we have seen, forged from a syntax particularly *other*. The alterations give, however, a set of rather familiar figures, ellipsis and hyperbaton at the head of the list. The singularity of journalisitc style is its great specialization in the uses of metataxes and the outlandish way it wears out the figures it prefers. The results can be a formula such as the dense one following:

On the eve of "Action day Walloons" (demonstrations at Mons, Nivelles, Verviers and Athus) Charleroi: 60,000 +! [*La Meuse*]

A single headline using all the operations. We can see the suppression of the verb as well as of the substantive *demonstrators* (which are implied by *demonstrations* and the number), the addition of the parenthesis, permutation, emphasis of the circumstantial *Charleroi,* and finally a suppression-addition marked by the colon and the plus sign. Truly, journalism offers metataxes at a price for everyone.

Chapter IV
Metasememes

0.1. General

To begin with, some warnings concerning the importance and complexity of this category of figures cannot be avoided. First, the neologism *metasememe,* which we adopted initially for symmetry and also because it indicates better the nature of the operations in question, totally covers what are traditionally called tropes, especially metaphor, the central figure in all rhetoric. Second, the study of "changes in meaning," which we could give as a first approximation, is a confrontation with the problem of signification, obviously the central problem not only of rhetoric but of every science and philosophy of language. The *signification of signification* brings up complicated questions that classical and medieval logicians had already refined, for these questions collected the crux of the theory of knowledge and also opened the way to many aporia that the most advanced linguistics had until very recently simply left within parentheses. We are not so presumptuous as to claim to handle in a few pages a whole field whose breadth we are only beginning to understand. The most rigorous attempts recently to establish a structural semantics do not fail to emphasize the fact that they are still at the level of initial stammerings.[1]

It is certainly not necessary to defend the primordial role that metasememes play in literary expression. The value of the spoonerism can be examined with a certain seriousness, but it would be an exaggeration to say that it has a high place in world literature. On the other hand, a poetics that excluded metaphor could hardly be imagined. No doubt there are exceptions, but they are rare, and, in fact, their deviation from the beaten paths may give them a certain value.[2] Concerning metaphor particularly, ancient rhetoricians have left us a number of observations; they are quickly exhausted, however, since they shamelessly cite the same examples and since the literary tradition of these treatises mitigates against specificity. But contemporary thought, especially Anglo-American criticism, has largely compensated for the lacunae in the historical legacy. Today the definition of metaphor has been the subject of colloquia, and a new and different work would be needed to provide a critical synthesis of these analyses.[3] We would also have to include in such a study everything of value that has been said on those tropes not yet classified. Bachelard, for example, following the stylisticians, was content to use the word *image* to describe phenomena that could be included in a rhetoric without difficulty. This allusion to the philosopher of poetic imagination makes us realize that concrete varieties of metasememic procedures lie outside our field of study. We are limiting ourselves to describing as objectively as possible the nature of the process in general, reserving for later the analysis of each figure in its kind and in its effects.

0.2. Definitions

In the first part of this work (sec. 1.2.3.), the metasememe was defined as the figure that replaces *one sememe with another*. But the sememe comes to us always through a word, and for that reason figures we classify as metasememes have often been defined as figures that replace *one word with another*. Taken literally, this formulation could just as well fit metaplasm through complete suppression-addition or even when substitution is only partial. By enlarging the sense of *word* and giving it the value of any element in the chain of signifiers, we could even say that every figure, every metabole, replaces "one word with another." This is nothing more than our original hypothesis: figured language is first of all revealed by the substitution of unusual elements for the proper elements of a given discourse. But this is the *initial* point of view of the decoder of the message: his first reaction was to see an alteration in the signifier. Because of the failure to make this very fundamental distinction between producer and receiver, ancient rhetoric—limiting ourselves to it only—confused alternation of meaning with alternation of form.[4]

Although Todorov does not make this duality explicit, he has proposed a schema for the two operations (see fig. 6). Triangle 1 represents the alteration

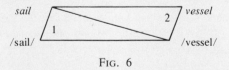

FIG. 6

between two meanings that can be attributed to the same signifier *sail* (polysemy). Triangle 2 shows that the same signified /vessel/ can be achieved through two different signifiers (synonymy). The diagonal common to both triangles represents the figure itself and the two relevant descriptions. Todorov considers, however, that the second one is more general.[5]

From this, one could imagine that the producer of this illustrious synec-

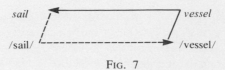

FIG. 7

doche started from the concept "vessel," which sent him back to the proper expression—that is, the word *vessel,* which disappears, yielding the word *sail.* While on the other side, the receiver of the word *sail* would shift from the proper signified to a nearby signified, the concept "vessel." In the first triangle, the decoder's triangle, the distance between the two signifieds is to be judged; in the second, the encoder's, the distance between the two signifieds is marked. Hence, we could try to indicate a dynamic schema using arrows (solid lines for the producer, broken line for the decoder) (see fig. 7).

But this representation would be incomplete because it does not take into account what is permitting the shift from *vessel* to *sail.* In reality, the producer moves to the word *sail* only through its meaning, by a process to be analyzed later but which we should indicate here (see fig. 8).

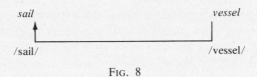

FIG. 8

We can, in fact, claim that in the strictest sense the producer starts from a signifier, since on the level of rhetoric the message at degree zero is already implicitly emitted. Figured language does not shift from the thing (not even from the concept); it works on already constituted signs.

To get back to the metaplasm by complete substitution (for example, using the archaism *con* for the more commonly used *understand*), it is clear that the rhetorician, even though following a similar course, does not end up with a modification of the denotative meaning of the term used. In principle, there is only an alteration of form. On the other hand, in the metasememe the change in form involves also a change in meaning, which is essential in the process. In one case, the figure derives from the ability of a signifier to refer to two signifieds; in the other, on the possibility that two signifiers have only one signified.

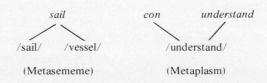

Finally, we may now make our first definition more precise: the metasememe replaces the *content* of one word with another word. But not simply any word: "To give a word a meaning that is not precisely the proper meaning of that word," to quote Du Marsais,[6] is a rule-bound operation. This is the sense of "not precisely." For Du Marsais this restriction was obvious, although in their claim to prescribe, the rhetoricians were not always in agreement on the cases of licit or illicit transfer (the limit was to authorize only a figure in use, one whose deviational value very generally indicated its literary qualities). We who have known Dadaist and Surrealist terrorism (at least in their formulated poetics) know that they claimed to replace the "not precisely" by "not at all." These experiments have been useful in liberating a formidable metaphoric potential, which has been justified each time that the relationship was not only "distant" but also "right."

0.3.   Types of Decomposition

The meaning of a word cannot be modified in simply any manner, except when allowed by explicit convention, as in a language with a key, which then makes it not a linguistic but a semiotic system. To correct once again our definition of metasememe, we say that it is a question of *modifying* the content of a word. As we shall see, there remains necessarily a *part* of the initial meaning. We have now designated in this way the foundation of the metasememic process. Like all metaboles, the metasememe rests on the articulation of the discourse. If the meaning of a word can be altered without becoming hermetic, it is because the meaning is plural. To use the terminology proposed by Pottier and Greimas, a terminology to which we shall not systematically limit ourselves, we consider the word, or rather the *lexeme* (minimal unit of discourse), as a collection of *semes* (minimal units of meaning), some of which are *nuclear,* others *contextual,* the whole producing an effect of meaning, or a *sememe.* In the same way as with the operations bearing either on the phonic arrangement of the signifiers or on their syntactic arrangement, it is the manipulation of the arrangements of semes that will produce figures. Nonetheless, an important difference can be noted immediately. The groupings of semes that constitute words are not provided with a linear order, even though there may be a hierarchy of semes. It follows from this fact that there is no reason to think of an operation upsetting the order of the semes. There are only two large types of operations possible—suppression and addition of semes or parts of semes, either separately or concurrently.

0.4.   Minimum Deviation

The necessarily *polysemic* nature of the lexeme (with the possible exception of "semantically primitive" words such as color names) is empirically seen in lexicographic use. To whatever extent they can, the usual dictionaires collect all the contextual classes of each lexeme, since the meaning of the word is the product of its possible occurrences. In the case of frequently used lexemes, such as the word *head,* analyzed by Greimas according to the entry in Littré,[7] the corpus of sememes can constitute a vast stylistic field. From what is given as the first meaning ("part . . . that is united to the body by the neck") to the figurative meaning indicated by *bare-headed* (where the reference is to the part of the head covered by hair), there is a deviation, which is enlarged even more by "the head of a pin" (where the first seme, an apparent one, is /sphere-shaped/). It is still a matter, however, of the *same* word and not of homonyms. Moving from the first meaning to the derived meaning, the semantic content has been necessarily modified but not totally replaced. If we consider that on the paradigmatic plane all the variants are equivalent (once lexicalized), every use of *head* in speech will constitute a metasememe. But certainly this way of speaking is not any more rigorous than is the formation by Jakobson whereby every paradigmatic selection is metaphoric in some way. It is important to distinguish here the properly rhetorical point of view from the semantic point of view. As we know, the first attempts to establish a semantic rhetoric based on the study of "changes in meaning" were able to do nothing more than make a study of the rhetorical concept of tropes while abandoning its terminology. In the simplest classification, the one proposed by Ullmann, everything was based on metaphor and metonymy, that is, on change by contiguity or by similarity, whether in the meaning or in the form (see table 7).

Table 7.   Associations with the Word *Hat*

	Similarity	Contiguity
Meaning	*helmet*	*head*
Form	*mat*	*topper*

The relevance of this schema can be discussed, especially since it confuses what is properly called metonymy with synecdoche (as Jakobson does also). For synecdoche itself has two symmetrically inverse forms. But this does not interest us at this moment. What is important is to restore to the rhetorical process its specificity in relation to the purely semantic process. When a word changes meaning, the first signified tends to disappear, giving place to the new signified. At the end of this evolution—since we are concerned with diachrony here—it disappears completely, allowing us to speak of an integral change. For example, *cape* has completely lost its original meaning of /head/. The same thing applies to lexical creation. If I use an existing word to designate a new, as yet unnamed object (the rhetoricians' catachresis)[8]—for instance, an example of the type "leaf of a book"—I can call this process that authorizes the extension of meaning analogical, metaphoric reasoning; but the comparison is no longer felt by the bookmaker any more than the dressmaker imagines that the head of her pin resembles her own head. One cannot sufficiently emphasize the fact that the poetic trope is a clear deviation, that it is marked, as we said above. For there to be a deviation, there must be tension, a distance, between the two sememes, the first of which remains present if only implicitly. To perceive this mark, we must necessarily be able to view the whole, to view it from the syntagmatic plane; that is, from a linguistic and/or extralinguistic context. If it remains true to say that the metasememe can be reduced to a modification of the content of a single word, we must add (for the sake of completeness) that the figure will not be perceived except in a sequence or a sentence. This does not imply that the tropes are then to be confused with metalogisms, for the latter modify the value of the sequence as an assertion, while the former act only on the value of the elements of the sequence to the extent that they are signifieds. To say this in the simplest manner, if a not very likable speaker calls me a *snake*, this will be a metaphor, because the animal signified coincides with only one aspect of me; but since the insult is also a word-phrase, it indicates the referent and becomes in this way a hyperbole.

In the case of metasememes, the context is necessarily linguistic, but this is not enough to make the mark patently clear. There must be in addition certain extralinguistic connectors, starting with a consciousness of rhetoric. Suppose that all the extrinsic conditions are met. We may choose either to examine sequences with purely poetic function or sequences in which the rhetorical function is subordinated to another function—for example, the conative, as in the case of advertising. In the once famous "Put a tiger in your tank," which had the uncommon honor of being cited by Jean-Luc Godard, the metaphor is as clear as in Aristotle's example: "He is a lion!" (speaking of Alexander or someone like that).* In the same way, in Apollinaire's poem:

> I know another little coney
> Whom I'd like to catch alive.
> Her warren's down among the thyme
> Of the valleys of the land of Love.†

we make out that it is a question of a well-known rabbit, though not necessarily one with four legs. The essential point is that *tiger, lion,* or *rabbit* be felt to have a modified meaning. Until the dictionary notes the definition of *tiger* as producing the signified "super gas" (or something like this), an explanation must be offered for why drivers struck by the message have not tried to put a wild beast in their tank. Since we have agreed that the exterior criteria are met, especially the preestablished belief that there now exists no motor with the ability to function by burning a tiger, we can admit that the message is

*[In fact, he was speaking of Achilles. *Trans.*]

†[In the French: "Je connais un autre connin / Que tout vivant je voudrais prendre. / Sa garenne est parmi le thym / Des vallons du pays de Tendre." *Trans.*]

received as linguistically improper. No doubt this impropriety presents a syntactical aspect, an ungrammatical aspect—since it is the use of a term without the ability to fill its function as an object complement—but in the last analysis this dissonance is of a semantic order. In the case of metataxes, as we saw above, the function itself is in question. In the case of metasememes, the deviation is between a "text" and its context, and only consideration of the meaning of the linked terms allows us to determine their incompatibility.

0.5.   Redundancy and Reduction

As we have insisted above, if "meanings" were monolithic, the receiver of the message could go no further and would have to decide that the message was simply absurd. In a language with no semantic redundancy, where blocks of meaning followed like beads on a rosary, no (semantic) figure would be possible. But, in fact, a certain level of redundancy is assured by the sharing of meaning in words (see chap. I, sec. 2.2.4). More precisely, it is the existence of *classemes,* that is, *iterative* semes or factors of compatibility between two semic nuclei, that assures for language a certain level of resistance to "base noise." If an advertising message sent out by a service station has interfering noise such that I read: "Put XXX in your tank!" there is a good chance that I will fill in the blank with something like *super gasoline.* In the same way, language being what it is—that is, men saying what they do—we can expect that the variable of the function "the sky is blue like————" might be *your eyes,* but few people would dream of completing it with *an orange.* In this case, the deviation is clearly considerable, and it is not certain that one could easily describe its reduction. The iterative semes, however, have not been totally suppressed. By contiguity, at least, the idea of color remains.

Unless we refuse the very principle of rhetoric and maintain that the poet is simply saying what he is saying, we are led to study how the correction of the voluntary error that constitutes the figure is to be made. We join here with Jean Cohen, who has very neatly formulated the complement of these two operations: perception and reduction of deviation. The first is certainly located on the syntagmatic plane, the second on the paradigmatic. However, we do not see the need to follow this author when he decides to call every paradigmatic deviation metaphor. Such a move would risk introducing new confusions into a field where there are already too many.[9]

0.6.   Some Models of Representation

To illuminate the processes at work in metasememic reduction, we will first of all recall a few large models capable of helping to describe the universe of representations. The first two are purely cognitive; one calls for nesting classes, the other for binary trees. Next we envisage models inspired by linguistics. According to the case, we are concerned with either the material analysis of the parts of objects or the rational analysis of concepts into their elements.

0.6.1. NESTED CLASSES

According to the *first model* (fig. 9.1), the objects that fall within our perception are grouped into classes of individual equivalents, themselves grouped into larger classes, which encompass them, or are decomposed into smaller classes, which show the details. According to the objects classified and the point of view of the classifier, one can end up with an indefinite number of pyramids, comprising classes more or less structured. Strictly speaking, as science confirms every day, the object does not exist; we agree to

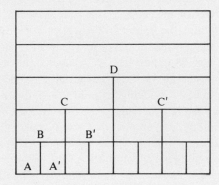

1. *First model:* Nested classes

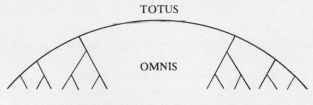

2. *Second model:* Disjunctive tree

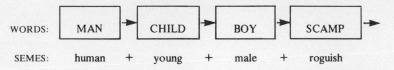

3. *Third model:* Endocentric series

FIG. 9

give the name to a group of phenomena forming a whole from a certain level
of observation. If the level changes, the object changes. Classification of
living beings is a well-known example of this model, but we can imagine
others, a limitless number of them, from no matter what area of observation,
no matter how restricted.

0.6.2. DISJUNCTIVE TREE

According to the *second model* (fig. 9.2.), the totality of the universe
(TOTUS) is decomposed by an unlimited analysis into its ultimate and
hypothetical elements (OMNIS). This becomes a tree whose every branch,
every bough, every twig represents more and more specific objects. This
dichotomic tree can be imagined, but we must carefully rid ourselves of a
more or less Linnean representation that could perfectly easily be applied to
the universe and would thereby take account of its structure. In fact, there is
an indefinite number of means of constructing such a tree, and the single
important aspect here is the operation by which it is built.

Nonetheless, among the innumerable "trees" and the innumerable
"pyramids" that can be conceived, there are some that are "truer" than
others simply because their hierarchy of grouping and differentiation better
matches what is observed in nature. However, there is no reason to suppose
because of this that nature conforms to the rational scheme that we conceive.
It is enough to note, for example, that the taxonomy of plants based on
phylogenetic differentiations is more effective and economical than a
classification that would take account first of the color of the flowers, second
of the number of leaves, and so on, even though such a model has been used
to construct a simplified though practically effective flora. Several contradictory or even mutually exclusive models can coexist. Every conceivable model
is at once speculative and realistic and for this reason remains at a place
determined by the distance between mind and things. The existence of such
classificatory schema receives testimony especially from those games in
which one is to identify an unknown object by means of a minimum number
of dichotomic questions.

The two models just described are cultural facts, products of the human
mind. Both are obtained by the same rational process whose two correlative
aspects they indicate. The model with nested classes stresses the grouping of
analogous objects (similarities), while the disjunctive tree insists on the successive differentiations by means of which the object is described with greater
and greater precision (differences). The two models differ in that one can be
seen as comprehensive, the other as extensive. On this, Piaget has written:
". . . a series of connected asymmetrical relations constitutes a linear set, and
nothing on the line is changed by cutting it at any section; a classification, on
the contrary, is a hierarchy or a pyramid whose summit or base is reached by
the most diverse paths."[10]

0.6.3. ENDOCENTRIC SERIES

Rather than consider the whole of the semantic universe and restrict ourselves strictly to linguistic terrain, it is useful to isolate series of successive words according to descending linear trajectories traced within the pyramid of nested classes or on the disjunctive tree. Each term of the series (called *endocentric*)[11] derives from the preceding one by the addition of one or more semes or determinations (see fig. 9.3) and reflects, finally, a new choice among the equivalent possibilities at this level.

It is easy to see, however, that it is always the semantic universe itself that is at the root of this structuring of vocabulary. It is the same with the following series, organized according to criteria other than specialization or generlization:

spring → *summer* → *autumn*	(cyclic and temporal succession)
one → *two* → *three* → *four*	(logical and noncyclic succession)
clouds → *rain* → *growth* → *flood*	(causal succession)
freezing → *cool* → *lukewarm* → *hot* → *burning*	(intensive series)

The terms of these series are united, therefore, by links of *contiguity*.

A third type of seriation, one which could be called *material,* since it is opposed to the semic series (which are conceptual), is achieved by considering the signified of a word and introducing it into the surrounding whole by adding it to other parts from this whole:

biceps → arm → man → family

All three types of series can be at work in the formation of metasememes.

0.6.4. TYPES OF SEMANTIC DECOMPOSITION

The application of the models just described leads to two radically different types of *semantic decomposition*. The *tree,* for example, may be considered as an organic whole, decomposable into coordinate parts that differ from one another:

tree = branches *and* leaves *and* trunk *and* roots, and so on

In this decomposition not one of the parts is a tree. The parts could appear to exist among themselves in a relationship of logical product Π (conjunction *and*), and we could designate the relationship between the parts and the whole *decomposition in mode* Π, which we shall do by convention. Strictly speaking, however, it is not the parts that have this relationship of logical product; rather there is an equivalence between the proposition (x is a tree) and the product of the propositions: (x has leaves) *and* (x has a trunk) *and* (x has roots), and so on. But it is essential to see here that such a decomposition is *distributive* in the sense that the semes of the concept corresponding to the whole are unequally distributed in the concepts corresponding to the parts (thus, the navigibility of the boat resides in the rudder, not in the cabin).

We can also consider the tree, or rather its concept, as a class of subclasses in some way interchangeable. The class of trees includes poplars, oaks, birches, and so on (the subclasses are interchangeable in that we can expect that their members possess at least leaves, a trunk, roots, and so on); but as a particular tree, any individual member of the class Tree will belong to one or other of the subclasses poplar, oak, birch. It will be either poplar *or* oak *or* birch, and so on. The mutually exclusive subclasses hold the same relation to class as species does to genus: they form a disjunction within the genus or a component of the exclusive type: (x is a tree) = (x is a poplar) *or* (x is an oak) *or* (x is a birch), and so on; or more simply: tree = poplar *or* oak *or* birch.

This time decomposition is no longer distributive but attributive, each part referring to a tree to which are attributed all the semes of tree plus some particular determinants. The parts among themselves are like members of a logical sum of the exclusive type and we designate by convention this kind of operation on the whole as a *decomposition in mode* Σ.

According to what is necessary, therefore, the *same* term can be decomposed in mode Π or in mode Σ.[12] In the first case, we will obtain an exocentric referential series (tree $\rightarrow$ branch), and in the second an endocentric semic series (tree $\rightarrow$ birch). All the figures we are going to describe in this chapter involve displacements through the length of such series. Since the series are exclusively ruled, as we shall see, by conditions bearing on semes (under these circumstances, we shall call the conservation of semes "essential"), we are justified in calling them semantic figures, or metasememes.

This brief incursion into the field of semantics (which is to be the base for our later logical constructs) convincingly shows us the possibility of considering vocabulary from two points of view. The first establishes endocentric series, which trace in some way the "successive" acquisition of semes according to a process of analysis and progressive differentiation. These endo-series exist *in posse* in the vocabulary; but it is we who trace their existence there, for each word or concept can, in principle, be the crossing point of as many series as it contains semes. These series are accompanied necessarily by decomposition in mode Σ (conceptual). The second point of view represents each material entity (each referent) as a whole of juxtaposed parts, the parts held simultaneously as parts of the entity. This mosaic translates decomposition in mode Π (material). We could name these elements *partemes*.

These two types of analysis are related directly to the model of meaning known as the Ogden-Richards triangle. The three angles of this triangle are, as we recall, the *signifiers* (which do not interest us in a description of semantic figures), the *concepts* (the semantic universe interpreted in mode Σ), and the *referents*, or things named (the brute material world perceived in mode Π).

Such considerations prove that the word is not, for the sender or for the receiver, a global entity of meaning. It is, in fact, instantly decomposable into semes or parts according to either of the modes demanded by the context. All the expressive or cognitive riches of discourse, and particularly the rhetorical ones, are based on this decomposition. We can affirm that the essential aspect of communication is established at the level of these atoms of meaning, which are semes, even if they are never named.

0.6.5. CONCRETE AND ABSTRACT

To complete our multilateral approach to mechanisms implied in metasememes, we must speak next of the broad categories of nouns: proper, abstract, and concrete. The proper noun will not be discussed here, for it presents an obvious anthropomorphic character: *sun* is a common noun designating a unique thing, while *Greek* is a proper noun designating a large number of individuals. For our purposes, we shall distinguish between concrete and abstract nouns. The word *concrete* is simply descriptive, labeling the objects of our perception: sun, Mediterranean, Paul Valéry, weasel. The word *abstract,* on the other hand, brings together concepts by which we intend to analyze these objects: white, lukewarm, transcendent, point. Without claiming here to analyze them rigorously, we judge that this distinction has a fundamental character. It seems quite clear that the first linguistic type of concrete vocabulary is the *substantive* noun, while abstract vocabulary, expressing the modalities of being, uses *adjectives* (the noun *patience* deriving from the adjective *patient,* and not the reverse).

The perfect definition of concrete words in the ideal dictionary would necessitate the interminable inventory of our understanding of the *referent* (the thing named). These words constitute our pocket cosmos, in the expression of E. Morin,[13] and translate the empirical world in our thoughts. On the other hand, abstract words cover only concepts, enactments of our analyzing will. They can be defined by a brief series of words, inalterable and definitive.

Under this distinction we recognize the empire of the modes Π and Σ, which we now feed into Piaget's scheme (assimilation / accomodation) in the reinterpreted Ogden-Richards triangle (fig. 10).

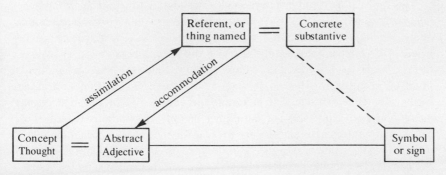

FIG. 10

Piaget calls assimilation the process by which we apply our schemes (mental or of action) to the real,[14] and abstract concepts are certainly such schemes. On the other hand, he calls accommodation the process by which we modify our schemes under the empirical pressure of our perceptive experiences. Concrete words are certainly the linguistic equivalents of these perceived realities.

Between these two categories of words, we can, ideally, conceive two movements in opposite directions. The first moves from descriptive or concrete words, which are, in fact, proper nouns in the true sense (for example, *sun*), and groups them into increasingly broader classes, each provided with a name. *Vegetation* would thus be the result of a process of progressive *abstraction* starting from observed plants. At each level of the operation, a part of the concrete character is lost; and to compensate, an abstract concept is devised that is occasionally detached from the grouping of objects in classes (compare the role of the words *aerial, terrestrial,* and *aquatic* in the classification of living beings). Reciprocally, the second movement starts from enactment words, monosemic lexemes (for example, *heavy*), which it builds into increasingly complex units, a movement of *concretization* by which, little by little, these lexemes approach empirical units (to form a kind of "reconsituted" reality). But from these double seriations, as much endocentric as exocentric, there result intermediary terms that are prone to both analyses. That is why we have been able to consider the tree, *at the same time,* as both an empirical conjunction with all parts (leaves, roots, trunk) and a rational disjunction of all its modalities (birch, linden, larch).

We are now in a position to explain the different categories of metasememes by following point by point the operators: suppression and addition.

1. SYNECDOCHE (General Table, Secs. C. 1.1 and C. 2.1)

1.1. Generalizing Synecdoche

The first category of metasememes corresponds to *synecdoche* and *antonomasis,* but only to the first type of them, the one going from the particular to the general, from the part to the whole, from lesser to greater, from species to genus. We must immediately insist on the nonrigorous character of these terms. As we said above, the "trees," or "pyramids," that are implicitly involved in the decomposition and recomposition of the semes do not necessarily coincide with a scientific picture of the universe. A primitive taxonomy also might do the job. This is what allows us to treat antonomasis (according to the tradition) as a simple variety of synecdoche. Cicero, when compared with the whole group of orators, is like a species compared with the genus.[15] We can be content with the criterion of the ancient rhetoricians: more for less.

In fact, one could find in any literary corpus only very few demonstrative examples of generalizing synecdoche (Sg). In *Des Tropes* of Du Marsais, we find hardly more than this one, threadbare example: "When *mortals* is used for men, the term *mortal* ought also to include animals, who are as subject to death as we."[16] Following is a more savory example, taken from John Barth:

> *En route* to Ocean City he sat in the back seat of the family car with his brother Peter, age fifteen, and Magda G——, age fourteen, a pretty girl an exquisite young lady, who lived not far from them on B—— Street in the town of D——, Maryland. Initials, blanks, or both were often substituted for proper names in nineteenth-century fiction to enhance the illusion of reality.

This is no doubt a sufficient illustration of the partial suppression of semes, with the effect of increasing the extension of a term, that is, making it more "general." Although we have put aside the question of the expressive nature of figures, it is easily seen that generalizing synecdoche will give an abstract, "philosophic" cast to the discourse, which obviously clashes in the case of naturalistic parody with the concreteness of the context.

If this process is pushed very far, we end up by replacing every word with *thing,* or *thingamagig,* or even by suppressing the word entirely, forming thereby a figure that ought to be called *asemia.* We are to remember, nonetheless, what was said in chapter I, section 2.4, about the invariant: figures of total suppression have no invariant and consequently may not be fitted into any of our four categories.

Alongside these examples that involve a semic decomposition of the type Σ, there are also more rarely some of the type Π. These synecdoches seem to be little "felt":

> The man took a cigarette and lit it

(*man* for *hand*). It is to be noticed that this type of synecdoche, Sg Π, is precisely one of those that make the construction of a metaphor impossible, a point we will return to later.

1.2. Particularizing Synecdoche

Particularizing synecdoche (Sp) and *antonomasis,* which is similar to it, make up, no doubt, by far the most frequent metaboles, especially in nineteenth-century fiction. Viewing this category of figures, which he confused with metonymy, Jakobson was able to speak of a predilection of the "realist" schools for metonymy. But, once again, we are interested here in only the logical structure of the synecdochic process. It appears to us, therefore, that slang expressions can be used as examples of synecdoche in mode Π without difficulty: "a tumble in the hay" for "making love"; or from old treatises (the famous example of *sail* for *vessel*).

Particularizing synecdoches of type Σ are theoretically possible and no doubt exist. But they are hardly "felt," because they are limited to introducing unanswerable questions about whether they approximate degree zero or not. To write *dagger* where *weapon* would suffice, is this a figure or not? Is it any more a figure to give names like Phylis, Silvander, or Lisette to the shepherdesses of the well-known piece by Dufresny?[17] Clearer would be this example from Dylan Thomas:

> Night in the sockets rounds,
> Like some pitch moon

(invisible → black → pitch). It is in any case to be noted that this type of Sp Σ synecdoche also makes the construction of a metaphor impossible (we will take this up later).

1.3. The Conservation of Essential Semes

An important question poses itself to us now, one which had already brought embarrassment to classical rhetoricians: "Although one might say *a hundred sails* for *a hundred vessels,* Le Clercq believes that it would be ridiculous to say, with the same meaning, *a hundred masts* or *a hundred oars*" (*Nouvelle rhétorique*, p. 275).* But supposing that the example were well chosen, the reason for it would be, not that we had shocked "ears accustomed to purity of language," but rather that to allow this deviation to be absorbed without equivocation, the substitute ought to keep the specificity of the word for which it substituted. Therefore, we must examine more closely the relationships of the part to the whole, species to genus, and so on, if we are to attach them to the representative models explained above.

The model with nested classes, in particular, remains quite heterogeneous, since at each level there is a change in the differentiating criterion. It is a question of a nonstructured classification, where we are faced with the two types of classes already described. (See the figure on p. 105.)

We must remember what was said (and what is easily verifiable by considering any semes, for example, *navigability* or *aggressiveness*) about the series brought about by these two types of decomposition: Σ: there is conservation of semes moving down from above; Π: there is distribution of semes among the parts.

A generalizing synecdoche of type Σ (*weapon* for *dagger*) or a particularizing one of type Π (*sail* for *boat*) ends up by replacing one seme by

*[The English translation of *Nouvelle rhétorique* reads at this point: " 'Let us simply note that if all figures are subject to certain cultural conventions (it would sound ridiculous, Dumarsais says, to say that a fleet of battleships is composed of a hundred masts[208]), figures based on the symbolic connection are the most precarious . . .' (Du Marsais, *Des tropes,* p. 85, n. 208)" (Chaim Perelman and L. Olbrechts-Tyteca, *The New Rhetoric: A Treatise on Argumentation,* trans. John Wilkinson and Purcell Weaver [Notre Dame: University of Notre Dame Press, 1969], pp. 336–37). *Trans.*]

Types of Classes

— those that group distinct individuals, identical from the point of view chosen.

EXAMPLES:

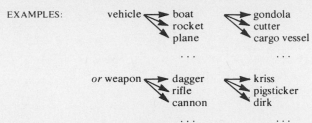

vehicle	boat	gondola
	rocket	cutter
	plane	cargo vessel
	. . .	. . .
or weapon	dagger	kriss
	rifle	pigsticker
	cannon	dirk
	. . .	. . .

— those that group different parts belonging to an organized whole.

EXAMPLES:

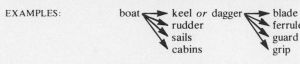

boat	keel	*or* dagger	blade
	rudder		ferrule
	sails		guard
	cabins		grip
	. . .		. . .

another where certain semes have disappeared. We call *essential semes* those that are indispensable to discourse and whose suppression makes discourse impossible. To maintain the intelligibility of the message, essential semes must be maintained.

Take for example a scene from a novel where a murder is being described (the reader may easily construct a like example of Sp II). The weapon may be called by the words *dagger, weapon, object.* The essential seme of the scene (call it, without further analysis, /murder/) is present in the first two words but not at all in the third. In the first, it is even clothed in supplementary, nonessential information, not redundant but *lateral.*

Thus we are led to distinguish two degrees of Sg Σ: one that plays on this lateral information but keeps the essential semes (/weapon/ for /dagger/), and also one which suppresses the essential semes (/object/ for /weapon/). The first degree is usually quite unfelt and appears only in the course of a semic analysis of the discourse. It is a part of a certain latitude left to the speaker concerning the level of the definition to be checked against his lexis. The second degree, on the contrary, is violently felt as a figure and can be used only if the essential seme is already present in the context in the form of semantic redundancy. Take the example of *iron* used for *dagger.* We can decompose it into three endocentric series, which converge two by two on the absent terms of the message (fig. 11).

We see the path taken: specialization of *dagger* into *blade,* then generalization of *blade* into *hard metal,* and finally the new specialization of *hard metal* into *iron.* Neither *blade* nor *dagger* is named; for the essential seme is /murder/, and we see that this seme has been lost along the road. The connection between the raw material (*iron*) and the finished product (*dagger*) obvi-

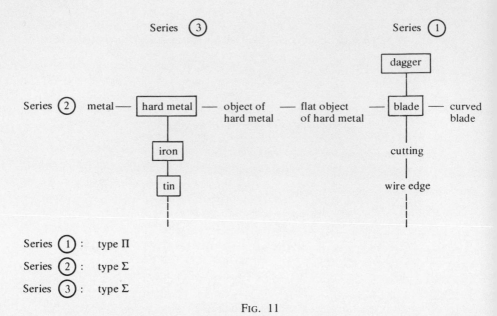

FIG. 11

ously does not suffice for reconstituting the message, since in other contexts *iron* could signify a nonaggressive instrument, as in:

> Iron better employed will plow the earth [Malherbe]

where *iron* (thanks to "better employed") has two zero degrees (/weapon/ and /plow/), or even in:

> Gold falls under iron [Saint-Amant]

in spite of the slight metaphoric coloring of this synecdoche. Therefore, only the context, the probability of transition of semes in narration, in other words the semantic redundancy, allows the reduction of the last two examples to their "agricultural" signification.

2.   METAPHOR (General Table, Sec. C. 3.1)

2.1.   Semantic Incompatibilities

This description of the mechanism of synecdoche brings us to the mechanism of metaphor. As we have shown at different points, metaphor is not, properly speaking, a substitution of meaning, but a modification of the semantic content of a term. This modification is the result of the conjunction of two basic operations: addition and suppression of semes. In other words, metaphor is the product of two synecdoches. We shall now describe in more detail this mixed operation. We start from an example chosen from Pater:

> To *burn* always with this *hard* gemlike *flame*, to maintain this ecstasy, is success in life. In a sense it might even be said that our failure is to form habits: for, after all, habit is relative to a stereotyped world, and meantime it is only the *roughness of the eye* that makes any two persons, things, situations, seem alike. While all melts under our feet, we may well grasp at any exquisite passion, or any contribution to knowledge that seems by a lifted horizon to set the spirit free for a moment.... Not to discriminate every moment some passionate attitude in those about us ... is, on this short *day of frost and sun, to sleep before evening*.

It goes without saying that the italicized syntagms are not the only metaboles in the text, still less the only factors of its aesthetic success. But they are certainly felt immediately by the reader as distortions of the lexical material. Attention is drawn to the message by these small semantic "scandals." Formally, metaphor reduces to a syntagm in which the identity of two signifiers and the nonidentity of two corresponding signifieds appear contradictorily together. This affront to (linguistic) reason gives rise to a reduction procedure through which the reader seeks to validate identity. It is very important to note that the reduction is always made in favor of the linguistic formation, one which is never contested. This is because we postulate that conditions extrinsic to rhetorical consciousness are present. Quite different would be the attitude of a receiver of a scientific message, where semantic incompatibilities could just as well be rejected (false or absurd discourse) as accepted (discovery of a new structure of the universe). As Jean Cohen has nicely remarked, such utterances are, moreover, indicated by remarks such as "science reveals that ... ," "contrary to received opinion, X has proved that...."[18] For a poetic reading, these warnings are without meaning, even though they could just as well be presented in an analogous form, but again with a twisted meaning. Admitting *a priori* that the code is the common code, the reader of poetry soon constructs representational fragments matching the model of the tree or the pyramid and seeks the level at which he can accept the equivalence of the signifieds. When we consider two objects, no matter how different they might be, it is always possible by running through the pyramid of nested classes to find a limit-class such that the two objects are both counted in together but remain separate in all inferior classes.

The terms *identical, equivalent,* and *analogous* have as their only goal the approximate designation of the relative level of the limit-class by comparison with those levels where the two objects remain individuated. Metaphoric reduction is achieved when the reader has found the third potential term, a link between the two others (for example, "intensity," "lack of refinement," "brief period of time encompassing all experience" in the example from Pater cited above). The reduction operates by explaining any tree or any pyramid

whatever, speculative or realistic. Each reader can have a personal representation, the essential thing being to establish the *shortest* route by which the two
objects can reconnect. The operation is followed until all the differences are
exhausted.

2.2. Intersection and Reunion

The first description of metaphor can be investigated even more
thoroughly. The limit-class mentioned above may also be described as an
intersection of two terms, the overlap in the mosaic of their semes or parts
(fig. 12).

FIG. 12

If the part held in common is necessary as a probing base for grounding the
claimed identity, the noncommon part is no less indispensable for creating the
originality of the image and for triggering the reduction mechanism. The ex-
trapolated metaphor is based on a real identity indicated by the intersection
of two terms to affirm the identity of the totality of the terms. It extends to the
union of the two terms a property that, in fact, is true only of their intersection
(see fig. 13).

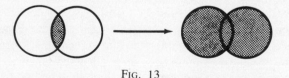

FIG. 13

We may express the metaphoric operation as follows:

$$S \longrightarrow (I) \longrightarrow R$$

where S is the starting term, and R the resulting term, the passage from one to
the other being effected by the intermediary term (I), always absent from the
discourse and which is a limit-class or a semic intersection, depending on the
point of view chosen.

Decomposed in this way, metaphor is revealed as the product of two
synecdoches, (I) being a synecdoche of S, and R a synecdoche of (I). This
close relationship between the two figures, generally thought irreducible, at
least in Jakobson's theory, is worth a closer examination. Can a metaphor be
formed by freely combining any two synecdoches, generalizing (Sg) or par-

ticularizing (Sp)? No, because since synecdoche modifies the level of the terms, we are obliged to combine one Sg and one Sp if we wish S or R to be at the same level (or the same degree of generality), as is the rule for metaphor. Thus there remain the two following possibilities:

(Sg + Sp) *and* (Sp + Sg).

2.3. Coupling of Synecdoches

Taking simple synecdoches and characterizing the type of decomposition they can perform, we can examine the relationship between their two terms looking for the operation (product Π or sum Σ) that allows us to pass from one to the other (see table 8).

Table 8. Types of Synecdoche

Synecdoche	Decomposition of the Type	
	Σ	Π
Generalizing	iron for *blade*	man for *hand*
Particularizing	pitch for *invisible*	sail for *ship*

To construct a metaphor, we must couple two complementary synecdoches that function in a precisely inverse way and that fix an intersection between the terms S and R. In mode Σ, the metaphor obtained will be based on the semes common to S and R, while in mode Π it will be based on their common parts. Therefore, the only two possible combinations will be (Sg + Sp) Σ and (Sp + Sg) Π. We see how little rigor there is in the idea of "generality" as we have used it until now: the material "part" is smaller than the whole, while the semic "part" is more general than the whole.

Table 9

General Scheme	$S \rightarrow$	$(I) \rightarrow$	R
a) (Sg + Sp) Σ *possible metaphor*	birch	flexible	girl
b) (Sg + Sp) Π *impossible metaphor*	hand	man	head
c) (Sp + Sg) Σ *impossible metaphor*	green	birch	flexible
d) (Sp + Sg) Π *possible metaphor*	boat	bridge	denture

The different possibilities are illustrated in table 9. In example *b*, we find that metaphor is impossible because neither S nor R is decomposable. Only in (I) do they coexist without constituting a conclusive intersection. In example *c* we find a similar case, where two semes coexist in an exemplary case (*I*). But this coexistence in a single object is not an intersection: for it to be an intersection, there must be an identical seme in the two different lexemes (case *a*) or an identical part in two different totalities (case *d*). Another example for case *c* would be:

The distinction between the modes of decomposition Π and Σ (conceptual and referential) has allowed us finally to distinguish two types of metaphors, the conceptual metaphor and the referential metaphor. The first is purely semantic and plays on the suppression-addition of *semes,* while the other is purely physical and plays on the suppression-addition of parts.

Is the referential metaphor, which is based on images (imagined representations) instead of on semes, still a semantic figure, a metasememe? For the moment we answer in the affirmative, specifying, however, that this type of metaphor could well be only a linguistic transposition of the pictorial or plastic metaphor that would be found when we generalized rhetoric to cover the other arts. Its close relationship with metasememes in the strict sense allows us to classify it under this rubric.

2.4. Corrected Metaphors

We have shown how metaphor attributes to the combination of the two collections of semes properties that, strictly speaking, apply only to their intersection; hence this effect of expansion, opening, amplification often noted by commentators. In fact, the passage of the metaphoric operation by way of the narrow bridge of the semic intersection may *itself* be considered an induced impoverishment, an exaggerated narrowing, like an insufficient justification. The author will then have the tendency to correct his metaphor, most often by a synecdoche taken from an unshared element, but also at times by a second metaphor.

Pascal has left us a famous example: "Man is only a reed, the most feeble thing in nature, but he is a thinking reed" (see fig. 14).[19]

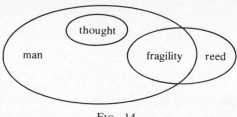

Fig. 14

We can examine the logical articulations of the sentence: the restrictive *only* introduces the metaphor as if it were a synecdoche (by the "narrow bridge" of "fragility"), while the adversative *but* introduces a generalizing synecdoche (always true by definition) as if it had to be proven. On this willed confusion of the true and the false is based one of the essential aspects of the corrected metaphor.

More trivial examples abound in slang or in the humorous speech to which this name is falsely given. A dachshund will be called a "sausage with feet" (metaphor corrected by synecdoche), the penis will be a "sausage with a mustache" (metaphor corrected by a second metaphor). We also know the metaphors of Saint-Pol-Roux, which were the pretext for a memorably mercurial one by André Breton: "crystal breast" (for a carafe), and so on.[20] Closer to us, Charles Tomlinson writes:

Crowding this beach
are milkstones, white
teardrops; . . .
chalk-swaddled, babyshapes,
tiny fists, facestones

Metaphor can be corrected by metonymy. This is the practice of Wallace Stevens on occasion.* Note that the metonymy here is a color; that is, one of those rare cases of a mono-semic lexeme that, precisely because of this fact, takes on the appearance of a synedoche:

the green freedom of a cockatoo

the yellow moon of words

John Hawkes writes in the same way: "the silken weave of Love's pink panorama"; and Shakespeare: "Life's but a walking shadow. . . ."

We have described two sides of this triangle: metaphor and synecdoche. The third side is, unquestionably, oxymoron (see fig. 15).

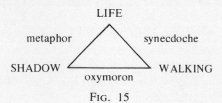

Fig. 15

Now *walking shadow* is given as the equivalent of *life,* the result of a legitimate transformation. By means of it, life, a biological process, is found suddenly bent into a contradictory expression, into incompatible parts. And in

*[The original reads: "This is frequently the practice of Maeterlinck, who was perhaps its inventor." *Trans.*]

this way, the play of the corrected metaphor is explained: to make the real burst forth, to create a shock by pulling a contradiction from an identity.

We still have this sentence to examine:

Rhetoric is the stylistics of the ancients. [P. Guiraud]

Although it is constructed on the same model as the corrected metaphor, it is not one. In both cases, however, we find the structure of a definition based (very structurally) both on an analogy (rhetoric = stylistics) and on a distinctive opposition (ancient / modern). This structure can be just as easily analyzed according to a classical model (a close genre, but with a specific difference) as according to the most recent model (Greimas: significant opposition on the same semantic axis). It is difficult to catch the difference, for it is more quantitative than qualitative and shows thereby how close rhetoric is to the habitual processes of using thought. Even a metaplasm can be analyzed as a function of its resemblance to certain proofs of phonetic change applied in the language disciplines. Guiraud's sentence remains rhetorical, however, at least in its use of the verb *to be* to link the two nonidentical terms. The example from Pascal cited above is in this consideration an intermediary between specifically literary and scientific operations. But both are equally rational (no doubt because language is constructed in this way), and we can view rhetoric as an *exasperation of the rational*.

In literary occurrences, the qualities of literature are signaled only by the context (extra- or intralinguistic) and by the precariousness of the logical articulations that abound. But the thinness of this explanation is certainly compensated by an aesthetic investment that takes the place of the failing noetic function.

2.5. Degrees of Presentation

It is clear that this description does not claim to exhaust the problem of metaphor, even in the limited theoretical frame we have constructed for this study. We have asserted that metaphor results from a double logical operation, but other questions remain in the air. Let us examine now the extent of these units. We have not spoken of this in the case of synecdoche, for it seemed clear there that the initial sememe, the one reduced or enlarged by the figure, is by its nature absent from the message. We could no doubt consider an example such as the following:

And the *salt* of their *tears* is still crystalizing

where there is a synecdochic relationship between the underlined terms. But it is clear that the message does not contradict the linguistic code. It is a simple determination. A figure would appear only if one of the terms were suppressed.

Strictly speaking, for the ancients true metaphor is *in absentia*. Such a presentation demands either a level of redundancy raised in the segment that contains the figure or a broad semic intersection between degree zero and the figured term. In the following example, in fact, only the context allows us to understand that:

Love in these labyrinths his slaves detains,
And mighty hearts are held in slender chains,

[Pope]

and in spite of the three metaphors, the topic is two locks of hair. This is why poets have had recourse, little by little, to the metaphor *in praesentia*, which makes possible more unusual juxtapositions:

My father's body was a globe of fear
His body was a town we never knew.

[Michael Ondaatje]

Lacking only the word *like*, we are faced here with comparisons. But intermediary degrees are possible when degree zero is present in the immediate neighborhood. This original example avoids the rather "equational" character of the metaphor *in praesentia*. Here is another example from Milton:

So, when the sun in bed,
Curtained with cloudy red,
Pillows his chin upon an orient wave, . . .

The relationship we see here are:

$$\frac{sun}{(\text{sleeper})} = \frac{cloud + wave}{curtains \text{ and } pillows} = \frac{(\text{nature})}{(\text{man})}$$

The use of metaphors *in praesentia* always assumes a grammatical form introducing relations of comparison, equivalence, similarity, identity, or derived relationships. At the limit, the most peremptory mark of identity is the simple substitution with which we obtain metaphor *in absentia*. We will analyze these grammatical forms in the section on comparison (below, sec. 3), theorizing that an unnoticed diachronic evolution has led from the rational comparison to the metaphor *in praesentia*, which certainly points to its paradoxical character.

The *in praesentia* form brings up another problem however. We know that tropes in Fontainer's sense involve one word alone. In our categories of metasememes, which encompass all of Fontanier's tropes, metaphors *in praesentia* would constitute an exception to this rule. In fact, this figure can just as well be analyzed as a figure by addition working on a single word, that is, like synecdoche. This is clear when comparing:

Spain—a great whale stranded on the shores of Europe

[Ed. Burke]

with the following in degree zero:

Spain, that country whose representation on a map is a swollen form lying at the borders of Europe.

There remains only one particularizing synecdoche (its shape as a whale) and *in absentia*. Despite the undeniable metaphoric functioning of the example cited, we believe that the synecdochic reduction is to be preferred for reasons of method and of generality. It has the additional advantage of insisting on the strict relation, discussed above, between metaphor and synecdoche.

3. COMPARISON

3.1. Different Types of Comparison

3.1.1. SYNECDOCHIC COMPARISONS

Let us examine a series of conventional comparisons:

Naked / jaybird	Simple / ABC
Clear / bell	Ugly / sin
Dull / lead	Mad / hatter
Pretty / picture	Cool / cucumber
Happy / lark	Deaf / post
Dead / doornail	Strong / ox
Deep / well	Quick / flash

Certainly these stereotyped comparisons, often used without being understood, are quite different from original creations. This type of cliché consists most often of expressions with intensive, hyperbolic, superlative value, expressions that function as semantic units. In metalanguage we can certainly split them into two parts, as above, to make clear that the first term always has a generalizing synecdochic relationship with the second, or more precisely, that the second term—the one being emphasized—particularizes the first by the addition of semes. Hence, one could be tempted to consider this kind of formulation as metasememes *in praesentia* by addition (or hypersememes). But in reality there is no semantic figure, since there is no infraction of the lexical code. It is for this reason, however, that traditional rhetoric sometimes classified comparisons with figures of thought (and not with tropes of meaning), and sometimes more precisely with figures of imagination, that is, in the series: *ethopoeia, topographia, prosopopeia,* and so on.[21] As a simple expansion of the description, the comparison "brings together diverse objects so as to emphasize one of them" or "brings together two distinct phenomena."[22]

3.1.2. METALOGICAL COMPARISONS

Before continuing, however, we must carefully eliminate a class of comparisons that we would call "true," as a way of recalling that all figures of rhetoric are always "false." For example, "he is strong like his father" or "she is beautiful like her sister" may simply be accurate assertions. Note, however, that if *he* is a weakling and *she* is an ugly duckling, the figure rushes back in. This is ironic speaking, and in our system this is a *metalogism,* thus a figure necessarily remarking on the referent of the message. A good number of rhetorical comparisons are metalogisms precisely in this way, most often hyperbolic ones. The shifting of metabolic categories is clearly perceived in a canonical example like "rich as Croesus" (hyperbolic in principle, even though the fortune of a millionaire might be as considerable as that of the last king of Lydia), compared with "he is a Croesus," which brings us back to antonomasis, that is, particularizing synecdoche.

Surrealistic language has accustomed us to still other comparisons, and Breton has brought our attention to a particularly interesting case, the one of "Beautiful like . . ." in Lautreámont.[23]

3.1.3. METAPHORIC COMPARISONS

We have been careful not to reduce all comparisons to the metalogical category. We shall see that another kind of comparison may be reserved as metasememic. Take the series:

(1) her cheeks are fresh as roses
(2) her cheeks are like roses
(3) the roses of her cheeks
(4) on her face, two roses.

Only (1) is eventually metalogical; all its terms are semantically normal and perfectly compatible with the lexical code. The second example already introduces an anomaly to the extent that the common attribute disappears. Since the limit-class is not designated, the reader will necessarily have recourse to the process of reduction described above. The *as* or *like* introduces an equivalence that is not totally assimilable any more than *peregrination* is complete in:

And then to awake, and the farm, like a wanderer white
With the dew, come back, the cock on his shoulder. . . .

[Dylan Thomas]

Examples (3) and (4) are, respectively, metaphors *in praesentia* and *in absentia.*

Since this is so, an important difference is made clear between the complete metaphor and the metaphoric comparison from the point of view we call *mark.* Metaphors *in praesentia* take us to syntagms where two sememes are

unduly assimilated, while the properly called metaphor does not show assimilation. In "Put a tiger in your tank," the metaphoric term is felt as such
because it is not comparable with the rest of the message. This incompatibility
then raises the comparison between the probable term and the asserted term:
super gas = tiger.

3.2. Copulas

Comparisons are introduced by the canonical *like* or *as*.* Metaphor *in
absentia* is a substitution pure and simple. Between the two extremes, authors
have used a wide variety of intermediary grammatical structures, generally as
attenuation of the rational character of *like,* which insists on the partial character of the similarity, consequently avoiding the affirmation of total commuta-
bility. We shall examine a few of them.

3.2.1. *Like* AND *As* AND THEIR DERIVATIVES

These terms introduce analogy, which is nothing other than weak equivalence, grouping individuals with few traits in common. Among the copulas of
this category, we find *such as, seems, even as, same as, kind of, just as*:

> . . . no, *even as* the trees
> That whisper round a temple become soon
> Dear as the temple's self, so does the moon
> Haunt us. . . .
>
> [Keats]

> If the moon smiled, she would resemble you,
> You leave the *same* impression
> Of something beautiful. . . .
>
> [Plath]

> A HEART alone
> Is *such* a stone,
> As nothing but
> Thy power doth cut
>
> [Herbert]

> Her fingers number every nerve
> *Just as* a miser counts his gold.
>
> [Blake]

> Hearts with one purpose alone
> Through summer and winter *seem*
> Enchanted to a stone
>
> [Yeats]

*[In French one word, *comme,* normally prefaces similes. *Trans.*]

I am a *kind of* burr; I shall stick

[Shakespeare]

An original variant is the use of *better than,* comparative by definition, which introduces a notion of degree into the common character:

Oh *better than* the minting
  Of a gold-crowned king
Is the safe-kept memory
  Of a lovely thing.

[Sara Teasdale]

3.2.2. PAIRING

Pairing is most often marked by terms of relationship, like *sister, cousin,* and so on. This copula is interesting in that it is itself a metaphor of *like:*

Blue! Gentle *cousin* of the forest green,
Married to green in all the sweetest flowers

[Keats]

It is even a metaphor corrected by synecdoche (*gentle* < *blue*) according to the schema described in section 2.4. We can also have:

He is made *one* with Nature

[Shelley]

3.2.3. *Is* OF EQUIVALENCE

This use of the verb *to be* is distinct from the *is* of determination: ''the rose is red'' is a process that is synecdochic and not metaphorical in nature. On the other hand, we find examples of *is*:

Nature *is* a temple where living pillars

[Baudeliare]

Death *is* the mother of Beauty

[Stevens]

3.2.4. APPOSITION

There are two degrees of apposition. The first is accompanied by a demonstrative, which attenuates the equivalence and brings it closer to simple comparison:

    and eke mine enemy, alas,
That is my lord, steereth with cruelness

[Wyatt]

And the larch that is only a column, it goes up too
    tall to see

[D. H. Lawrence]

The higher degree suppresses the demonstrative, juxtaposing the terms directly or by the intermediacy of a colon, comma, dash:

City of spring, the governed flower,
Turns in the earth

[Dylan Thomas]

The apparition of these faces in the crowd;
Petals on a wet, black bough.

[Pound]

... when the moon hangs on the wall
Of heaven-haven

[Stevens]

Reason your viceroy in mee, mee should defend

[Donne]

By making the same grammatical function share several terms, apposition puts these terms in a comparable position and makes the whole into a paradigm. The definition of paradigm is, structurally, identical with that of metaphor; as a result, it is possible to consider the metaphor as a paradigm deployed as a syntagm.

3.2.5. SUBSTANTIVE AND VERB

The comparing and compared may also be found in a syntagm where they fill different functions, subject and verb, for example. By the rule of isotopy, they must fit, say, by sharing iterative semes. The shared semes form a semic intersection, which gives the syntagm in question a structure proper for the formulation of a metaphor:

The sky rejoices in the morning's birth

[Wordsworth]

Time in the sea eats its tail

[Ted Hughes]

Authority forgets a dying king

[Tennyson]

Given the structure of the English verb, the reduction of these metaphors generally allows the choice of two solutions, as in the first example:

The sky rejoices like a man rejoices

with the metaphor *sky = man*

The sky glows like a man rejoices

with the metaphor *glows = rejoices*.

3.2.6. GENITIVE AND ATTRIBUTE

The genitive is frequent in poetry:

And yet this great wink *of* eternity

[Hart Crane]

Yet still he fills Affection'*s* eye

[Samuel Johnson]

A stupid clown *of* the spirit'*s* motive

[Delmore Schwartz]

As its name indicates, the genitive (example: *the roof of the house*), allows the movement from species to genus, from the part to the whole. It is a synecdochic operation, the inverse of attribution, which is a determination (example: *the man with the broken ear*):

Time, *with* a gift of tears

[Swinburne]

. . . far from the grey shores
that fringe *with* shadow all the world's existence

[D. H. Lawrence]

The brown enormous odor he lived by
was too close, *with* its breathing and thick hair

[Elizabeth Bishop]

As we see it, the most economical reduction of these two types makes of them metaphors *in absentia,* where the genitive and attribute are present only to attract degree zero better through redundancy. *Man's eye* would be degree zero, and *affection* a simple metaphor for ''loving man.'' Inversely, at degree zero *melancholy-creating time, a gift of tears* would be the metaphoric substitute for ''creating melancholy.''

Just as the subject + verb syntagms, the determinant + determined syntagms presume a semic intersection (classemes). These classemes, or iterative semes, can in certain cases be relayed by the attraction of stereotyped syntagms like the fine title of a collection by A. Cantillon: *The Music Heart (Le Coeur à musique).* The mind recalls the music *box* and immediately makes the metaphoric parallel between heart and box, then between music and the expression of sentiments of love, which are the subjects of the book. In such a case it becomes impossible to decide if degree zero is ''music box'' or ''the loving heart.'' The two metaphors cross.

4. METONYMY (General Table, Sec. C. 3.2)

4.1. Contiguity

We know already that metonymy, a figure radically opposed to metaphor in Jakobson's famous theory, is ranked in the system proposed here in the same "square" as metaphor. Everything we have said about synecdoche, which includes a good number of the metonymies proposed by Jakobson, no doubt makes that which justifies this partial assimilation already apparent. We know also that ancient rhetoric was not able to formulate a satisfying definition for metonymy, the majority of these treatises simply enumerating the types. It is said generally that "metonymy consists in taking the cause for the effect, the container for the contained, etc." Domairon risked the remark that between the proper term and the figured term was "a relationship of a relationship" [!].[24] Among modern semanticists (Ullmann's theory mentioned above, for example), metonymy is "a transfer of the noun by *contiguity* of meanings," this contiguity being "spatial, temporal, or causal." Seen this way, there would be little difference between metonymy and synecdoche, for in both cases "the thing receives the name of another thing with which it is in close contact."[25] We do not argue that in the notion of contiguity there is the beginning of a satisfactory theory of metonymy, but we see that the problem is not well formulated by this reference to a "thing."

Du Marsais, one of the rare classical rhetoricians to have asked himself summarily about the difference between metonymy and synecdoche, remarked that in the first figure the "relation between the objects is such that the object whose name is borrowed remains independent of the thing whose idea it wakens and does not form a whole with it ... while the union found between objects in synecdoche assumes that the objects form a whole, such as the whole and a part."[26] Within the vagueness of this formulation, we can find, believe it or not, metonymy's specific character.

In fact, Du Marsais means that metonymy is a figure operating at a constant level where the word being substituted is related as the logical product of the word substituted for. In other words, while metaphor is based on the semic intersection of two classes, metonymy rests on a void. In reference to the logical analysis of metaphor given above, we can say that in the metonymic operation, the passage from the first starting term (S) to the resulting term (R) is made via an intermediary term (I) that includes S and R in either mode Σ or mode Π, that is, via a nondistributive class. Therefore, we have the two excluded cases of metaphoric operation, either Sg Σ or Sp Π (see table 10).

Analyze as an example the sentence "Take up your Caesar," spoken by a teacher to tell his students that they were to continue their study of *De Bello Gallico*. The intermediary term will be the spatio-temporal totality, including

Table 10

Metaphor	Metonymy	Mode
$\overline{S \;(I)\; R}$	$(\widehat{(S) \; I \; (R)})$	
co-possession of semes	co-inclusion of semes in a whole	conceptual Σ (semantic plane)
or of parts	membership in a material whole	material Π (referential plane)

the life of the famous consul, his loves, his literary works, his wars, his times, his city. In this totality of type Π, Caesar and his book are contiguous.

4.2. Connotation

Table 10 brings out the complementarity of metaphor and metonymy: in metaphor the intermediary term is encompassed, while in metonymy it is encompassing. And at this point it is proper to raise the two ideas of denotation and connotation, ideas valid only on the semantic plane but which have their analogues on the referential plane.

Metaphor brings out denotative semes, nuclear semes, included in the definition of terms. Metonymy, on the other hand, brings out the connotative semes, that is, those contiguous to the array of a larger grouping and combining to define this grouping.

According to Yoshihiko Ikegami,[27] whose theory resembles and reinforces our own, there are two sources of connotation: (1) the association of the word with other words (in fact, for him it is also a question of signifiers and signifieds) and (2) associations of the referent of this word with other entities of the actual word (therefore extralinguistic). Linguistic connotations of a word lead to all forms

a) whose phonological structure is partially identical;
b) that can be substituted for it in a given context;
c) with which it can be combined;
d) of which it is a constituent part;
e) whose semantic structure is partially identical;
f) whose graphemic structure is partially identical.

This broad web is potential and differs according to the hearers.

Since any context whatever has the effect of suppressing a part of the forms and meanings of a word, we can say that the *primary* web of association will move toward those forms and meanings eliminated by the immediate context. The *secondary* web will be revealed by applying rules a through f, the *tertiary* web by applying them a second time on the results obtained the first time, and so on.

According to our model of interpretation, the procedures described by Ikegami are not all connotative. Rules *d, e,* and *f* are, in fact, basic to the operations of suppression-addition, rule *e* being precisely basic to metaphor. Rules *c* and *d,* on the other hand, are quite like what we call connotation, and we can see that they apply directly to our analysis of metonymy.

The "species" of metonymies usually in the manual inventories (container/contained, producer/produced, matter/final product, cause/effect, and so on) are nothing other than the broad categories of connotation between terms. Put in the situation of having to reduce a semantic incompatibility neither synecdochic nor metaphoric, the receiver of the message will rely on one or the other of these types of relationships.

This brings us to hypothesizing (to be verified by careful experimentation) that the reader has recourse first to analytic procedures to reduce metasememes. He will first see whether the figure is synecdoche, metaphor, or antiphrasis. It is only when the consideration of the semic datum (nuclear and coded and therefore certain) has failed that he will seek connotative extrapolations that will allow him to identify metonymy.

Connotative categories have rapidly become conventional and have led to the production of series of metonymies more or less cliché, such as the following series of "signs": frock, crown, scepter, shepherd's crook, sword, judge's gown, sail, . . . It is perhaps because of this propensity to cliché that one finds them less and less in modern literature, where they do seem quite rare. A cliché deviation is no longer deviation. Here are some pure metonymies borrowed from the language of sports:

The Fords picked up their feet [Report of the twenty-four-hour race at Le Mans]
The Fords: instrument-agent. *Picked up their feet:* cause-effect.

Here is another example, taken from Victor Hugo, which we shall examine later to analyze antithesis:

You will bring to my *tomb*
What I made for your *cradle.*

Just as metaphor can tend toward no intersection at its limit, metonymy can tend toward an infinitely enveloping whole. The two figures thus join each other, without any intrinsic or extrinsic justification. This possibility (we were about to say "this danger") is widely exploited in advertising, which creates by the encompassing slogan the needed totality, in an operation that is related to *petitio principii.* Take an advertisement metonymically representing a man of action by a powerful sports car with the saying: "SPRINT, the cigarette for the man of action." If the link between "SPRINT," fast car, and "man of action" is obvious, the link between SPRINT and a cigarette is absolutely arbitrary. Far from using an existing link, this advertising formula creates the link from whole cloth.

5. OXYMORON (General Table, Sec. C. 3.3)

Our table of metaboles has the advantage of classifying in the same square oxymoron and antiphrasis, while the usual analysis (Morier) considers oxymoron as a kind of antithesis. Léon Cellier analyzed very well the difference between these two figures from the point of view of their ethos: antithesis as a kind of tragically proclaimed contradiction, paradisiacally assumed for oxymoron.[28] On the formal plane, our analysis will be quite different and will lead to a careful distinction between oxymoron, paradox, and antiphrasis.

Oxymoron is the result of a contradiction between two close words, generally a noun and an adjective: "cloudy clarity," "burning snow." The contradiction is absolute because the negation takes place in an abstract vocabulary: "harmonious discord," "black sun." We have, therefore, a figure in which one term is a nuclear seme negating a classeme of the other term. For example, *darkness* imposes the classeme *obscure,* which is canceled by *visible.*

But there is a real question whether oxymoron is actually a figure, that is, whether it has a degree zero. As Cellier has brought out well, the oxymoron is a *coincidentia oppositorum,* in which the antithesis is denied and the contradiction fully assented to. Therefore, it would be irreducible to any degree zero. Any examination of its occurrences shows, in fact, that very few oxymora are truly irreducible.

And love's the noblest frailty of the mind

[Dryden]

What is noble on one scale of values is only frailty on another scale. As for "... yet from those flames / No light, but rather darkness visible" (Milton), the visible and the darkness do not emanate from a single object, but only from neighboring zones of the flames ... unless *visible* is hyperbole for *dim.*

In the most general case, then, there is a degree zero of oxymoron, just as there is a degree zero of paradox. This is not, however, an absolute rule, and we emphasize this, for such a rule would mean the impossibility of constructing sentences semantically contradictory, an impossibility that any sensible linguist would not risk formulating given the present state of our knowledge.

In respect for our general principle, the reduction of the oxymoron ought to consider the figure *in absentia.* Degree zero of "darkness visible" will be *obscure darkness,* and the shift from *obscure* to *visible* is effected by negative suppression-addition. Certainly "obscure darkness" already constitutes a figure—the epithet, as understood by J. Cohen.

The relationship of oxymoron with antiphrasis is striking, as it is also with paradox. The connection between oxymoron and antiphrasis proposed by certain authors is pure fantasy, since the latter is a metalogism by repetition (*A* is not *A*). Oxymoron violates the code and belongs *de facto* to the class of metasememes. The same is true of the example that Morier classifies with antiphrasis and which is in reality an oxymoron:

> Well then, Madame, since we must use *harsh words,* what will you do with *your wit and your talents* if your Highness has not half a dozen persons of good taste who appreciate them? [Voltaire]

Wit and *talent* are quite the opposite of "harsh words," and there is no need to consider either referent or context to be sure of it, but a dictionary is sufficient. On the other hand—and here lies the interest of this example—if the sentence is addressed to a foolish Highness, there is antiphrasis on *wit* and *talents;* and in the contrary case, there is nothing at all.

6. ATTELAGE—ANTIMETABOLE—ANTANACLASIS*

In this section we will group three figures that are less important but which pose particular problems. Fontanier had already clearly perceived the difficulties, since he grouped them in the category of syllepses or mixed tropes. But the mixture is not precisely defined, as G. Genette correctly stresses in his introduction.[29] According to Fontanier, syllepsis consists (first figure) in using the same word in its proper and its figured meaning at the same time (second figure). The second figure is generally classed as metaphor, synecdoche, or metonymy, and Fontanier's analysis remains perfectly valid from this point of view.

The true difficulty resides in the fact that the second use is not *necessarily* figured, and there exist syllepses that are not mixed just as there exist metaphors not corrected. This is often the case with antanaclasis, called by Fontanier a "childish play on words," that is, a pun.

We know how difficult it is to decide whether two homonyms are or are not different words. The arguments most often used are diachronic, and by this fact have little to do with the rhetorical use of language, which is essentially synchronic (the deviation perceived in the here and now). Rhetoric, therefore, is placed *de facto* in front of the polysemy, at times quite broad, of the vocabulary. To grasp the effect of this polysemy, there is no need to distin-

---

*[We use the French word *attelage* here, as there is no real equivalent in classical rhetoric. In fact, confusion about how to treat this figure seems rife. Leech, for instance, treats Pope's "Here thou, Great Anna! whom three realms obey,/Dost sometimes counsel take—and sometimes Tea" as syllepsis; that is, a metasememic figure that we here call *attelage* (see Geoffrey N. Leech, *A Linguistic Guide to English Poetry* [London: Longman, 1969], p. 211). Richard Lanham, in his *Handlist of Rhetorical Terms* (Berkeley and Los Angeles: University of California Press, 1969), cites the same lines as an example of zeugma, a metataxic figure. The deviation here operates out of word meaning, not word order. *Trans.*]

guish the first or proper meaning from the second or figured one (those already recognized in the code), or more radically, new tertiary meanings. All that is necessary is to consider the rule of isotopy, studied by Greimas, which controls the normal usage of language, that is, degree zero. Attelage, antimetabole, and antanaclasis draw their effects from a controlled polysemy.

The weakest degree of the group is *antimetabole:*

I pretty, and my saying apt? or I apt, and my saying pretty? [Shakespeare]

The two meanings of the word *pretty* (or of the word *apt*) appear in different syntagms (coupled by symmetry) and without any feeling of incompatibility. The incompatibility or the paradox is, on the contrary, basic to *antanaclasis:*

The heart has its reasons which reason does not know. [Pascal]

These two figures, truly quite close, twice use the polysemic vocable, and only the proximity of the two occurrences brings out the metasememe. On the other hand, in *attelage* we have two meanings assumed at the same time by the same word:

Miss Bolo went home in a flood of tears and a sedan chair*

or

I dwell here in the skirts of the forest, like fringe upon a petticoat. [Shakespeare]

In and *skirts* have two meanings simultaneously that one usually calls proper and figured. But if "skirts of the forest" or "in a flood of tears" is in itself a figure (in this place a metaphor), the specificity of the attelage is connected to the fact that it forces us at the same time to consider the proper meaning in "in a sedan chair" or "skirts ... upon a petticoat." We can then consider that *petticoat* or *sedan chair* is there only to reinforce the first, or literal, meaning, that it is not part of the figure, and that every metaphor invites us to perceive simultaneously a first and a second meaning. Syllepses would then only be a variant of metaphor, synecdoche, and metonymy, as Fontanier foresaw.

This reasoning, however, no longer applies to antanaclasis nor to antimetabole, where the two new meanings form an equally acceptable degree zero. The dictionary enumerates meanings that exclude each other: these two figures transgress the code by creating a sort of archilexeme absent from the dictionary and also by grouping semes with two distinct meanings or even opposed meanings. In this last case (the example from Pascal) the figure is close to oxymoron.

We are in the presence of metasememes by addition, and not by suppression-addition as with metaphor, where we are also given a word to be

---

*[Example from H. W. Fowler, *A Dictionary of Modern English Usage*, 2d ed., revised by Sir Ernest Gowers. (New York and Oxford: Oxford University Press, 1978), p. 610. See the article on syllepsis for some discussion on the difference between this figure and zeugma. *Trans.*]

taken in two different meanings. In metaphor, one of the senses has disappeared *from the message* and is called up only on our reflection. It is quite a different case with attelage, puns, antimetabole, and antanaclasis, where the message fully carries the two meanings at the same time and is careful only to isolate them in two different syntagms. We certainly have, therefore, addition of all the semes composing the two distinct meanings, brought together under the "archilexeme" *created* by the particular context that the figure affords it. The term *archilexis* could serve to designate at the same time attelage, antimetabole, and antanaclasis.

Chapter V
Metalogisms

0. GENERAL

Whatever might be its definition, and even if we argue about its "reality," the "real" appears to the scientist as the "paradise of adult love," which must be found or rediscovered endlessly, its faithful image fixed in a language whose supreme quality is its objectivity. The literary man, like the man in the street, has difficulty respecting this sacrosanct objectivity. Either he is unthinkingly attracted to it or he feels its restraints and dreams of escaping it. Either he denies it or he violates it. At times he plays with words, at other times with things.

Metasememes come to his aid when it is a question of passing from one signification to another. Metasememes "pervert" the meanings of words, making us think that a man is not a man but a lion, a crab, or a worm. A cat is not a cat but an emperor, a sphinx, or a woman. The poet, then, whether poet of the streets or literary poet, makes us believe what he himself believes, he makes us see what he wishes to see, and he uses rhetorical "figures" only to "defigure" signs.

Instead of "perverting" the meaning of words in this way, instead of fashioning the language, the rhetorician, whether professional or amateur, can use the objectivity of reality as it "is" so as later to separate himself from it clearly and achieve his effect by this very distancing.

0.1. Metasememes and Metalogisms

There is certainly nothing less "figured" than an expression such as "A cat is a cat." Yet we can see here the motto of the sensible man. For common sense and good usage go together, and it is easy to show how the poet, unwittingly or as a professional, can infringe on either or both thanks to metaboles. We can, for example, follow a "fine strong gentle cat" through the brain of Baudelaire. We see immediately that the cat of Mr. Commonsense would hardly recognize his progeny in it.

A fine strong gentle cat is prowling
As in his bedroom, in my brain;
So soft his voice, so smooth its strain
That you can scarcely hear him miowling.
....
Familiar Lar of where I stay,
He rules, presides, inspires and teaches
All things to which his empire reaches.
Perhaps he is a god, or fay.[1]

It is true that in certain socio-cultural contexts to make a cat divine is not a metaphor. In the same way, we see the cow as something good to milk, while for the Hindus it is a divine being. We could say the same of any animal that figures in a sacred bestiary. In the West during the nineteenth century, nonetheless, according to that common sense so fond of the literal, Baudelaire's expression would certainly qualify as metaphoric in spite of its interrogative form. Metaphor becomes patent when one says "The cat is a god" (A).

We can move next to an expression similar to the last one, with the exception that there is an intervening demonstrative or, as judicious logicians say, an "egocentric particular."[2] In "This cat, it's a tiger" (B), the metaphor is also a hyperbole. Metasememe and metalogism are joined in a single expression. That there is a metaphor is beyond doubt, since we are at present at "analogical transfers of designations,"[3] which would modify the meaning of the words as they are imposed. But it is also clear that the use of the demonstrative refers to the ostensive situation, that is, a situation outside language. At this point, if the analysis of the referent shows that the being in question is, in fact, a cat, except for those who wish to mark its exceptional qualities, the metalogism is clear. If possible, it is even clearer in the paradox "This is not a cat" (C), if it is true that to appreciate this paradox we must on the one hand consult the referent and on the other discover that the being in question is certainly a cat in the current meaning of the term.

These three examples ought to permit us to understand better what distinguishes the metasememe from metalogism, even if, as (B) shows, they can in practice be found in the same expression.

(A). The "fine strong gentle cat" of Baudelaire was neither "fay" nor "god" except for him. We have gotten in the habit of thinking since that time that the cat *is* fay or god. But if the experience to which Baudelaire refers was common, if it had escaped the particular circumstance, the concept "cat" would have been affected, and we can say that the metaphor was imposed as it was in the other cultural contexts to the point of becoming a proposition of fact. In (A) the metaphor plays the role that linguists assign it. As Benveniste points out, it is certainly "such a powerful factor in the enriching of concepts"[4] because it redistributes signifiers and signifieds. That is, if usage were to accept it, it would by this fact impose a semantic modification.

(B), (C). It is quite different for the metalogism, whether "pure" or associated with a metasememe. It can change our way of looking at things, but it does not upset the lexis. On the contrary, it is defined in a state of language that it does not question. At the same time that it is perceived, the necessity of taking words in the meaning some call proper also appears. In spite of paradox (C), a cat remains a cat in the same way that a pipe remains a pipe, whatever Magritte might say about it. That a fearsome sea can be called favorable does not change our ideas of benevolence. And if for Theophile Gautier "the sky is black, the earth is white,"[5] the antithesis made from two hyperboles changes nothing in our concept of colors.

Finally, metalogism demands a knowledge of the referent to contradict the faithful description that could be given of it. By way of the associated metasememes, there can be an accident by a modification of the meaning of the words, but in principle it goes counter to the reputedly immediate data of perception or consciousness. This is why it seems that metalogism, as it differs from metasememe, ought to contain at least an egocentric particular, which is the recognition that there are metalogisms only of the particular. In (B), which is a mixed expression according to our distinction, one can deduce a universal judgment of the metaphor, but this could not be done for hyperbole, since it exists only relative to the state of fact it challenges.

0.2. Ancient Rhetoric and General Rhetoric

Comparing our terminology with the terminology of ancient rhetoric, we can say that metasememe is a trope as Fontanier understands trope in his *Manuel classique pour l'étude des tropes*.[6] But metalogism is not the equivalent of what he names "figure" if the criterion for figure is the substitution of one expression for another, for every metabole is in this way a "figure."[7] Whatever its form, metalogism necessarily has as its criterion reference to some extralinguistic given. In *Figures*, Gérard Genette has recently proposed a definition of figure as "a deviation between sign and meaning, like an interior space of language."[8] However we understand what this "space," metaphoric of course, consists of, it does not define the metalogism. Speaking as Genette has, metalogism would need an *exterior* space, one between the sign and the referent. Genette's definition is too narrow, for it conceives a rhetorical "defiguration" only by comparison with linguistic usage. Within its context, the speech act proves that it is possible to make a paradox without making any deviation within the code. It is not necessary that there be "two terms to be compared, two words combined, a space where thought can operate."[9] Nor is it necessary that the "reader be able to translate implicitly a given expression by another.''[10] Change in meaning and substitution, the criteria for trope and ''figure,'' respectively, do not account for metalogism. The famous paradox by Magritte (''This is not a pipe'') is an empty surprise: it asks for no translation, and if it compares two terms, one of them is a state of fact, not a state of language.

One can say that thought does not exist without language and that, consequently, Magritte's remark is paradoxical because it contradicts a factual proposition: ''This is a pipe.'' But we certainly see that in this circumstance it is the fact that predominates, and the proposition is in no way the literal meaning of the ''figure,'' if one agrees to recognize with ancient rhetoric what the author wanted to say in the literal sense. This proposition is certainly what he could have said if he had tried to describe the situation rather than questioning reality.

If the linguistic signs are not sufficient to indicate metalogism, the traditional ideas of a literal meaning, of usage, and even of deviation are not sufficient to explain it. Metalogism plays, therefore, an essential role in a rhetoric that attempts to be general and to rid itself of epistemological obstacles that have hindered the development of traditional rhetoric. We know how useful it would be to be able to speak rhetorically without at the same time being forced to recognize in the metabole a literal meaning that is always elusive. It is pointless for the followers of Croce to be ironic about ''primary'' or ''proper'' meaning, since the usage on which this meaning is based and from which the metabole is supposed ''to deviate'' is itself made up of innumerable deviations.[11] The study of metasememes, however, already gives us the chance to escape the reproaches of those (Croceans or surrealists) who refuse to admit that a metabole is translatable. We know very well that only the most banal metasememes give an indication of what their literal meaning is. The metasememe refers only in exceptional cases to a *single* proper meaning. It often indicates, however, that it is possible to discover through the ''figured'' meaning different related meanings that proper usage would more easily accept. When we read ''This peaceful roof, where doves walk . . . ,'' we are not forced to admit, following principles of ancient rhetoric, that Valéry wanted to say *sea,* but he could have said *sea, ocean,* or whatever else.[12] If, however, we go along with the surrealists' school and take the metaphor ''according to the letter,''[13] we are mistaken about Valéry's intention. The ''roof'' he gives us is a roof that ''palpitates.'' We miss the meaning of the poem if we remain unaware that he is speaking of the sea, but it is a sea that is to be ''upright,'' as he reminds us later, in front of the contemplator.

Croce, Breton, and their disciples would no doubt have been less violently in revolt against the imperative of rhetoric if rhetoric had not itself been so imperative. When it was mixed with the art of speaking and writing, it was in a position to prescribe and proscribe. But it is possible to construct a rhetoric that does not simply advise the speaker or writer but is used to indicate in discourse what psychiatrists would say were "manifest" in the "latent" meanings that metaboles suggest in denying those meanings.

In ceasing to be a normative discipline, rhetoric can appreciate not *the* deviation but deviations that separate the metabole, not from the "proper" expression, but from expressions closer to received usage. This correction of the theory of deviation (which could, perhaps, save catachresis from the fate that Fontanier and Genette reserved for it[14] by emphasizing that the literal meaning is never anything more than one possible meaning) does not suffice for the study of metalogism. Rhetoric should no longer ask the eternal question, neither of the writer nor of the marketplace rhetorician, so dear to Du Marsais, What did he mean? Nor should it limit itself to asking, What could he have said if he had obeyed the norms of the language in which he is expressing himself? The infraction of the usual norms, in fact, which can be a sufficient condition for a metabole, is not its necessary condition.

If we call an "ace" anyone who excels in a discipline, the meaning of the metaphor is so clear that it has subsequently moved into the language. Even at the time it was "fresh," only a ninny would have mixed an exceptional man with a playing card. Its literary aspect is transparent in the metaphor, since the idea of supremacy serves as the mediating term between the received expression and the metaphoric expression. But even today, if we called an obvious cretin by this name, no recourse to usage would make the antiphrasis felt. The metasememe can indicate in what terms it would also be expressible, translating it by periphrasis, if the language has no equivalent, as is usually the case. On the other hand, one can seek in vain through lexicons without ever finding an equivalent, not even an approximation, of a metalogism, the reason being that it is in principle circumstantial. This is not a play on words, because even if one were to suggest for it a "proper" meaning, this meaning would only be a middle term between the metalogism and the appropriate situation.

By applying Occam's razor to ancient rhetoric, Gérard Genette has properly denounced the "rage to name" that motivated it.[15] In fact, Lamy, DuMarsais, Fontanier, and their fellow workers like Linnaeus spent the best of their efforts in endlessly inventorying the "species" of rhetoric, without ever being able to bring their respective taxonomies into agreement, since it is always possible to discover or to invent new "species." Proof of this is that we in our turn are proposing neologisms for rhetorical analysis. But our goal is different from theirs: it is not a question of discovering the missing link but one of defining the fundamental operations of which figures and tropes are the particular cases. Trying for an exhaustive taxonomy, the ancients failed to see that it is often impossible to "translate" a metabole, or if one prefers, to reduce it to others. This is particularly true in the field of metasememes, since a metaphor, for example, can be interpreted as the product of two synecdoches. The single translation admitted in ancient rhetoric was the reduction of the literal meaning, conceived as a "substance" of which metaboles were "accidents." This substantialist prejudice is responsible for still another error. Once recognized, once given the name said to fit them, these "accidents" themselves appeared to be "substantial." Their nature is fixed once and for all, and the only further question is to find the place in the inventory where they fit. This is a way of forgetting that metaboles have no existence as such, that they are not natural beings and that one can cease constructing them for the pleasure of classifying them. Language becomes this "fourth kingdom" that Bréal contested,[16] and metaboles, endowed with an independent existence, cover up the laws that govern them by their very number.

This verbal inflation of the ancients has particularly complicated the problem of making distinctions between tropes and figures. To clarify the problem, however, it is sufficient to consider language in its referential function. It makes little difference that a metasememe at times has the value of a metalogism. It even makes little difference that the metalogic procedure can be applied to every metasememe. In a given expression striking because of its equivocality, the essential thing is to be able to distinguish one from the other. Metaboles are neither "species" nor "monads." Metalogisms in particular are procedures, operations, or maneuvers that can double a metasemantic operation and can also, although less frequently, work without any metasememe.

We all know, to use an example as demonstration, how difficult it is to know what a silence "says." If certain silences, however, are more eloquent than words, they are not always a simple absence of words. Silence is a respectable metabole. Its mark and effect are often recognizable, but it is more difficult to say what it is. When it is deadly, understood, or obstinate, it has a certain sense; it can even say a lot. It is, however, rarely translatable in the manner that the ancients understood this operation. Its "proper" meaning always remains only a possibility, and often we are unable to explore that possibility. When this can be done, however, most of the time it is by recourse to a referent. Certainly, we can defend the existence of metasemic silences that a knowledge of the usage and strictly linguistic content takes into account. When in a text *ad usum delphini*, for example, certain terms are omitted as too crude, the alert reader reestablishes the original easily, for usage admits such maneuvers and we can hardly speak of metabole. But in the majority of cases, silence unveils what it wants to say only through the referent. To understand the silence of a lawyer, of an accused, or of any babbler, it is often necessary that the referent indicate what it could mean for the metabole to be perceived. It does not modify the code. How could it? It does not modify usage, for usage has not yet rigorously established when it is "normal" to remain silent. Perhaps this is when there is nothing to say, but then silence is not a metabole in this case. There is only a metabole if silence indicates an omission, and it is to be understood as a metalogism only if the omission does not keep us from considering what could have been said. Its "proper" meaning, then, if we can still speak in this way, depends essentially on the ostensive situation imposed.

The same holds true for litotes, which we consider a metalogism. By passing into usage, the words of Chimène came to be a metasememe. For the initiated, "not to hate" can mean "to love."* It is nonetheless true that what is a litotes in the mouth of Chimène is so only because we know of her love for Rodrigue. The litotes would be empty even in the terms Corneille used if one did not know the sentiments to which the expression referred. It is true that metasememes can necessitate the same knowledge. Metaphor *in absentia*, especially, does not appear as metaphor unless the referent is known. "It's a tiger" is a metaphor only if the being referred to is a man or a certain gasoline. To stand in front of a cage of felines and say "It is a tiger" does not shift us into rhetoric. In the same way, if it happens that the metasememe requires moving outside language, this is only a maneuver to reveal metabole. If Pascal were still alive and could communicate his "thoughts" to a friend, he could say of a passerby in a tone mixed with sadness and pride: "That man you see there is perhaps only a reed, but he is a thinking reed." He would be using here a metalogism, but with the unique goal of imposing a semantic modification. The metaphor of the man/reed has been freed from any ostensive situation, the concept of fragility serving as a mediating term, without the necessity of passing by way of the referent.

In his *Exercises de style*, Raymond Queneau relates the same happening in a hundred different ways.[17] One of the recountings is titled "Litotes," and we could well believe that these litotes, according to ancient rhetoric, have a literal meaning, since in his "Notations" at the beginning the author takes this as his task. It is quite clear, however, that these notations are meant only to present the happening; they are not themselves literal. Queneau is giving here simply another point of view among many, one that can be taken conventionally as the "common and simple" description of the events reported. In fact, it is not certain that if the expression of them is "common and simple," the faithful description of the facts in question can be recognized, according to the views of Du Marsais. To be sure of that, one would have to be present at the happening. There is litotes only because Queneau wants it so. Without a referent, we can only infer that there is neither hyperbole nor paradox. On the other hand, when the fellow in the "Notations," the young man who "didn't seem too intelligent" in "Litotes," is presented in "Metaphorically" as a "chicken with a long neck," we recognize the metaphor because we know, without need of verification, that a man is not a chicken. Finally, that some people are "chickens" in slang confirms here again that this is a question of

*[The reference here is to Corneille's *Le Cid*, act 3, sc. 4, line 963. *Trans.*]

words, because neither do we have to witness an act of courage to know that a man is not gallinaceous.*

It is not impossible that someone might take Queneau's metaphor literally and consider that the hero of *Exercises de style* is, in fact, a chicken. If, on the other hand, one accepts "Notations" as a faithful account of the events, we can say that "Litotes" warrants its name. However that may be, these examples show that measuring the "deviation between the sign and the meaning" is not always sufficient and at times is not necessary. The literal meaning, which was an obsession of ancient rhetoric, can be only a stage where one does not necessarily find the meaning of the metabole. Metasememes and metalogisms are in practice so closely tied that there is a tendency to confuse them, but we have no less an interest to distinguish them.

0.3. Logic and Metalogism

Whatever their theoretical stance, logicians agree in admitting that there are syntactically correct enunciations that are nonetheless devoid of meaning. Take

(1) Quadruplicity drinks temporalization [Russell]

(2) Caesar is a prime number [Carnap]

Since logicians are interested in meaning only, utterances of this type do not hold their attention any longer than it takes them to show that they are devoid of meaning. If this is true, according to these authors, it is because they transgress logical categories. " 'Prime number' is a predicate of numbers; it can be neither affirmed nor denied of a person."[18] On the same situation, Gilbert Ryle, in his *Concept of Mind,* speaks of "category mistake."[19] What the logician condemns is precisely what interests the rhetorician. In particular, it is not an accident that the theories of Ryle are basic for the study of metaphor for several English-language authors. His "category mistake," which is used to denounce the absurdity of Cartesianism, is rebaptized "category confusion" by Turbayne, who opposes it to "category fusion,"[20] in which he sees the process by which metaphor is constructed. In any case, it is a question of presenting the facts "as if they belonged to one logical category . . . when in reality they belonged to another."[21] The process is the same; but what logic condemns rhetoric recognizes, working to distinguish metabole from error and from nonsense.

Rhetoric has, perhaps, the right to make an assertion concerning the attribution of meaning to expressions that "say nothing" to Carnap. Categories of the logician can be judged metaphoric. And if they are not metaphoric, it is

---

*[The original here operates on the slang sense of *poulet* in French: "cop." The last sentence literally reads: "Finally, that some people are *poulets* in the vulgar sense, and that public order reign, confirms here again that this is a question of words, because neither do we have to see a policeman to know that he is not gallinaceous." *Trans.*]

because they correspond to categories of reality. If with Breton, one believes "in the future resolution of those two states that are so contradictory in appearance, dream and reality, in a sort of absolute reality, a surreality,"[22] it is then conceivable that expressions seemingly devoid of meaning acquire one according to the point of view adopted toward them. Without calling up "surreality," there can be a meaning found for Carnap's sentence. In a certain *Sprachspiel,* or "language game,"[23] it is possible to give each prime number the name of a person. If we do not prejudge the "reality" to which (1) and (2) refer, we cannot affirm that they are devoid of meaning. One can even argue their ambiguity. It is this ambiguity that for the logician is the sign of non-sense. He has no need to busy himself with it. On the other hand, it is of prime importance for rhetoric.

At first sight, all rhetorical utterances appear ambiguous. It is true that man is a reed since he is fragile, but it is false since he is not a plant. It is not enough to say that utterances are false. They are at the same time true and false. More precisely, they are at the same time able to be verified or proven false. The logician is right to consider them "pseudo-propositions," because they answer none of the criteria of truth. They have no logical "meaning," but they nonetheless express different meanings among which they do not oblige us to choose, but among which they forbid us a choice. If choice were possible, verification would be also.

There exist, however, utterances that are of interest in logic as well as in rhetoric. The logician may refuse to follow the poet when he says that there are perfumes "green like prairies" or that the earth "is only a giant unfolded newspaper." The "category mistake" allows the logician to decline. We must notice, however, that "logical possibility" varies with the author. A sentence that Carnap condemns is taken by Russell as logically possible.[24] The commentator of Wittgenstein, Max Black, does not refuse to consider the remark of Chamfort, according to whom "the poor are the Negroes of Europe."[25] This is because it is, in fact, difficult to decide precisely when the "fusion" of categories becomes "nonsense" and therefore precludes logic from being interested in it. As long as Caesar is presented as a prime number, the "category mistake" can appear clear. But if we say that he is a lion, a black, or an ace?

It is impossible to say whether Chamfort's phrase is true or false until we have decided what poor and what blacks he is talking about. Without the ostensive situation, the logician cannot assign it a truth value. But within the situation, he can. The problem is then to know when such a situation holds. The commentary we gave for (2) leaves this as a possibility, but only on condition of constructing a "language game" starting with the message in question and boldly modifying the meanings of words. Without this, such utterances have at most a metaphoric meaning, a possible meaning for those who admit transgression of logical categories.

The distinction constructed between falsehood and nonsense can be useful in rhetoric. It allows us to distinguish two types of utterances that include what we have been calling until now metasememes and metalogisms. Metaboles, no doubt, do not always present themselves in a predicative format, but it is always possible to reduce them to it. In this case, the metasememe is always a ''pseudo-proposition,'' for it presents a contradiction that logic disallows and that rhetoric accepts. This is true of metaphor; it is also true of the other metasememes. In the predicative format, metasememe uses the copula in a manner the logician considers illicit, because *to be* signifies in this case ''to be and not to be.'' To grasp the metaphor in Chamfort's expression, it is necessary first of all to know that a poor person is not a black and next to disdain this distinction in order to admit that if he is not, he nonetheless is. In this way, we can reduce all metasememes to the formula proposed by Harrison

$$(\exists x) \, (fx. \sim fx),$$

which is the formula of contradiction,[26] with the exception that this is not a contradiction.

Metalogism, on the contrary, is of direct interest for the logician because it offers an ostensive contradiction. The metalinguistic process to which the logician has recourse for establishing the truth or falsehood of a proposition is the same one used by rhetoric to establish the necessary falsehood of the metalogism. The ''Leave! I do not hate you at all'' by which Chimène dismisses Rodrigue is not devoid of meaning. Analysis of the referent shows simply that in this way Chimène hesitates to speak the truth. While metasememe is unaware of logic, metalogism is accepted as false in the truth function dear to certain logicians. By applying the metalogic procedure to Chamfort's metaphor, we can now establish that he is exaggerating or that he is saying too little about the situation.

Notice once again that metalogical analysis is not prescribed. For anyone who knows, for example, that *black* in French (*nègre*), can designate a ghost writer, often poorly paid, the qualifier (the other side of the Atlantic) is no obstacle. For him alone the linguistic signs propose a metaphor that usage has at least prepared, if not expressly ratified. In this usage, as Whitehead has said, we can ''take a vacation from reality'' by recognizing either that a certain ambiguity remains or even that a metaphor is absent. On the other hand, to find the eventual metalogism, we must invoke reality and confront the signs with their referent. To note the metalogism, we must in addition be assured that the signs do not give a faithful description of the referent.

0.4.   Metalogisms and Figures of Thought

It seems that we are not able to remove metalogisms from the table of metaboles. For each one of them, in fact, we can establish a protocol that gives the truth of the facts that the metalogism contests. This protocol is not a literal meaning, since it goes counter to usage. It is an *a posteriori* construct that causes the metalogism to appear as a contradiction imposed on the truth function. This protocol is not what one wanted to say; it is what truth would oblige one to say.

One can admit, along with Genette, that although translatable in principle, the metasememe is never translated without the loss, if not of meaning, at least of certain connotations that it contains. The metalogism is translatable, but whether translated or not, it conserves its meaning. But it might just as well be called untranslatable, since without putting the code into question, it "contradicts" a state of fact, if this can be said. Hence, it resembles the canonical figures of thought that Fontanier said were "independent of words, of expression, and of style and stayed no less the same basically, in terms of substance, even when the style, expression, and words were quite different."[27]

0.5.　Range of Metalogisms

The range of the metasememe derives from its definition. Replacing one group of semes (or sememes) by another, it concerns one word. We did justice at the appropriate place to the illusion created by figures *in praesentia* and those that seemed to invoke several words. It is always possible to reduce them to figures *in absentia* (as in the cases of metaphor and oxymoron).

The definition of metalogism, on the other hand, entails no limitation of range, except that concerning units of meaning equal to or higher than the word. If the metalogism affects only a single word (true for example in numerous hyperboles and litotes), its semantic content appears altered, but that is because a metasememe is then doubling as a metalogism. In itself, metalogism only transgresses the "normal" relation between the concept and the thing signified. The norm invoked here is the one of a veridical language, a truth mirror.

At the time of a visit by a prince, the welcome reserved for a prince being what it is, say, cool, it will be judged by observers as "warm" or "icy." A group of students demanding rights of self-determination in a university are judged in the same way, according to the nature of the judge, as "isolated groups," a "new class," a "party," a "power," if not "for the revolution" itself. Their actions are taken by some as "stirring up," or at best as "arousing" opinion, while for others they are "demanding" or "constructing" the world of tomorrow.

For these reasons, the symmetry of the following general table (table 11) will be given only a didactic value, for the number of units of meaning does not have a discriminating value here. This is less true, however, for certain metalogisms, like allegory, which can be claimed in principle to call for a collection of signs, since its role is to develop a metaphor. Even in this case, however, it is quite difficult to claim, unless *a priori,* that a metaphor is limited

**Table 11.   Differentiating Criteria of
Metasememe and Metalogism**

Criterion	Metasememe	Metalogism
Linguistic 1. Field of alteration	Code	Relation to the context and/or to the referent
2. Range	One word	One or several words
Logical 1. Value	Neither true nor false	False
2. Quantity	Universal or particular	Particular
Ontological	Not circumstantial	Circumstantial

necessarily to an isolated sign, while an allegory appears as soon as at least two signs come into play.

0.6.   Decomposition

If every rhetorical operation rests on the possibility of decomposing discourse into units, we can ask what the units in question are in metalogism if it is true that it distinguishes the referent or the context. But we certainly understand that the decomposed elements cannot be other than linguistic, because the only manner of acting on the referent is to act on the language that renders an account of this referent. The operation concerns, therefore, the sememes, but without leading to any alteration of the code.

1.   SUPPRESSION

1.1. With *litotes* the arithmetical character of rhetorical operations appears clearly. One says less so as to say more; that is, the extralinguistic datum is considered as a quantity in which certain parts may be suppressed at will. True litotes, which according to Fontanier "more or less *diminishes*" a "thing"[28]—as does hyperbole, but in the opposite direction—is a displacement along an intensive series (cf. chap. IV, sec. 0.6.3). It is certainly a question of semic suppression or addition. Thus, through shyness or to control the other, we can say, "I like you" or "I feel a certain affection for you" when what we want to say, in fact, is "I love you." Other litotes, ones appearing more frequently, work by suppression-addition and will be considered later.

1.2. Rather than continuing with litotes, which has hardly suffered from the discredit into which other metaboles have fallen, we ought to consider that if the "lessening" that Fontanier speaks of is pushed to the limit, we arrive at *silence*, for at times the best way of saying less is to say nothing at all. Thus we see that in certain situations the silence of a government, the press, or right-thinking persons has the value of litotes. Silence, the metalogic equivalent of ellipsis, confirms that the number of units of signification is not the criterion for clearly distinguishing metasememes from metalogisms.

If litotes works through a partial suppression of semes, silence works through the total suppression of signs. In this way, however, lies the path to conjectures, allowing adventure on the part of the decoder who is obliged to choose an addition, if not of signs, at least of semes. Silence is one of the four invariant figures spoken of in chapter I, sec. 2.4. It can be analyzed as a figure belonging at the same time to each of our four categories.

When it coincides with a rupture in the discourse, silence takes the name *aposiopesis.** If it is only provisional rupture, we call it *suspension*. In the three cases, the code is not broken, but, in fact, eliminated. Certainly a look at the context can at times indicate what sequence has been omitted, at times allowing it to be reconstructed. Nonetheless, three metaboles, which are really only one, most often draw their signification from the state of fact about which they are unwilling to say anything. Certain aposiopeses have the value of "etc." We can see this as the limit of synecdoche, where even the smallest part of the seme is judged superfluous. But others, where conjecture is enjoined about the suppressed sequence, may be interpreted as a refusal to proceed even to the most enigmatic alteration of the code. They disqualify the code to the benefit of silence. They refuse metabole, and precisely for this reason they are metaboles that economize the code no matter what it is as a way of indicating its insufficiencies, of showing that it offers nothing or is, in fact, even a danger.

2. ADDITION

2.1. Hyperbole

Arithmetical operation is as flagrant in *hyperbole* as in litotes. More is said as a way of saying less, or as Fontanier says, things are "augmented,"[29] that is, the intensive semes are modified. If litotes can lead to silence, hyperbole seems to have no assignable limit. We can imagine Cyrano exhausting all

---

*[*Réticence* in the original. *Trans.*]

languages to celebrate the sublimity of his nose. There is, however, a hyperbolic way of treating litotes; for example, the Pharisee who could spend his
life in the temple repeating "I am but a poor sinner," when he knows that he
is a rich apostate.

Even silence can be hyperbolic. Faced with certain sights, or under the
stress of strong emotion, a speaker who suddenly keeps silent or an author
who closes his discourse with suspension dots says more than really exists
about the spectacle or emotion and lets us believe that he is nonetheless
thinking about it. Silence is in this way hyperbolic every time that it is what
one could say in addition (see the General Table, sec. D.2, for another kind of
silence).

2.2.   Repetition, Pleonasmus, Antithesis

Addition can be purely *repetitive*. It becomes then *repetitio* or *pleonasmus*. Repetition is certainly not necessarily a metabole. When a professor
repeats for the poor student who never understands, he is not necessarily using
rhetoric; but if he blindly trusts to the precept *bis repetita placent,* the good
students can notice that he is saying too much.

Our goal in general rhetoric is not to find an exhaustive taxonomy of all the
"species" of metabole known through the past, and at least provisionally we
can allow some figures like expletion and epiphenomena (which, however, do
work by addition) to remain in the ancient repertories. The essential thing is to
emphasize that in the category of metalogisms through addition could be
included metaboles that, if we can consider the referent from a quantitative
point of view as an assemblage of units, add units, by a linguistic operation, to
this group that does not contain them. Looking at it this way, that pleonasmus
is a metalogism could be challenged, because it adds nothing useful. The
signifiers it offers are empty. When a witness whose words are suspect repeats, "Me, I saw him, with my own eyes, saw!" he would have to be a bat at
least to surprise the person he is addressing. Pleonasmus seems to be directed
only at the receiver of the message, without concern for the referent. When
reduced to its degree zero, the referent can be described as "an *I* has seen it."
Then the *I* that is speaking, like the *seen,* is a referential unit that it is not
necessary to repeat. To see pleonasmus as a metalogism by addition, one must
not, as does the linguist, see in the *I* only "the person who is uttering the
present instance of the discourse containing *I.*"[30] The *I* must be taken as a
fragment of space-time that can be questioned and need not be mentioned
twice. If not, the pleonasmus that we evoke will move into the category of
metaboles of interlocutors who acknowledge the *I*. On the other hand,
equivocation disappears if we consider pleonasmus or repetitio without personal pronouns. "My cat, my cat!" A mother Macree can repeat these two
words without stopping. Is she only piling up redundant terms? This is not

certain, because she makes us understand that she has not simply lost a cat, but *her* cat, and *what* a cat! her *dear* cat!

Like pleonasmus and hyperbole, repetitio can "enlarge" the event, can "augment" things. It can also add semes and phonemes, but it marks above all the distance established concerning the referent, which it treats as a sum of ontological units to which language adds supplementary units.

Antithesis can seem to conform to these facts. It is a figure using repetition in the sense that instead of uttering "A," it adds: "A is not non-A." We read, for example:

... neither the one *hurt* her, nor the other *help* her

[Sidney]

or

He *raised* a *mortal to* the skies;
She *drew* an *angel down*

[Dryden]

The condition of such an antithesis is the possibility of a lexical negation and the abstract terms, often opposed two by two, that fit it particularly, like *love / hate, beautiful / ugly,* while concrete terms often lack opposites. As Kibédi Varga emphasizes, we can oppose *love* to *hate,* but not *streetlight* to *cheese.*[31] The same author recalls, following Lausberg, that opposite terms ought to present a common element—common semes with an acceptable isotopy—or there is the possibility of dropping into comedy, as follows:

Prices get on and travelers get off.*

Whatever else it may be, comedy is only a particular ethos. It does not concern the general structure of antithesis, but we see in these examples, reputedly poetic, that the common element is decidedly present. In the example from Gautier cited above, "The sky is black, the earth is white," this element is the simultaneous and contiguous presence of sky and earth in the same countryside. The effect of the following would be totally different:

Chinese ink is black, snow is white.

The example is complicated, however, by the fact that it opposes two hyperboles, as do many antitheses. If we believe Morier, who cited this example, the sky "was perhaps only gray. . . ." But besides its naiveté, such a commentary is wrong in understanding *black* in the sense of "gray," while Gautier's whole effort is to persuade us, against experience, that the sky was black. Even if he asks us to imagine a sky "of deepest gray," the first of the hyperboles making up the antithesis has meaning only by the deviation it

*[In French, "Les prix montent et les voyageurs descendent." *Trans.*]

emphasizes between a sky that might be gray while the earth is white and the truly black sky that Gautier's verse imposes. Antithesis is, then, the result of two hyperboles, neither of which modifies the sense of the words, but both of which, as well as the resulting antithesis, play on the deviation suspected between a referent that is not to be lost sight of and language that adds to a description of realistic intent some occasional semes.

Take an example from Hugo:

> . . . and you will bring to my tomb
> What I made for your cradle.

Leaving aside the metaplasms (*tomb/your cradle*)* and the metasememes (the two metonymies, *tomb* and *cradle*), we find here five antitheses:

you	future	bring	my	tomb
I	past	make for	your	cradle

The antithetic series are, however, united by the same semantic axis: the link addresser-addressee, on the one hand, and especially the relationship of equivalence *that/which*, which ties together the two single non-antithetical and indefinite terms of the distich. This *what* or *that which* functions in the same way as the x of an algebraic equation. Taken alone, *tomb* and *cradle* have no hyperbolic value. The simple juxtaposition, however, has the effect of simultaneously reinforcing the two opposed terms. Thus, although the antithesis is not necessarily based on a combination of two hyperboles, nonetheless it itself has a hyperbolic character.

3. SUPPRESSION-ADDITION

3.1. Euphemisms

Consider three persons leaving a play they judged painful. One of them, following proper and expected behavior, will say, "That wasn't bad"; the other, "That was magnificent"; and the third, "That wasn't devoid of interest." But we know that it was devoid of interest. Proper and expected behavior apart, they could agree to saying: "That was painful." Such a remark takes the place of degree zero for their *euphemisms,* different in their formulation but identical in their function and functioning. The form of the euphemism can vary. It can be a litotes or a hyperbole. It can say more or less, but most of the time it says more and less at the same time, suppressing in a remark reputedly objective the semes judged cumbersome or superfluous and substituting new ones. An invariant remains that allows us to guess the

---

*[The metaplasms are perceived only in French, of course: *tombe/ton berceau*. *Trans.*]

euphemism, but linked with adventitious semes that, while not hiding it completely, partially defigure it.

3.2. Allegory

With *allegory,* substitution appears total. We read in "On First Looking into Chapman's Homer" by Keats,

Much have I travell'd in the realms of gold,
 And many goodly states and kingdoms seen;
 Round many western islands have I been
Which bards in fealty to Apollo hold.
Oft of one wide expanse had I been told
 That deep-browed Homer rules as his demesne;
 Yet never did I breathe its pure serene
Till I heard Chapman speak out loud and bold. . . .

In reality, the substitution cannot be total on the semantic plane because on the rhetorical plane the invariant is there with the mark to allow us to grasp the allegory instead of seeing in the expression only a travelogue.

Since antithesis is often composed of hyperboles, allegory, like parable and fable, is often made from metaphor. But it can also be supported by particularizing synecdoches, as is the case in numerous novels that function as propaganda for certain ways of life or in those cautionary ballads, a kind of popular song that was once quite popular in the United States. However that may be, if at the lower level of allegory, parable and fable are composed of metasememes, we can show that at a higher level these genres constitute a metalogism. It is clear that they are used often to disguise through an unexpected and charming anodyne exterior realities whose crude expression can disturb or which in literal formulation appear inacessible to the understanding of the audience. As such they are close to euphemisms. But we cannot bring in the ethos of a figure this way without denying our methodological attitude. On the contrary, we must show that by their very structure allegory, parable, and fable are metalogisms. The example indicates this. Having served as a metaphor in Western tradition, "Apollo" is an allusion (another metalogism) that suggests that the islands in question can designate a body of literature rather than geographical locations. As for the first nominal group, it takes its meaning by reference to the later one, and the literary fortune of "Apollo" lets us understand that "the realms of gold" can certainly be literature also. This said, the complete sentence may be read for whatever value at degree zero and present an acceptable meaning, although of little interest. It is precisely this deception concerning the first meaning that prods us to see if a second and less banal isotopy, might not perhaps exist.

Suppose that the lines appear in isolation, as lines inserted in a journal. However thin it might be, the context is a base inviting us to seek a second meaning in literary events rather than in sea voyages. The association of "Apollo" with Greek poets lets us suppose, on the other hand, that it is a question of a certain kind of literature. Thus the invariant appears: "islands," "bards," "bold," which through their connotations are just so many indicators to determine our final choice.

The same analysis is valid for parables and fables. Taken literally, they furnish an inadequate meaning, which is itself a mark. In addition, they always operate in the same restricted semantic fields, and for this reason partially coded ones: pastoral life for religious parables, animal life and manners for fables. As for true allegories, they have reached such a level of codification that dictionaries of them have been constructed. This constitutes a second mark. Context is another, to the extent that it prepares us to find the literal meaning insufficient. While context is necessary for understanding the lines of Keats, it would be much less so if "Apollo" pointed to religion instead of to literature. That is, in the figures we are now analyzing, the context and codification having the same marked value, they make each other superfluous—a single one would have sufficed.

When we state that the first meaning is insufficient, we ought to justify our impression. If we agree to call *transformeds* the constituent elements of degree zero (as a general rule for characters, abstract institutions, and so on), and *transformates* these same elements after their rhetorical transformation, we obtain the following schema, valuable for the transformeds *i:*

$$\text{metasememe}$$
$$\text{(transformed) } i \xrightarrow{\hspace{1.5cm}} \text{(transformate)}$$

The metasememic transformation is generally a metaphor (king $\longrightarrow$ lion) or a particularizing synecdoche (wily $\longrightarrow$ fox; worker $\longrightarrow$ bee or ant). At the same time, the relationship existing between the transformed is transposed to the level of the transformates, either as it is (in fables: judgment, pleading, language) or by the intermediary of a metasememic transformation (bad action $\longrightarrow$ devouring). But these relevant relationships at the level of the transformeds are not true at the level of the transformates: it is in the truest sense that one can say that the ant "is not a lender." A resumé of this appears in figure 16.

We can now explain our formulation more precisely: when the first isotopy appears to be insufficient, it is because of the irrelevance of the relationships compared with the elements to which they are connected (for example, absence of a court or tribunal among the animals). When the irrelevance is exaggerated, it seems ridiculous, as in expressions like, "The car of state sails over a volcano."

This analysis gives sufficient emphasis to the role of metasememes in the

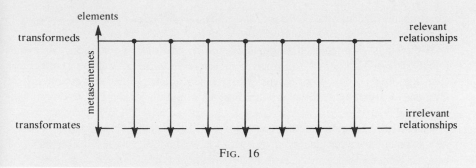

F<small>IG</small>. 16

figures observed: it can play a role in the transformation of each element. Metalogism, nonetheless, appears to be a figure of the whole and can be understood only by knowing the particular referent—human society in La Fontaine's fables, Greek literature in Keats's words.

We can understand the metaphor of literary activity as Apollo if we suppress from the signified "literature" some troublesome semes and add to it certain semes contained by *Apollo*. But when allegory is developing, it is often necessary to consult the referent to distinguish the figured formulation from another, presumably naive formulation, into which it is not truly translatable (in which case the metaboles would only be "vain ornaments"), but in which the protocol of the event under consideration is recognizable.

In time of war, "The myosotis are in flower" could mean "The allies have landed." If we see here an allegory, we also see that knowing a secret code is enough to decipher it. It is somewhat difficult to speak of metabole here, since degree zero is certainly unknown to some. In fact, this is like giving an account in a foreign language. For the person unaware of the code, however, there is the possibility of such an expression appearing to be allegorical if certain elements in the adopted language recall the event in question. If, for example, the message still retains suggestive terms, if it is poorly translated, if the terms are not arbitrarily chosen, an occasional receiver, say a spy, could "get to the facts" through the allegory. Such cases are frequent in daily life. In the present case, too explicit an allegory points to the event it ought to hide. It reveals certain aspects of it; and after suppressing the deceptive semes, the protocol of the considered event can be composed simply by adding the descriptive semes to the ones remaining. Substitution is then only partial, but our starting point indicates well enough that it could be total.

3.3.   Irony

Euphemism comes close to *irony* when substitution is made to enhance negation. Using irony, one can say of a mediocre author that he is esteemed. The same thing can be said seriously as euphemism. Formally, the two metalogisms can become confused, but irony shows better how the facts can be distanced, for it almost always denies them.

Antiphrasis is hardly distinguishable from the above tropes.* "Fine mind!" can be said today to stigmatize a deplorable attitude. Such an expression does not always demand consulting the referent. If the expression is frequent, it can be understood as a metasememe, but at times it can be forced into metalogism.

Take a mother saying to her progeny, "Little monster!" The code is in no way violated; whether the designated child is, in fact, a monster or not, and whether or not the mother is speaking in a hostile or affectionate context, the figure will appear in the one case and disappear in the other. Thus we perceive the deviation according to the context, linguistic or extralinguistic. Without such recourse, one possible solution would be to have a special punctuation mark, such as the ironic point (ζ) invented by Alcanter de Brahm to mark the inverse value of the remark.[32]

But intermediary cases exist, two canonical examples of which are Daddy Warbucks and Cape of Good Hope. To find the figure here after it has been buried under centuries of conventional lexicalization, we must know that the first is a generous philanthropist and the second a place of constant storms. All Daddy Warbuckses are philanthropic, and only high seas and danger are to be found at the Cape of Good Hope. The next problem is to know whether the code has been violated. What is a truly nuclear seme, that is, a coded seme? We broached the question in section 0.6.5 concerning concrete and abstract words, concluding that concrete words escape the code. For the amateur of crossword puzzles, the code is contained in the *American Heritage Dictionary,* where we find that the sun is a "star that is the basis of the solar system and that sustains life on earth." But the *Oxford English Dictionary* accepts other semes, and the *Encyclopaedia Britannica* even more. Between the code and the thing, several levels of description are possible, so that the limit between metasememe (alteration of the code) and metalogism (alteration of the extralinguistic context) is seen as relative. But taking everything into

---

*[In a recent article, Group μ has added to its account of irony and antiphrasis: "In *A General Rhetoric* irony was 'hardly' distinguished from antiphrasis. The reason for this lack of rigor is to be found, no doubt, in the intuitive acceptance of irony as ethos and not as a formal structure. It is precisely by taking into account the cleavage between these two planes that we can propose a tentative general definition of irony: as *ethos* (or figural effect), irony is an affective category to be classified in the series of values of derision, from sarcasm to black or genial humor; as *structure* (or empty metabole), it is confused with antiphrasis, a particular case of suppression-addition bearing on the logical value of the utterance. This double aspect is to be maintained: irony will be understood here [in the article] at the same time as figure and as the effect of figure. To isolate just one of these data is to risk error, ambiguities, confusion. Finally, we note that a definition of irony is possible only at a 'molecular' level and not at the 'atomic' level: it is nothing other than the intersection of an antiphrastic structure and a mocking ethos" (Group μ, "Ironique et iconique," *Poétique* 36 [1978]: 428). *Trans.*]

consideration, this is only the rhetorical view of one of the essential problems of semantics.

Certain very frequent *litotes* proceed by suppression-addition:

Go, I do not hate you!

[Corneille]

        I did endure
Not seldom, nor no slight checks. . . .

[Shakespeare]

These are close to irony and antiphrasis, but they obviously merit a particular treatment in that they result in a double, even triple, negative. Todorov correctly remarks that litotes is "emphasizing the difference between a grammatical negation and the lexical negation that is its opposite."[33] Antiphrasis and irony proceed to simple negation. They are noted because of the irrelevance of the relationship between context or referent, on the one hand, and the apparent meaning of the figure on the other. Once these are noted, in order to understand the figure's real sense it is enough to understand the words in a meaning opposite to the one they seem to have and which they do in fact have in the code being used. The litotes that we are examining here are more complex. The original utterance undergoes two simultaneous negations that at first glance, it seems, ought to cancel each other. But this is not so. The first one, the lexical negation, the one accounting for the antiphrasis, starts from a precise term and ends up at another precise term according to a coded, perfectly symmetrical semic opposition (hatred / love). The second one, the grammatical negation, would do the same if it corresponded to the logical negation in a system with two values. But the intensive seriations that are the domain of litotes carry a number of degrees. In Chimène's remark, these are what are counted off in the petals of a daisy. In such an assemblage, to deny one element is the same as posing at the same time all the others, not simply one of them.

We have all the more reason for classifying these litotes in this category, since we have until now considered negation as the suppression of a positive seme and its replacement by the corresponding negative seme.

Among the metalogisms that deny expressly that things are as they are we can mention those that ancient rhetoric knew under the names *occupatio, asteismus,* or *epanorthesis.* We could also indicate a metalogism not in the ancient tradition even though it is related to what was once designated as *praeoccupatio* or *procatalepsis.* It concerns *denegation (Verneinung),* * by

*[This translation of Freud's *Verneinung* originates with Lacan. It is usually translated as "negation," *négation* in French. For the entire background, see Anthony Wilden's note 11 in his translation: Jacques Lacan, *The Language of the Self* (Baltimore: Johns Hopkins University Press, 1968), pp. 95–96. *Trans.*]

which a subject avows what he is by saying what he is not. Even though this figure comes from a rhetoric of the unconscious, denegation is open to an analysis similar to what we proposed for allegory. Suppose that a man has repressed a drive toward parricide, which comes to light gradually during psychoanalytic sessions. It can happen that this desire will be expressed negatively as in the following utterances:

(1) "Don't think that I hold a grudge against my father!"
(2) "If there is one thing I've never wanted, it's certainly the death of my father."
(3) "I hope to God my father lives a hundred years!"
(4) "The man I was killing in my dream was certainly not my father."

Remark (3) is not negative in its expression, and we have chosen it expressly because it still has the same function as the others. At least in the eyes of the psychiatrist in the psychoanalytic relationship, it is the single one where the value of denegation is to be grasped. For an analyst sufficiently aware, these different formulas can mean precisely the contrary of what they appear to say. To discover this meaning that eludes the consciousness of the patient, the analyst ought to be sensitive to the marks that make the peremptory words of the patient suspect. In other words, to grasp their rhetorical value, that of a rhetoric that escapes the speaker, he ought to proceed to a reduction of the deviation conforming to what we have several times described.

Utterances (1) and (4) have more than a single mark to be noticed by the rhetorically conscious analyst. First of all, they are striking by the inadequacy of the meaning they propose and especially by the irrelevance of the relationship between the remark and the "context of the situation."[34] Finally, the psychoanalytic universe has alerted him to similar expressions so that he sees in them "something of a mark, a certificate of origin comparable to Made in Germany printed on an object."[35]

Certainly, the psychoanalyst can be fooled when he suspects the veracity of a patient's remarks; but if the direction of the cure proves him right, remarks (1) and (4) appear as rhetorical utterances proceeding by negative suppression-addition. At that point, his presumptions about the existence of a disguised invariant are justified by the figures of the unconscious found in the patient's remarks. This invariant that exists in the figured expression is the desire for parricide of a sort that the patient would have expressed if he had not already suppressed it. But the invariant is also the patient's inability to recognize his desire, and thus degree zero varies according to the point of view of the analyst or of the patient.

The analyst is helped in his reduction by the relative codification of the expressions of denegation. He knows that in certain contexts a desire is invariably expressed through formulas that mean just the opposite of what they appear to mean. Therefore, he has no trouble reestablishing what he knows to be the degree zero of a figure. Utterances such as the ones cited all signify to him: "I want or have wanted to kill my father."

As long as he remains in ignorance of this repression of desire, the patient remains unaware of the metalogism that strikes the analyst. He is persuaded to express himself literally, in conformity with the facts. There is no question about his reducing the deviation. When he can do this, when he discovers for himself the real meaning of his words, he is led toward an invariant that is not the one made by the analyst, because the patient must include a mention of the repression.

Finally we can reduce the cited remarks in two ways, by taking as an invariant either the expression of the desire or the expression of the repression of the desire. But however that is done, metalogism appears because the very expression of the repressed desire ought not be expressed as the negation of a desire.

In the analysis of denegation, if we remain with the problematics of desire, we can summarize it in the schema in table 12.

Table 12. Denegation

Figure	Deviation	Degree zero
Expression of the negation of desire	Unconscious position ←- - - - - - - - - - - - - - Conscious reduction - - - - - - - - - - - - - - - - →	1. Expression of desire 2. Expression of repression of desire

Close to denegation, so close as to allow for confusion, is *disavowal (Verleugnung)*, whereby psychoanalysts consider that a subject refuses "to recognize the reality of a traumatic perception—most especially the perception of the absence of the woman's penis."[36]

Disavowal may remain tacit and thus be of interest for the psychologist. It is obvious that to be interesting for rhetoric, it must find expression in one way or another. In this way, we see its structural identity with denegation. The single difference is that it is usually easier for any addressee to perceive the reality that he is shielding. If a woman who holds that the absence of a penis is a reality fails or refuses to indicate this crushing reality in her language, anyone can readily understand that her disavowals are rhetorical. But if the disavowal concerns the question of castration, we realize that her perception of reality can lead to discussion. We shall not, therefore, insist on this difference, which in practice may be illusory.

Since our intention is not to set down a complete list of metalogisms, we shall simply say one more word about *paradox*. Do you see this pipe? "All right," Magritte tells us maliciously, "This is not a pipe." If he had asked us to see in his drawing "something like a pipe" (a shepherd's pipe, a chimney, or a phallus—it makes little difference, since we are all somewhat music-mad, workers, or Freudians), we would have caught the play on words, the play between words, whose goal could be to make us forget that words can have a precise meaning. We would have seen that he was eliminating certain semes from a linguistic sign so as to add others and thus form a new signified. But his paradox is more than a play on words. Its value comes from the directional indications it imposes—from language to referent and back. There is no simple substitution of semes; but using the bent of language, there is suppression of elements of the real that *we must not see*. Everyone is free to add what he chooses to see. Magritte could have chosen as a title "This is a lighthouse" or "This is a bird," instead of leaving the addition for the viewer to supply. The important thing is that he makes us believe that things are not what they are, that the linguistic operation does not concern language. His paradox "cancels" reality. Nevertheless, if the "this" is something, by giving it a name we add to the universe some object, if only mentally.

One can take Magritte's word as a truth of artistic common sense. It is true that "this is not a pipe," since it is a representation of a pipe. But the so-called paradox remains nonetheless a metalogism, whatever the name given it. In fact, if we see here a profession of faith in the unreality of art or in the surreality of whatever objects, it remains true that a "reality" is put into question.

To deny that metalogisms exist, one must deny that "reality" exists. To recognize these metalogisms, it is enough to admit that a certain "real," whatever it might be, is imposed on the language that postulates it, even if that language transcends the "real" or claims to change it. It is by paying this price that we salute the inventor of the "knife without blade, lacking a handle." We would not be surprised if a lion or a wall had neither blade nor handle. This is certainly proof that if Lichtenberg had invented an object whose existence were strictly linguistic, we would appreciate his humor and ingenuity only because under, through, or behind the language we would perceive a particular "reality" without which the word of Lichtenberg would not have the meaning it does.

When Baudelaire claims:

> I am the wound and yet the blade!
> The slap and yet the cheek that takes it!
> The limb and yet the wheel that breaks it!
> The torturer, and he who's flayed![37]

we see in it only the expression of his quite real masochism. But if we consider these verses outside their psychological context and hold instead to the letter of the text, we find in them a paradox all the more scandalous because the "reality" glimpsed through the words is itself also to be taken "according to the letter." The metalogisms can hardly do violence to the "reality," can hardly render it simply hypothetical, cannot even deny it, for to do so would be, in fact, admitting it by trying to negate it.

4. PERMUTATION

It is difficult to cite examples of metalogical permutation. Perhaps one would be to shift the words into reverse order. Caesar could have shown himself in a role other than his general's role if he had said, *"Vici, vidi, veni."* Film gives examples of it all the time by permuting elements of the real. If the physical universe, however, works so that effect always follows cause, the same is not necessarily true in language. It is often quite natural to present the effect before the cause. Metalogism is not flagrant unless we try, for example, to recount the life of a person from the grave to the cradle. It is conceivable, in the same way, that a daughter might give birth to her mother or that the sea might be held in a drop of water.

That this is rare outside surrealistic language does not destroy its interest for metalogical permutation. On the contrary, it seems to be indispensable for the poet who is not content with singing of nature, but means to change it.

> Once I was very nervous. Here I am now on a new path: I put an apple on the table. *Then I put myself in the apple. What peace!* [Henri Michaux]

Perhaps some day we shall see in Michaux's magic only a process. The experience that he recounts will serve as an example to writers without talent, each of whom will have his apple into which to slip himself, even if it happens to be a pear. Today already surrealistic rhetoric has lost its freshness, but we shall surely see the day when metalogical permutation, which can still hold surprises for us, will appear as exhausted as are epanorthoses or epiphonema for us now.

Chapter VI
An Approach to the Phenomenon of Ethos

0. GENERAL

0.1. The reader who has followed us thus far in this essay may well feel a certain unease at this point. If the assigned goal of this study of rhetorical mechanisms is the total elucidation of poetic phenomena, we must certainly admit that the analyses we have been pursuing are, in fact, far from rendering a complete account of that complex reality. This criticism can be made even more precise: in the same way that *Homo sapiens* can be apprehended only through the repeated examination of numerous individual humans, poetic reality also must be grasped through the unique objects we call "texts" (it is of little importance here whether the message be perceived as poetic be oral or written). Thus the question now is, Are the results we have obtained up to this point operative at the level of the text? Such has not been precisely our claim, and for the moment we subscribe to the famous remark of Valéry: "Even if we measure the footsteps of the goddess, noting their frequency and *average* length, we are still far from the secret of her instantaneous grace."[1]

Hence, can we say that our study is licit? Or better, has it a meaning? If we can agree with M. Juilland that the literary fact does not remain after shredding and that its essence resides in an indissoluble, integrated whole,[2] every operation that breaks it down seems condemned *ipso facto*. Others have already spoken better than we are able to of the evils of "atomizing texts" or of "analysis by notecards." And if the work itself is, as S. Dresden has suggested, a sort of absolute at the same time independent and incomparable, critical activity—as it is concerned with rendering an account of all the dimensions of the text—rests on an internal ambiguity: "Its purpose is to characterize a work that by its nature is incommensurable, to appreciate it finally according to common and objective criteria, using a method both universal and rational."[3] Faced with this ambiguity, we are strongly tempted to abdicate totally and renounce the ambition to apprehend poetic reality except by the path of intuition. This is the attitude defended by some followers of Croce, who refuse all analytical concern. We are confronted here with the

sacralizing—therefore scleroticizing—concept of the work of art. In his valuable preface, Jean Cohen has shown nicely the minimal operation value of
some of the too lyrical definitions of poetry.[4] In turn we find other, somewhat
disturbing ideas in the following passage:

> The only way to enter the enclosure is through a fortuitous leap, an intuition. All
> intuition is affection, is an act of love or that which presupposes love. . . . The ulti-
> mate uniqueness of the literary object is only understandable through a blind and
> dark leap.[5]

Even when the total conception of the work of art is accompanied by wide
knowledge and sharp sensitivity, as was the case with Leo Spitzer, this condemned ambiguity is not mentioned, and intuition—with all the lack of rigor
that concept can have—reigns as uncontested empress.

It seems that this empire will remain as long as the misunderstanding
remains, in poetics as in other sciences, that the adage "divide and conquer"
is again awarded a value that morality does not allow it. We know quite well
that linguistics was not able to develop seriously until the day that the substantialist hypothesis was rejected, when the object of the linguistic sign was
carefully defined and divided into signifier and signified. In the same way,
every history of stylistics contains one central lesson: if this discipline is the
Babel so often condemned, it is because each stylistician (or almost) has made
the claim of offering a total explanation of the phenomenon of style, failing to
note first the need to approach piecemeal the immense field he has chosen.
"Criticism" will never be able to free itself from the web of complex relationships enclosing it until it rejects a good part of its claims. If the work is a
strongly individualized unit, can it be reduced, to start with, to smaller individualized units? Each man is also unique and incomparable, but there could
be no advancement in his knowledge until he realized that individualism had
to be put aside. Why would argue, today, with the right to exist of cytology,
osteology, and neurology? Each of these disciplines represents a small section
of the large discipline of the study of medicine, each commensurable with the
others, and the progress thus realized brings a better clinical comprehension of
the individual.

In undertaking this work, therefore, we have tried to "divide" the literary
problem as a way of understanding it better. We begin with the statement that
the poetic phenomenon has a linguistic dimension and an extralinguistic dimension. In the form-substance problem, expression dominates: "things are
not poetic except in potential and . . . language allows this potential to move
into act. . . . Clearly, therefore, the specific task of literary poetics is to question, not content, which remains the same, but expression, by learning what
constitutes the difference."[6] On the other hand, what are called "aesthetic
categories" and which certainly constitute an essential part of the work of art
are finally independent of the medium chosen, since identical sentiments can

be raised by works deriving from different disciplines.[7] We do not accept the simplistic views of Elsa Dehennin, who in criticizing Jakobson says, "Examining a non-linguistic characteristic, there is need of a non-linguistic method."[8] It is nonetheless true that the linguistic aspects of poetry demand a linguistic study, leaving aside for the moment other considerations.

0.2. If the literary phenomenon is complex, it is because notions of value and effect hold a predominant place in it. Our future analyses will be concerned with this point. We know that the specific value of an assembly of stylistic facts is not simply a function of pure structural mechanisms working at the level of small units; numerous other elements come into play. For this reason, we shall have to decompose, distinguish, and establish hierarchies.

In the following pages, we shall use the word *ethos,* commonly used in modern aesthetic terminology. Ethos is close to what Aristotle called $\pi\alpha\theta\circ\varsigma$ in his *Poetics* and to the *rasas* of classical India.[9] We define it as an affective state raised in the receiver by a particular message and whose specific quality varies as a function of a certain number of parameters. Among them, a large place is reserved for the addressee himself. The value attached to a text is not pure entelechy but a *response* of the reader or hearer. In other words, the latter is not content to receive an intangible aesthetic datum but *reacts* to certain stimuli. And this response is an appreciation. In physiology, sight and hearing are not the "virtue" or "properties" that the ancients believed they had defined but the response structured by an organism subjected to certain physical stimuli that may be described objectively. Like sight or touch, the effect depends at the same time on the stimuli (the metaboles) and on the receiver (reader or hearer).

The result of this is that if the idea of effect is psychologically first when it is a question of literary fact, this question (and *a fortiori* the question of the value of this effect) passes to the second plane on the epistemological terrain. Michael Riffaterre has understood very well that in the first operation it is necessary to dissociate judgment from its stimuli[10] and that the aesthetic properties recognized in certain facts and the psychological reactions raised by them are for the linguist first only simple signals.[11] *Mutatis mutandis,* it is these stimuli, these signals, that we have catalogued and described in our study—an incomplete but indispensable operation, since ethos, a subjective impression, is always motivated, in the last analysis, by objective data.

To conclude these remarks, what remains is to describe the conditions of a specific ethos. In what follows will be found only a simple sketch of the directions that our future analyses will take. The reader will be able to grasp a more detailed knowledge of these views in a later work that will constitute in some way the continuation of this one.[12]

It is impossible to respond immediately to the question, What constitutes style? The word *style* designates, in fact, "one of those complex abstractions that has been compared to polyhedrons: they present a multiplicity of facets each of which can serve as a basis for a definition."[13] To reduce our im-

Table 13. Constitution of Ethos

	Constituents	Effects
1. Nuclear ethos	Structure of the metabole	In potential
2. Autonomous ethos	Structure + substance	In potential
3. Contextual ethos*	Structure + substance + context	In fact

*[*Ethos synnome* in French. *Contextual* seemed more appropriate in English. However, *contextual ethos* should not be taken to mean "ethos of the context," but "ethos communicated *by* the context." *Trans.*]

mediate task to ethos, we shall try to enumerate and establish a hierarchy of its components. Table 13 comprises the elements that come together at the creation of an ethos in a certain context-bound metabole.

1. NUCLEAR ETHOS

1.1. Rhetorical Function and the Nonspecificity of Metaboles

By an analytical operation, it is possible for us to conceive of an empty metabole, that is, a figure that would exist only in its structure, no verbal material giving it body. It could be objected that this reality has no existence in daily life; we know also that no linguist has ever been able, in fact, to isolate a signifier from its signified, but this distinction is promising. Does this empty figure, which only the mind can apprehend, possess an ethos?

The primitive effect of a metabole, whatever it may be, is to unleash the perception of the literary quality (in the broad sense) of the text in which it is incorporated. It is, therefore, revelatory of that function Jakobson called poetic and which we prefer to call by the less marked term "rhetoric." This function puts the stress on the message as such, on its form as much as on its content; it promotes "the palpability of signs."[14] In his short essay on tropes, Tzvetan Todorov notes that "the single quality common to all figures of rhetoric is . . . their opacity, that is, their tendency to have us perceive the discourse itself and not only its signification."[15] That is where it all stops. Our work here demonstrates, in fact, that there is almost no necessary relationship between the structure of a figure and its ethos. The examples we have given, examples we have tried to choose widely, prove it. Jakobson had already indicated precisely that "the poetic function" went far beyond the frame generally assigned to poetry. Moreover, the most striking of his examples were, we remember, borrowed from the fund of invective and political propaganda. Until now, the rhetorical analysis of messages has allowed what constitutes the specificity of poetry, a quality that other dimensions indicate as the opposite of slang and advertising slogans, to escape. The metabole, therefore, is the necessary condition of an ethos, but not the sufficient one. Table

Table 14. Examples of Polyvalence of Metaboles

Activity	Function	Metaplasm	Metasememe
Literature	Lyricism, etc.	Through ec*r*ipse of the moon low black clou*n*ds [Th. Koenig]	Eyelids, *shores* of sight
Advertising	Persuasion	I like *Ike*	Put a *tiger* in your tank
Slang	Derision and/or hermeticism	*Smeelch* = coins, [small change]	*Squaw patch* [fertile land]
Linguistic evolution	Necessity, economy	Miniature (minium-minimum attraction)	A traffic *bottle-neck*
Crossword puzzles	Ludic function	"Phonetically: dusk." Rep: *EV* [= eve]	Whale road worker (= sailor)
Liturgical language	Sacralization	*Temurah* of the Kabbala	*Lamb* of God

14 (which uses figures from only columns A and C of the General Table of Metaboles) will illustrate better than a long discussion the broad independence of figures and their possible values. It goes without saying that this schema is meant to be illustrative only.

Each column of the table gives examples whose operating structure is identical and interchangeable. Neither traditional rhetoric nor the disciplines grouped under the flag of stylistics nor, until now, our general rhetoric furnishes formal criteria for permitting the distinction to be made between, for example, a slang metaphor and an advertising metaphor.

We conclude from this that metaboles are not to be distinguished on the operative plane. Whether it is a question of the promotion of values (a certain kind of poetry) or of their destruction (slang), whether it is a question of persuading (advertising) or of some game (crossword puzzles), whether it is even a question of activity without evident ethos (to find a name to designate a new reality), the same identical structures are used. Therefore, it is vain today, if not childish, to condemn any further metaphor or metonymy as double agents in the service of a more or less suspect metaphysics.

1.2. Variability of Nuclear Ethos

There is, however, reason to be prudent and not to refuse *a priori* the existence of a certain link between the structure of the metabole and the affective state it raises. For this reason, we are not satisfied to say that the empty figure is a designation of rhetorical discourse. Each species of figure differs from its neighbor by its operator and/or its operand. These distinctions, which no doubt can be structured into binary oppositions, entail several consequences on the plane of ethos: metaboles will be distinguished by their force and at the same time by their specific aesthetic potential.

1.2.1. DISTANCE

The strength of the metabole can come from the degree of its abnormality: the amplitude of its deviation can be quite variable and thus depends, as we have suggested, on the greater or lesser fixity of the elements it started from. We borrow the term *distance* from information theory. It designates the number of units of signification by which a poorly coded message differs from the same message correctly coded. Without going into details, we can call on the reader's experience: he knows in some vague way that metaplasm consists in general of a more flagrant break in the code than does metasememe. But this is not all, for if distance varies with the operand's column, it depends as well on the level involved within the column. In the field of metaplasms, we can arrange the following in an increasing order of distance: synonymies, substitutions or additive affixes, antistrophe. But the effect of strength achieved by this distance can be reinforced or corrected by other variables that concurrently make up the effective ethos of the figure. This is why nuclear ethos involves only possibilities and not realities.

1.2.2. SPECIFIC AESTHETIC POTENTIALS

It is well known that Roman Jakobson sees metonymy as the privileged figure for arts with realistic tendencies, while the metaphoric process seems to him more proper for romantic and symbolist aesthetics.[16] It certainly does seem, in fact, that certain figures agree better with certain broad classes of mental attitudes than do others. Apocope, ellipsis, and, more generally, all figures achieved by suppression can (but are not obliged to) reveal a certain impatience of speech. Generalizing synecdoche seems to favor abstraction, while its opposite seems to favor a kind of myopia. Others have shown that the classical arts made frequent use of litotes, while hyperbole was one of the elements of baroque aesthetics.

But it is clear that we could discover a hundred hyperboles in classical works, a hundred baroque works peppered with litotes, realistic films using metaphor, and romantic paintings utilizing metonymy. At the nuclear level, figures have, therefore, a purely potential ethos. Still, these ethoi do not have fixed tendencies.

2. AUTONOMOUS ETHOS

The autonomous effect is a function of the nuclear effect on the one hand and of the material used by a precise metabole on the other. Take two metaphors using slang vocabulary and technological vocabulary, respectively.

Their effects will be quite different. Whether lexical or syntactic, linguistic elements are in fact marked by general stylemes. Independently of contexts in which they can be used, *squawk box* is pejorative, while *phonograph* is striking by its formality. In this way, a synonymical series can be established following the directions of Bally.[17] Examples would be *dead, deceased, passed on, croaked, kicked the bucket, threw in the sponge,* and so on. Around each essential notion, a series of expressions gravitates, each giving its particular value (more or less emphasized) by a comparison (implicit or explicit) with all the elements of the paradigm that can be classed with it without change of denotation. It goes without saying that the concept of synonymy can be extended from the lexical field to the syntactic one. The two expressions "I want to come visit you" and "I would like to pay you a visit" certainly form a synonymic pair, although the first one presents a neutral term, while the second term is marked.

But what do these stylemes correspond to and where is their origin? It is clear that the verbal material does not *in itself* have the ability to evoke a level of language by the decree of some imminent power; the value of the term represents rather the sum of linguistic experiences gathered by the receiver. If *hark* and *bedew* evoke for him a "poetic style," this is true for the most part because he has hardly encountered these words except in texts given as poetic. It is here, therefore, that we must advance the idea of *ecology,* referring to the discipline of the natural sciences that studies the milieu in which certain types of life develop. The general styleme may be defined as a process of memory or reference that can place the unit in the more or less specialized milieu where it is commonly found. The particular coloring of this value comes above all from the relationships made by the speaker with the identified milieu. We shall rapidly list, taking care not to predetermine the direction of our future research, what these evoked values could be:[18]

    a) Localizing component
        (1) Precise literary genre (burlesque, poetics, etc.)
        (2) Historical epoch (archaism, etc.)
        (3) Geographic milieu (peasant patois, creole, etc.)
        (4) Socio-cultural milieu, classes
        (5) Professions and other fields of human activity
        (6) Natural relationships (between persons of the same sex, of different ages, whether tied by blood or not, etc.)

    b) Frequency of the unit
        (1) Frequency in high, low, or middle language (determined empirically)
        (2) More or less strong disposition to derivation, composition, etc.
        (3) Filled metaboles in the process of fixation, residual archaisms, traditional comparisons, neologisms ending their stylistic term, citations, foreign words, worn filled metaboles being renewed, etc.[19]

Such a study would no doubt bring us to the point of opening again the venerable *Traité de stylistique* and give new luster to the idea of "choice," so dear to stylisticians. Bally was interested in the affective value of acts of organized language, in the reciprocal action of acts coming together to form the system of means of expression in a language.[20] But he was wrong when, in a paragraph often unwittingly cited, he wanted "to separate style and stylistics forever,"[21] since it is also true that however voluntary and conscious the use of language may be when used by a literary man, it is from that language that he borrows his material. The Genevan master, moreover, was aware of his ambiguity, reserving for "natural language" the right to be always "potentially beautiful,"[22] which may be translated as the ability to be used in literary works and to exercise there a function.

In the present state of our knowledge, we are unable to formalize with any certainty all the nuances of frequency and of a localizing component. The sketch above is to be understood more as a list than as an organization; moreover, the classification is arbitrary and infinitely divisible. There do exist, however, attempts at structuring ecologies. The studies of Eugenio Coseriu (which distinguish "linguistic zone" and "objective milieu," "structured lexicon" and "nomenclature lexicon," "technique of discourse" and "repeated discourse," "synchrony of language" and "synchrony of structures," and especially "architecture" and "structures" of language) are of great interest for this reason.[23] The same is true of Trier and Weisberger's famous theory of the *Begriffsfelder;* the report by Hjelmslev on lexical structuring in the *Actes du huitième congrès international des linguistes* also contains some very worthwhile suggestions.[24]

It is true that these theories carry numerous para-linguistic elements. But here we are obliged to leave the purely linguistic field: autonomous ethos depends not only on structural mechanisms but also on psychological and sociological data. In an article with views that are at times arguable, Jean Mourot reopens the dossier of stylistics "to wonder if the truly scientific approach to literature, once in possession of all the historical and philological preliminaries, has not entered the sociological study of the constitution of literary values."[25] If the value attached to a literary act is also the function of an individual, himself integrated into a socio-cultural context, it is only right that attention turns to these two elements, which create and destroy the normative and analytic systems through which the literary object is perceived. We remember that in *Brave New World* the character called "the savage" has learned to read English in the complete works of Shakespeare, the only literary work available. Sprinkled with citations, shards of replies and images quite Shakespearean, his language can only be a surprise in Huxley's aseptic world. The shock of man against society, which destroys this world, is all the more moving, since for this "savage" the genius of Shakespeare is both norm and code of good usage. This outlandish example allows us to understand that in the analysis of autonomous values, it is absolutely necessary to bring out certain cultural data that are at times difficult to grasp.

On this subject, it has no doubt been noticed that there is a new strand of rapport between our work and the rhetoric of the ancients. In fact, the notion of ecology has some remains of the theory of the three styles, which post-classical commentators formalized as the "Wheel of Virgil" and which all rhetoricians used until the eighteenth century, refining and redividing it, but conserving especially its dogmatic form.[26] We owe to Bally the first efforts toward a liberation leading to a new rhetoric that would not be normative and aprioristic, but descriptive.[27] We claim that these stylemes have nothing permanent about them. The replacement of values, looked at diachronically, can be quick and complete: certain archaisms that could produce an effect of nobility in the Romantic era might well have been low and burlesque in the seventeenth century. On the synchronic plane, however, we can say in principle that there hardly exists any unique ecological component, excluding certain technical vocabularies, whose linguistic state is sometimes difficult to determine.

Thus, at its autonomous level, the stylistic mechanism possesses a certain polyvalence, and the link existing between this ethos and the specific effect of the figure integrated into a context remains loose. Even in cases where the intrinsic autonomous value of a metabole seems fairly characteristic (which is far from being a general rule), this value is not restrained from taking on a new level through the context. In itself it still remains only a potential.[28] Therefore, this simple remark, which is certainly almost a truism, condemns all static approaches to the literary work, all those operations that consist of a description without any hierarchy of the mechanisms grasped at their autonomous level. The "work," we say, not the "poetic phenomenon" as such.

3. CONTEXTUAL FUNCTION

If style is "more than the sum of its elements,"[29] this something more comes, it seems, from the hierarchical workings of the mechanisms. We are generally in agreement with Pierre Guiraud in recognizing that "every work is an autonomous universe"[30] and that in this perspective "the 'combination' is important, just as is 'selection' ".[31] The third level, that of the work, integrates the first two. Every stylistic phenomenon occupies a place in the structure of a text containing other metaboles, themselves endowed also with autonomous ethoi. And it is by this play of reciprocal influences, of interaction and relative proximity in the text, that the selection of the potential ethos is at work—all of which then move to the plane of realization.

The relationships that the linguistic features create among themselves are of the highest complexity. Rhythmic, metric, phonetic, and phonological relations make up the conventions of verse as well as the phenomena of alliteration and assonance. These structures are built up in very refined ways, as Nicolas Ruwet has indicated in his analysis of a verse by Baudelaire.[32] The reality of a work's ethos is to be sought in the integration of all the elements—in the interferences, convergences, and tensions created in it.

The dense field of contextual function has been explored by more than one stylistician. Among all the works this problem has given rise to, we are happy to point to those by Michael Riffaterre, whose has constructed a rather rigorous theory of the linguistic context using certain concepts made available by communication theory.[33] One of the most useful distinctions Riffaterre has proposed is that of the micro-context and the macro-context.

We need not expound at length on the first of these, since in chapter I, section 2.1.3, we described it as the most useful empirical method for determining degree zero. In verbal sequences with a rhetorical function, some elements are in contrast with what redundancy and distributional relationships would allow us to expect. Riffaterre has shown nicely that the *stylistic device* (which in all cases is a metabole) was by definition inseparable from its context. That is easily understood if we know that the reduction of the deviation is always made at the level of the higher unit of which it is a part. This remark is important because it makes the following fact clear: unmarked linguistic elements (micro-context) participate as well as do marked elements (the stylistic device) in creating style. This alone ought to suffice to eliminate the warnings of detractors from the idea of deviation.

The macro-context is "that part of the literary message that precedes the SD [in our system, the metabole] and which is exterior to it."[34] The extent of this context is, of course, quite variable. It depends at the same time on the type of text being examined, on its difficulty, on the quickness or slowness of the reader, on his memory, his knowledge, his literary experience. We are thus in the realm of imponderables: to what extent do the first words of Stephen Daedalus influence the reader once he has come to the last chapter of *Ulysses?* We realize that certainly there can be no complete answer to questions of this sort. The study of *patterns* gives promise of a fruitful future here. We can say in any case that in the course of the reading, a shifting literary norm is imposed on the reader. Take a text written in modern English. Starting at a certain moment, the artist can decide to write in the language of the fifteenth century. At first the linguistic features of Middle English will obviously be a figure. But the deviation is absorbed little by little. If the sequence is rather long, it can even become an actual convention. And then a return to the language of the twentieth century would seem a deviation. In all cases, a phenomenon of adaptation operates for the receiver in order that messages be perceived. *Piers Plowman* is not read in the same way as Faulkner's novels; and among the latter, *As I Lay Dying* and *A Fable* are to be viewed in different lights. According to the context, therefore, there is a constant displacement of a local degree zero being imposed on absolute degree zero. This is what Paul Imbs suggests when he proposes that we represent the idea of style in the form of a nested hierarchy.[35] At the summit are the broadest areas, at the base the most narrow but most immediately perceived.

Style —of a group of languages:
    —of a language;
    —of an epoch;
    —of literary genres; styles proper to certain subjects;
    —of a school or literary milieu;
    —of a writer;
    —of a moment in the life of a writer;
    —of a work;
    —of a part, a paragraph, a movement, etc., of a work;
    —of a sentence.

Therefore, each level constitutes a type of context, is the creator of a norm, orienting toward an effective realization all the autonomous ethoi that are developed at a lower echelon.

In reading, it is necessary to be attentive to the repetition of phenomena that present identical features (metaboles with comparable autonomous effects, logical concatenations, and so on). Around these metaboles is constituted little by little a true "stylistic field," the sum of the literary values with which they are charged throughout their occurrences. In some ways it is a question of a new kind of localizing component, no longer working, this time, on the plane of language, but on the plane of the text. What makes the study of these fields complicated is that they are not, any more than the macro-context, constituted immediately, but in the process of decoding the message. It is at this point that the reader's tendency to synthesize the groups of metaboles is fully activated.

In this way, one arrives at a picture of the text as a space where the aesthetician is to study the multidimensional webs of interdependencies, of correspondences, of syntagmatic or paradigmatic relations that have been established among the different metaboles, ending finally in the creation of contextual effects. The problem is certainly complex. This is all the more true as the linguistic metaboles move to join with contextual ethoi, thus creating a fourth level (until now hardly explored), the ethoi appearing through figures belonging to other semiological systems: metaboles of narrative, of persons, of support, and so on. Before we can closely examine research on literary ethos, therefore, we will have to determine the rhetorical condition of these new figures and describe their functioning.

4. ETHOS AND JUDGMENT

In the preceding lines, we have carefully distinguished ethos and value judgment. It is acknowledged, however, that every text can arouse a certain appreciation. But this effect is metastylistic; it is logically posterior to the recognition of an ethos derived from the entire text. In any case, it must be noted that this distinction leaves an even greater share to the receivers of the message. The act that consists of expressing, manifestly or not, aesthetic satisfaction or discontent before a particular text indeed supposes the presence of a scale of values that until now have escaped any precise measurement. In fact, it depends on several variables (psychological, cultural, sociological, and so on), and it can be contaminated by other scales of values (ethical, political, and so on) existing in the individual. A serious study of this response that constitutes appreciation is, therefore, "of another order" and calls for methods and concepts radically different from those we have been using until now.

Part Two
TOWARD A GENERAL RHETORIC

Preface

It is, no doubt, superfluous to repeat here what we have already told the reader in the introduction—that the second part of this work does not claim to be anything other than a first exploration into the almost virgin regions of a rhetoric meant to be applicable to all modes of expression. Just as it was relatively easy to describe with precise care figures of language for the most part well-known for centuries, so it was also perilous to propose a system of metaboles for other fields, so to speak, that have until now hardly been released from the embrace of intuition. Passing from linguistics into semiology, one necessarily runs the risk of being approximative and incomplete.

Precisely because of the novelty of the matters treated and the value they indicate for the formulation of a modern rhetoric, it seemed useful to offer two essays in this direction. The first essay is concerned with the transformation that the rhetorical function imposes on the supposedly normal ordering of communication understood as an interpersonal relation seen from the point of view of the actors in the process. Here we shall certainly pick up some figures already described by classical authors, but so as to bring them together in a homologous group, as in the model established in the first part of this work. For obvious reasons, this chapter will again treat linguistic matters in set order, but now, theoretically, what we say about linguistic communication ought to allow for transfer into nonlinguistic communication systems. The painter is to an extent a person addressing other persons about things or persons.

As for the second essay, the last chapter, it clearly moves away from the linguistic field, at least if we consider that "linguistics stops at the sentence."[1] It is obvious that sequences of sentences, in a literary exercise just as in daily or scientific exercise of speech, are organized, or can be organized, according to rules that are not those of language. Roland Barthes goes so far as to say that the actual ambition of classical rhetoric was to be that "second linguistics" treating "discourse" (or what we have called "developments").[2] However that may be, there remains much to be done if we are to master the

[1] Roland Barthes, "Introduction to the Structural Analysis of Narratives," in *Image-Music-Text,* trans. Stephen Heath (Glasgow: Fontana, 1977), p. 82.
[2] Ibid.

categories proper to different kinds of discourse, assuming that these might be differentiated. The general hypothesis of our theory will rest in its application: given a norm, or degree zero, of any type of discourse, the user of rhetoric deviates from it to produce specific meanings or effects.

Of all types of discourse, story (*récit*), or narration,* is no doubt the most interesting one from the aesthetic and especially the literary point of view. But we must keep in mind that plastic arts and cinema, for example, may also tell stories (*histoires*). As a result of assembling several reflections on metaboles of the story (*récit*), we are also placing ourselves "beyond the sentence."

*[French has a slightly different vocabulary than does English to indicate narrative, which creates problems for the translator attempting to distinguish between *récit, histoire, narration,* and *discours*. These "ordinary" words have been further defined by formalist and structuralist criticism. In the following pages, we translate *discours* as "discourse"; *narration* and *narratif* as "narration" and "narrative," respectively; *histoire* as "story"; and the troublesome *récit* sometimes as "plot," sometimes as "story." Where ambiguity may exist, we have cited the French word. Briefly, a story (*histoire*) is embodied in plot (*récit*), which is presented in a narration (*narration*). The same story, then, might have different plots and be presented in different narratives—a truism of oral narrative study extended to literary criticism. *Trans.*]

Chapter VII
Figures of Narrative Voice

0. GENERAL

Some might ask if there is any justification for isolating a group of metaboles related to narrative voice. Narrators and their satellites appear in the message only through words and relations between words. As such, they appear in the general system of language (*langue*) and can be the figured object of any one of the four types analyzed in Part One.

On the other hand, Jakobson's theory of functions expresses the risk that there could be complete independence of these four types among themselves. In fact, the message is the result (or the place) of their interaction, since they are all definitely manifested through words. From the point of view of communication as such, it would thus be arbitrary to isolate addresser and addressee, even though the emphasis on one or the other does give birth to what Jakobson calls expressive and conative functions. These personae are named by means of words and form referents, therefore, in the same way as the referents of any sign whatever are formed.

The very nature of the communication act, however, linguistic or not, confers on the addresser and addressee a privileged and symmetrical role and imposes on the semantic universe a certain number of cleavages forming systems. The structure of persons in our language (*langue*), as we shall present it here, using E. Benveniste's work,[1] can be put in the shape of a very simple disjunctive tree, constructed from six binary oppositions (see fig. 17, in which we have framed the species that can be realized in utterances).

At the top of the table is a category in which the very notion of person does not exist. All the specifying oppositions have at this point been neutralized. This is no doubt the place to remind the reader that person is always specified in relation to a verb, which itself may carry the mark of person, as does the pronoun.* The *apersonal* (we prefer this term to *impersonal* for reasons to be given presently) is the domain of the verb used in non-personal modes: infini-

*[The inflected verb is more a feature of French than of modern English. *Trans.*]

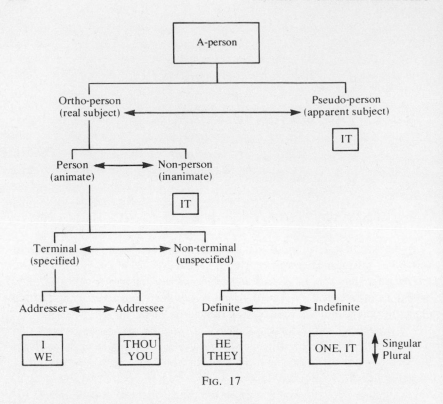

Fɪɢ. 17

tive and participle. The category traditionally called impersonal appears to us to carry in fact *pseudo-persons,* that is, entities not able to assume the function of the subject. In this way, it is opposed to the category of real subjects, or *ortho-persons.* In the sentence "It is raining" or in "It is drizzling," the parallelism with forms such as "he is speaking" or "he is chatting" could well reflect an underlying ideology, an anthropomorphic conception of nature.* In this case the impersonal *it* would be a deviation compared with the norm demanding the apersonal category. We shall leave this delicate problem aside and concentrate our analyses on the other oppositions of the table.

We see clearly that at the top this table moves into purely semantic categories: animate/inanimate. Just as with the general tree (chap. IV, sec. 2.2), some vertical endocentric series can be traced that can be examined, thanks to additions or suppressions. Horizontal displacements (suppression-

*[This passage, as well as others below, is complicated by the differing pronominal systems of French and English. The French *il* subsumes both the English *he* and *it* (when *it* is masculine). Therefore, the French for "it is raining" employs the same pronoun as does "he is speaking." The example from Verlaine of person/non-person commutation (see below, p. 173) reflects the same French pronominalization, impossible to capture in English. Hence, in French the pseudo-person pronoun is *il* ("he", which is both "anthropomorphic" and virifocal. *Trans.*]

addition) are also possible, but they present a peculiar character because of the perfect dichotomy of the system and its great stability (it belongs to the code, and its degree zero is without ambiguity). These horizontal deviations are to be carefully distinguished from permutations (where if an *I* takes the place of *you,* the *you* in its turn will take the place of the *I*), and we shall call them *commutations,* considering them particular cases of complete suppression-addition in binary systems. A suppression-addition takes place here only by adding the inverse seme of the seme suppressed.

Person has as well two other determiners: gender and number. We first thought (perhaps wrongly, but it had to be demonstrated) that we ought not introduce gender into the analysis. It does not, in fact, allow specific deviations of person (even though figure 17 is asymmetrical from this point of view; only the *he* and the "object" are given gender).* Number, on the other hand, is certainly relevant, for the addresser of the message is *by necessity singular.* Number is simply translated by doubling all the slots of the table in the third dimension, making possible a third kind of deviation. Deviations of number are only possible (in our language, at least, since some idioms allow a dual) between the two poles of a pair, which itself may have commutations.

We must not, however, lose sight of the fundamental remarks of Benveniste on the special nature of terminal persons. In the *we* there is an *I* dominant (and in the *you* a *thou* [*tu*]) that is in some way the spokesman of this group. According to Benveniste's formula, the *plural is a factor of limitlessness, not of multiplication.* We add that *I* is a gear, or shifter,† which specifies a person in the act of communicating, making that person "responsible," in the full sense of the word. This is the source of the ethos of every figure of person.

A final remark is needed before moving to the inventory of figures. Writings, we know, are divided into *genres,* which have norms concerning person. It is possible that this norm already constitutes a deviation when compared with ordinary spoken language; but there is no need for us to consider this deviation, since we are concerned only with secondary deviations in comparison with the norm of the genre.

1. PERSON / NON-PERSON COMMUTATION

If it is "normal" to speak familiarly or formally with another, it is frequently enough, however, that the familiar disappears from discourse. Scientific publications eschew familiarity, just as they do the *I* that is hidden behind

---

*[True only for the French *il,* meaning both "he" and "it" in English. The English neuter, obviously, is without gender. In French, everything has a gender, either *il* or *elle* ("she") (see immediately preceding translators' note). *Trans.*]

†[The word *shifter* is in English in the original. *Trans.*]

scientific objectivity. Treatises on geometry or physics are addressed to audiences in the same way as letters or calls to arms. But the norm in the one is precisely the opposite of the norm in the other. We would be surprised to find a mathematician writing: "You take a two and a three . . ." or "Now, I have here two parallel lines. . . ." We would be just as surprised if a lover wrote his fiancée using only scientific or professional terminology. This is because the norm in lovers' language, a personal relationship if any exists, calls for direct personal address, the *I* or the *you / thou*. In scientific language, on the other hand, a deviation has been established that has become "normal" and which makes the *I* and the *you* unlikely, a true stumbling block were they to appear. It remains true, nonetheless, that a treatise on geometry is addressed to someone, just as a personal journal, even one in code, is addressed to the one who reads it.

For rhetorical reasons, however, we could reestablish a *you* by finding a prescientific language like that of the alchemist who could speak in a confidential tone as to an apprentice:

> If thou put the root of it brayed upon the eye, it will make the eye marvellous clear, because the light of the eyes. . . . [*The Book of Secrets of Albertus Magnus (1550)*]

Once a norm has been established—and no matter what the deviation from which it might derive—every violation of this norm has a rhetorical effect. Descartes provides an example of this. Although everyone had known for a long time that philosophy existed by and for philosophers, when he decided to write his philosophical work in the first person, he went against a norm that reason may well judge "abnormal," but one that custom had ratified. At that moment, he created a deviation of language for anyone surprised that an almost novelistic recounting could be the introduction to a method for a careful direction of the mind. The *I* of the *Discourse on Method* is as legitimate as the *I* of Augustine's or Rousseau's *Confessions*. But it is far from being natural or "realistic," as Butor said,[2] for it has the effect of surprise in the same way that the appearance of Hitchcock in each of his films is surprising until one gets used to it.

In large measure, literary genres regulate the uses and exclusion of *I, you,* and *he*. But since these genres are only conventional manners of writing, a day will come when, for example, the essay can take the form of the novel, the novel the form of the essay.* Persons will then change their roles, and a deviation will at first be perceived that will later become "normalized," since a critic (Claude Roy) can declare (to the surprise of no one) that he read *Being and Nothingness* "like a novel." In a philosophy like existentialism, which attacks the *I,* it is, in fact, its absence that is surprising.

When Shelley's "Ode to the West Wind" begins, "O wild West Wind,

---

*[Nabokov's *Pale Fire* already has realized this prediction. *Trans.*]

thou breath of Autumn's being,'' we can hardly speak of metabole, since it was Romantic poetry that brought in the mode of conversations with nature. However, before these conversations had become a rule of the poetic genre, they must have been surprising, just as later the opposite commutation by Verlaine was surprising:

Il pleure dans mon coeur	It is weeping in my heart
Comme il pleut sur la ville.	As it rains on the town.*

A Christian can address his personal God in the consecrated words: "Our Father who art in heaven . . . ,'' but these same words would have a rhetorical savor in the mouth of a deist or a pantheist. If biologists still do not know precisely when life starts and ends, we have no reason to be surprised at the frequency of such commutations, all the more so since the fabulists, friends of talking beasts, and the philosophers who are concerned with the rise of consciousness in plants and even in matter have their numerous disciples.

Rarer is the ortho-person / pseudo-person commutation, by which a subject called "apparent" by the grammarians becomes "real," as in the following plaint:

It is the fault of those who rain

[A. Blavier]

2. TERMINAL / NON-TERMINAL COMMUTATION

We have spoken often enough about the *he* in the manner of Caesar to emphasize the role usurped by the third person for rhetorical ends. Examples are not lacking. In *The Education of Henry Adams,* the *he* is an *I* who is too shy to speak his name. The same thing is found in the work of Gertrude Stein, especially when she describes her own character from the point of view of Alice Toklas.

Her bookish life commenced at this time. She read anything that was printed that came her way and a great deal came her way. . . . She read them all and many times. She and her brothers began to acquire other books.

When Henry Adams writes, "One sought education in order to adjust the dose," we can bet with certainty that *he* was the seeker. The *he* is an *I* held at a distance, as is so often true also for Henri Michaux's work, which is like a challenge thrown at rhetoric. In the latter's work, "what separates persons is of less import than what unites them, and the essential thing will thus be to reject the formal proofs discovered about their differences."[3] If, however, norms are constantly overturned in this poetry, and the most diverse de-

---

*[See note at bottom of p. 170. *Trans.*]

viations constantly "normalized," Raymond Bellour has shown nicely that substitution of persons obeys vague and only slightly imperative rules in Michaux's poetry, but at least certain of them are firm enough so that processes can be discovered in them that relate to rhetoric. In particular, there is the habit he has of speaking to himself in the third person, a feature we also find in Berryman's *Dream Songs*. We find this process in Beckett as well, who combines the two commutations terminal / non-terminal and definite / indefinite, in such a way as to put his own individuality into question.

On the other hand, laws of genre for a long time have forced the critic to speak of the author in the third person singular. Today, under the influence of Bachelard, a criticism of "identification" is imposed that tries to deny the distance separating the critic from his author.

> To what fire am I then to devote myself?
> In what flame am I to revive myself without destroying myself at the same time?
> Nerval looks around himself; there he discovers the sun.[4]

Who is speaking? J.-P. Richard in the name of Nerval? Nerval in the language of Richard? We really know too little about this process. The *I* of the critic is confused with the *I* of the poet.

> It is not I who guide my soul to heaven. It is I who am guided by my own soul along the open road, where all men tread. Therefore, I must accept her deep motions of love, or hate, or compassion, or dislike, or indifference. And I must go where she takes me. For my feet and my lips and my body are my soul. It is I who must submit to her. This is Whitman's message of American democracy.[5]

Who is speaking? Lawrence or Whitman? It does little good to call on phenomenology and its postulates and methodological consequences, for no one can deny that Lawrence, like Richard, is having us accept an apparent subject as the real subject. Whether he lends his voice to Cooper's or Whitman lends him citations, by the conscious confusion of the *I* and the *he,* Lawrence has given us works that can be read as both novel and essay at the same time. By "marrying the other," the critical *I* becomes the narrative *I.* Whether he has the right to do this is of no consequence. Rhetoric that is on the lookout for deviation and norm notices in modern criticism that persons are no longer "in the place" that tradition has assigned them. The sacred *he* of earlier "objective" criticism can give way to the *I,* which can appear normal once we perceive that this new function is meant to represent a hybrid being—half-critic, half-poet or novelist.

The *you* or the *I* can also appear when least expected; for example, reducing the distance between the writer and his creations. With the attention of an entomologist, Butor describes in *La Modification* a *he* who is traveling, but he speaks to him formally, as if he wished the conversation to be only with him, excluding the importunate reader.[6] It is at this point that the ordinary

reader is "changed." The same connivance, minus the familiarity, is found in
Moby Dick when Melville addresses his character, "Take heart, take heart, O
Bulkington!" (In section 5 of this chapter, we shall consider the commutation
thou / *you* [*tu* / *vous*].)

Advertising often uses the opposite commutation. In principle, it ought to
"be direct," or at least use direct address. But often it uses the third person to
relieve the addressee, who is after all only a prospective client, of what is
called his "responsibility." "The man with good taste dresses at Z"; "The
woman in the know finds her shoes at Y"—in such formulas, deviation
appears only on analysis because they have become very common. A simple
mind, or a malicious one, however, may well see nothing in them for himself,
which proves that concerned persons feel the deviation only if they reduce it
immediately. Without the hint, without the rhetorical effect, such expressions
would truly say only what they do say.

Similarly, in the therapy by "symbolic realization," instituted by M.-A.
Séchehaye, it is "normal" for the therapist to address the patient in the third
person singular to allow him to avoid responding, or better, to answer in the
same form.

> Now Mama is going to feed her little Reneé. It's time to drink some good milk from
> Mama's melons.[7]

To give the patient confidence, he is treated royally, as a mother might say to
a fussy child: "Does Marie want a little more soup?" Any third person not
used to rules of language in the infantile mind would catch the deviation that
escapes the child and the patient in this usage, that escapes even the doctor or
the mother.

In this category of commutations, we can also place all shifts of direct
discourse into indirect discourse (and inversely), which create a "deviation"
and whose goal is to leave the circle of "responsibility" or, conversely, to
reenter in.

3. ADDRESSER / ADDRESSEE COMMUTATION

According to the linguistic norm, *I* designates the one who is speaking and
implies at the same time an utterance that fits *I*: in saying "I," I cannot fail to
speak of myself. This norm is, however, broken at times, not only in poetry
but even in current language. If a father says angrily to his son, "What's this!
I don't do my work! I come to meals without washing my hands!" it is clear
that his reproach is not addressed to himself. He is simply commuting the
signs that normally designate the interlocuters. In this instance, the *I* equals
you. The process derives from rhetoric, even if normal usage of the language
allows the *I* to appear in discourse referring to the person addressed. In fact,

to use Benveniste's terminology, the *I* and the *you* are "reversible," because they are in "subjective correlation."[8] A sentence of the type:

> You said to me: "I came to see you yesterday"

has nothing to do with rhetoric. There is no ambiguity to hinder identification of the *I* because we know that the addresser of the message, from the moment he speaks, must call himself "I."

This inverse commutation (*I* ⟶ *you*), which acts, in the example, to reduce the deviation, may in other sentences indicate the position of the deviation. This is the case in interior monologue, so frequent that it surprises no one. The *I* is divided into parcelled *I*'s that refer to each other and permit the speaker to combine the conative function with the expressive function of the language. Sully made systematic use of this commutation in his *Mémoires,* done in the second person. But it is not necessary to be Sully to use it. We have recourse to it all the time—every time that we want to hold ourselves at a distance. Wallace Stevens uses it often.

> And for what, except for you, do I feel love?
> Do I press the extremest book of the wisest man
> Close to me, hidden in me day and night?
> In the uncertain light of single, certain truth,
> Equal in living changingness to the light
> In which I meet you, in which we sit at rest,
> For a moment in the central of our being
> The vivid transparence that you bring is peace.

We could say that in this prologue to *Notes Toward a Supreme Fiction,* the addressee of the poetic message is the poet's own poetic, the poem itself, which implies a person/non-person commutation. Interior monologues are then interpreted in two ways, based on whether one considers them real monologues or dialogues between the *I* and the parcelled *I,* be this a corporal or a spiritual *I,* and the *I* who suffers or the one reflected in the mirror. This double interpretation is valid for the conversations Baudelaire holds with his heart, his soul, or his sorrow. It is valid also for those conversations Stevens holds with his "interior paramour."

> . . . out of the central mind,
> We make a dwelling in the evening air,
> In which being there together is enough.

If we opt for the dialogue, a synecdoche necessarily arises in the person / non-person commutation.* If not, we would have an addresser / addressee commutation.

---

*[See Harold Bloom, *Wallace Stevens: The Poems of Our Climate* (Ithaca: Cornell University Press, 1977), p. 167, for Stevens's *you* as synecdoche. *Trans.*]

Returning to the commutation *you* ⎯⎯⎯→ *I*, we can note that it is frequent in propaganda literature. In principle, it derives from the conative function, but this function can be masked in an expression that appears to rise from the expressive function and where the *I* replaces the expected second person. Some years ago, "Vote for Eisenhower" or "You ought to vote for Eisenhower" were generally translated as "I like Ike." It is clear that the numerous addressers of this message did not refrain from expressing an opinion. Saying "I," they expressed "you" and gave confidence to the crowd, so that all the *you*'s concerned recognized themselves as the subject.

4. DEFINITE / INDEFINITE COMMUTATION

Definite / indefinite commutations are frequent in French,* and it is often difficult to determine at what point these become rhetorical. English, though less frequently oblique, sometimes presents the same difficulty. Even in the least sophisticated uses of French, *on* can substitute for any of the other persons. English prefers to attach "one," when used indefinitely, to an enclitic. If some unidentified persons have torn up the pavement during the night, it would be normal to say, "On a dépavé la rue" (or "Someone has torn up the street"). Familiarly, however, in both languages one says, "They've torn up the street." The line of deviation is thin and perhaps not perceived. Nonetheless, there is still definite / indefinite commutation, since the anonymous tearing up is attributed to unknown but definite persons or at least ones definable by inquiry. It is true that the rhetorical value of the commutation appears more clearly when *on* ("one") is substituted for the second person in sentences such as "One is taking a walk?" or "Has one eaten well?" which are the respective equivalents of "Are you walking?" and "Did you eat well?" In this case the definite / indefinite commutation is clear, especially in English, where we might expect, as a deviation, the use of the solicitous *we*. Such commutations are banal, however, since they appear in dictionaries. Therefore, a commutation of the sort *one* / *I* would be necessary for the deviation to appear flagrant—at least in French. To an employer accusing him of incompetence, a man could reply: "One does what one can." In this case it is clear that he is talking of himself, and in English as well as French the rhetorical effect is clear, even if the deviation is not so great as in second-person substitution. In certain proverbial expressions, *one* is the equivalent of *I*, but the *I* does not exclude the other persons, as in "It takes

*[Up to now we have had to make only such emandations in the original text that would bring English-language examples into line with the French commentary. However, the French indefinite *on* ("one" or "it") is used in ways that have no easily defined English counterpart. In translating this section, therefore, we have made additions that would clarify the concepts as they apply to English, while trying to leave out nothing in the French original. *Trans.*]

one to know one'' or "One can't unscramble eggs," although *one* is not frequent in English proverbial expressions. In any case, this is not a clear deviation, and *one* can be considered as having the meaning that is most current. It is still true that *I* and *one* are opposed to each other both as terminal / non-terminal and as definite / indefinite. Therefore, we can appreciate the deviations Samuel Beckett created in *Molloy;* we can also compare how we are forced in English to respond to the French *on* by looking at the two versions:

Un peu plus et *on* sera aveugle. C'est dans la tête. Elle ne marche plus, elle dit, Je ne marche plus. *On* devient muet aussi et les bruits s'affaiblissent (. . .) De sorte qu'*on* dit, J'arriverai bien cette fois-ci, puis encore une autre peut-être, puis ce sera tout (. . .) Si l'*on* pense aux contours à la lumière de jadis c'est sans regret. Mais *on* n'y pense guère, avec quoi y penserait-*on*? Je ne sais pas. Il passe des gens aussi, dont il n'est pas facile de se distinguer avec netteté. Voilà qui est décourageant. C'est ainsi que je vis A et B . . .

A little more and *you*'ll go blind. It's in the head. It doesn't work anymore, it says, I don't work anymore. *You* go dumb as well, and sounds fade. . . . So that *you* say, I'll manage this time, then perhaps once more, then perhaps a last time, then nothing more. . . . If *you* think of the forms and light of other days, it is without regret. But *you* seldom think of them—with what would *you* think them? I don't know. People pass too, hard to distinguish from yourself. That is discouraging. So I saw A and B. . . .

In French Beckett describes the loss of individuality by means of the *je/on* commutation; in English the deviation is *I / you,* made operative, no doubt, by the fact that the English *you* subsumes both the singular and plural second person. Hence in English the singular / plural commutation, to be discussed in the next section, does not exist in the second person, and the second person becomes a vehicle for depersonalization. In the Beckett example, the *I/on-you* deviation we are analyzing does not exist for his hero. It is nonetheless flagrant for the person who is not alienated, depersonalized, or, if one prefers, indefinite, as Molloy is. He is not, though, the only person in the novel to be this way, since the woman who receives him is also designated by *on*. The following passage is remarkable in that the indefinite is used with three different values:

On trouvera étrange que j'ai pu faire les mouvements que j'ai indiqués, sans leur secours (des béquilles). Je trouve cela étrange. *On* ne se rapelle pas tout de suite qui on est, au réveil. Je trouvai sur une chaise un vase de nuit blanc avec un rouleau de papier hygiénique dedans. *On* ne laissait rien au hasard.

It may seem strange that I was able to go through the motions I have described without their help [the crutches]. I find it strange. *You* don't remember immediately who you are, when you wake. On a chair I found a white chamber pot with a roll of toiletpaper in it. *Nothing* was being left to chance.

The English here must use three separate indefinites to translate the flexibility of the French *on*. If the second *on* introduces a remark applicable to anyone (hence the general *you*), the first is unequivocally the reader, and the third is Molloy's landlady, who is left far more as an implied presence in English than she is in French.

French authors like Fontanier have distinguished an interesting commutation called *enallage* of person. It consists especially in using a *vous* ("you") for an *on*, as in this example of Lamartine's verse:

> *Un seul être vous manque et tout est dépeuplé.*
> [*"You lack a single person, and the world is void."*]

We note that this commutation is precisely how *on* usually is translated into English. The English equivalent, no doubt, would be the substitution of *one* for *you*.

> That's the time
> One looks at the elephant-colorings of tires.
> Everything is shed; and the moon comes up as the moon
> (All its images are in the dump) and you see
> As a man. . . .

> [Wallace Stevens]

5. SINGULAR / PLURAL COMMUTATION

The most common of these commutations is the one that has passed into usage, but which remains perceptible when one is attentive: plurals of majesty or of politeness.* The plural thus offers to the *I* of the learned a diluted anonymity, while at the same time it confers on the *I* of majesty the amplification such pride demands. A subtle play becomes possible, coded into the languages of familiarity and majesty:

> The tide of blood in me
> Hath proudly flow'd in vanity till now.
> Now doth it turn and ebb back to the sea,
> Where it shall mingle with the state of floods,
> And flow henceforth in formal majesty.
> Now call we our high court of parliament. . . .
> [*Henry IV, Part II,* act 5, sc. 2, lines 129–34]

In English the royal plural is not used in the third person, perhaps because this is excluded from the cycle of "responsibility." German, however, does not hesitate to treat the addressee as a person (unlimited by the plural) from whom a response is not even asked.

---

*[Once again, the polite distinction in French between *tu* and *vous* does not apply in English. *Trans.*]

Outside the plurals of politeness and royalty, some authors have used rhetorical plurals. This is the case in the example already cited regarding psuedo-person / ortho-person commutation:

It is the fault of those who rain.

Less clear but operating on the same mechanism is this example from Beckett:

The policeman has dispersed.

The opposite commutation, from singular to plural, can be found in debates between politicians and among adherents of different religions. "What does the Marxist think about it? What does the Christian think?" The spokesman of the particular group will respond, "I. . . ." If, as Benveniste emphasizes, the *we* contains a dominant *I,* it is nonetheless true that the use of *I* creates a deviation to the extent that it eliminates in favor of an individual the group of *I*'s forming the *we*.

Preachers often have recourse to Biblical language when they address the community of faithful saying, "You are a sinner." Thus they adopt forms by which they address each and all:

Thou art dust, and into dust thou shalt return.
Thou shalt honor thy father and thy mother. . . .

Again the commutations of *he/they* furnish the clearest examples. We think that we can keep the collective singular of the type:

The boss, he doesn't care about the worker's demands.

6. REMARKS

Our analysis has been concerned primarily with suppression-additions of commutations of the binary system of persons. We see in these that one person has been used to replace another. When the two persons are kept, we have a structure of suppression-addition complementary to oxymoronic structure (in which terms are excluded by negation and not by complementarity). Perhaps from this angle we can reconsider the inexhaustible sentence by Rimbaud: "I is another."*

In the realm of additions, we must also mention the *repetitive addition*, which has given Queneau in his *Exercises de style* the heading "Moi je."†

Finally, vertical displacements in the disjunctive tree of persons correspond to synecdoche. The most extreme generalizing synecdoche is common—

---

*[In French, "Je est un autre." *Trans.*]
†["Me, I . . . ," A common if stylized usage in French, it has no close equivalent in English. *Trans.*]

the one that rejects even the relevance of the very notion of person by calling on the impersonal, using at times the participle, as in the variant proverb:

Findings, keepings

or the past participle, as in:

Forewarned, forearmed

or the infinitive, as in:

To sleep—perchance to dream

[Shakespeare]

or in this last example, from Milton, which is interesting because in itself it reduces the deviation:

To suffer, as to do,
Our strength is equal. . . .

It is true, as J. Dubois has pointed out, that the infinitive and participle are related, respectively, to substantive and adjective,[9] the possible correlatives being found in the corresponding marked forms.

7. CONCLUSIONS

Here we must repeat that not all substitutions of person are rhetorical. When Italians use the third person singular as direct address in formal speech, this is current usage. The same procedure in "Fritalian" is normal speech, as in English, only in certain expressions appropriate to certain contexts: "His Majesty is served!" or "Does His Excellency wish to both himself . . . ?" Outside these fixed usages, what is a common expression of politeness becomes in English, however much the context might seem proper, a figure that is noticeable to anyone able to distinguish the language of kings from the language of the street.

If ideas of deviation and norm correspond to reality, it is clear that there exists no absolute norm in speech and that rhetoric ought not to claim to establish it. If it is "normal" to address another person using formal or familiar language, the norm in question will always be only a convention, one able to be changed as soon as we abandon what Wittgenstein called *Sprachspiel,* the "language game" in which that norm is imposed.

Examples could be added at will, and they show that there are only potential figures. Substitutions of person, their suppression or addition, become rhetorical only when it is clear that they break a convention or do not fulfill an expectation for the one using them or noticing them. To recognize a rhetorical operation in a substitution of person, it is first necessary to know the norm from which it deviates and then to make certain that there is a deviation. This is why, when considering work such as Michaux's, the rhetorician has difficulty finding figures, since it is not at all "normal" for Michaux, for example, to speak of himself in the first person. It is saying little to say that he objects to rules. He is unaware of them, or if you like, he finds it "normal" not to take them into account. The use of *he* for *I,* to which he frequently resorts, can pass for a figure if he is being judged in comparison with current language, but the commutation is no longer a figure for the person considering the total work of Michaux. An author of this importance has his own "language games," and it can even be true that use of persons conforming to common usage is paradoxically rhetorical in this work. And, conversely, the use of certain nonconventional language is not necessarily rhetorical here.

But now we are faced with the contextual function of the rhetorical feature. In the play of contextuality at this level, deviations can be normalized, allowing then the possibility of creating new deviations.

Chapter VIII
Figures of Narration

0. GENERAL

The most noticeable "developments" of sequences of sentences, at least from the literary point of view, what is called story (*récit*) or narration, constitute, no doubt, a privileged field for the generalization of rhetoric, to the extent that "structurally, narrative shares the characteristics of the sentence without ever being reducible to the simple sum of its sentences."[1] We must say that miniature stories do exist that are complete in one short syntagmatic whole (*Veni, vidi, vici*). But narration cannot be described within the categories of grammar. It is found also in nonlinguistic systems: in plastic arts (Trajan columns, stained-glass windows, comic strips, and so on), in the theater as scenic representation, in film.

As we shall see in a moment, there is reason here to call on the famous distinction proposed by Hjelmslev between the form and substance of expression and the form and substance of content.[2] Nicolas Ruwet had already noted, in 1964, that this theory "allows us to approach systems of signs other than those in natural languages."[3] The Saussurian sign becomes here a unit of form "constituted by the form of the content and expression, and established by the solidarity that we [Hjelmslev] have called the semiotic function." It is "a Janus-like perspective in two directions, and with effect in two respects: 'outwards' toward the expression-substance and 'inwards' toward the content-substance"[4] (see table 15).

If during our wait for a universal semantic theory, which would be "in some way the science of concepts able to figure in human languages,"[5] we

Table 15. Structure of the Linguistic Sign

	Substance	Form	
Expression	phonic field	sound signs	SIGN
Content	semantic field	concepts	

Table 16.   Semiotic Structure of the Story

	Substance	Form	
Expression	novel, film, comic strip, etc.	narrative discourse	NARRATIVE SIGN
Content	real or imagined universe, real or fictive stories (*histoires*)	story (*récit*) properly so called	

could put off until later an examination of possible figures of content-substance—supposing that these were conceivable—it seems important to say here some words about expression-substance, given that the story can handle different substances either in isolation or concurrently. Table 16 can be proposed for narration.

We need to explain immediately certain terminology. The narrative sign is constituted by the relationship between storytelling and the story told, or in other words, between what we often call *discourse* and *story* (*récit*).[6] It is clear that there is also descriptive discourse, didactic discourse, and so on. On the other hand, current language defines *story* as "oral or written relation (of true or imaginary facts)" (Robert's *Dictionnaire*),* which for us corresponds to the discourse of a story.

1.   FIGURES OF EXPRESSION-SUBSTANCES

1.1.   Support and Substance

Hjelmslev has already explained that it is important to distinguish substance from matter, "physical or psychic support of a nonlinguistic nature."[7] The expression-substance is the phonic field as it exists in a state of possibility in a particular support: the articulating apparatus for sound emission. Each language imposes on its users a particular phonological system, distinct from the others; but in principle each individual can assimilate phonemes that do not exist in his own language. Substance always has need of a support. But substance itself is susceptible of being made manifest in different modalities. A text may be *spoken,* and between the different speakings could be distinguished different modalities, from monotone to expressive diction. But a text may also be *sung.* Support and substance have not changed, but a norm of substance has been determined by this modality: a text is normally spoken. In

---

*[Paul Robert, ed., *Dictionnaire alphabétique et analogique de la langue française* (Paris: P.U.F., 1953-), s.v. "récit." *Trans.*]

itself, this alteration has no repercussion at the higher level of relationship, expression-form / content-form.

If we turn now to the written word, we find the same distinction. Substance is graphic; the support can be a manuscript, but it is usually printed—a book or magazine. Also the same text may be printed with different covers, for books do not all have the same format. The same support, the same substance, different modalities. The same is true for film (8, 16, 35, 70 mm, "standard" format or "scope" format). Modalities of support, no doubt, can become modalities of substance: just as a film is shown in different formats, a typeface 8 bold contrasts with a typeface 8 condensed in a printed text. The book receives two substances—writing and image. We have spoken of modalities of the first; the image can be drawn or photographed, or it may be an amalgam. Drawings and photos can be in black and white, in simple colors, in composite colors. There are so many modalities of substance.

Traditional theater is founded on theatrical representation, on the simultaneous and differentiated presence of characters and spectators. This is its support. It involves two substances: one phonic, the other visual. But the visual representation can be Chinese shadow play, marionettes, actors. The phonic substance may have different modalities and may even be absent, as in mime.

We find the same substances in film, whose support is what is projected on the screen. The support is achieved by a continuous sequence of images on a given surface. The realization of the visual substance has three principal modalities: drawing on the film itself (as MacLaren has done), sequential drawings photographed (designs and animated objects), and continuous filming.

1.2. Norms and Deviations

First some remarks on stories using two substances, as is the case especially with the illustrated book and the film. If we take the book without illustrations as the norm, we can generally consider the use of illustrations as so many additions. If the illustrations contained precisely the same matter as the text, then we would have repetition. But the more interesting fact is that at times the illustration anticipates the text, as in the case of Boz's engravings, which preceded the episodes recounted by Dickens. We can even envisage a kind of negative suppression-addition, as when Lapoujade illustrated simply with images of a woman the novel *Gèneviève* by Jacques Lemarchand, in which—except in the title—the heroine is never named or present. In the same way, we could study the evolution of norms in the comic strip, comparing the relationship between image and text. First, commentary was separated from the picture, then there was a movement to dialogue in balloons, and then the rediscovery of stories without words.

Silent films of the 1920s used a deviation by suppression. The rule was to insert titles or explanations, anticipating the images, but in *The Last Laugh*, Carl Mayer and F. W. Murnau tried a film with no titles. On the other hand, when Godard, in our time, reintroduced the title (*A Woman is a Woman, The Soldiers*), the effect was felt as an addition. Normally, the film with sound uses several channels: noises, dialogue, music, commentary. In filmed stories, the intervention of commentary often becomes a figure, as the suppression of music or dialogue does also, even the substitution of music for natural noises or commentary for dialogue (*Privilege* by Peter Watkin).

Taking into account simply the iconic substance, figures can be created by the use of two or several modalities in the same substance. Thus, in a film-musical Gene Kelly once danced with an animated-cartoon mouse. Other film modalities are related to the speed of the film (slow-motion, speeded motion, running the film backwards); to the use of special focal lenses (long or short focus, narrowing or enlarging the visual field); to the use of double-exposure, of negative prints, of color. On the distributional plane of the relationship between modalities of substance these effects appear as so many suppression-additions: a sequence in color breaks the continuity of black and white; accelerating the projection alters the normal speed.

1.3. Distribution and Integration

One phenomenon spoken of earlier occurs here also: from substance we move to form; from the relationships uniting them, we move to the relationship uniting discourse and plot. On the plane we are concerned with in this chapter, it is the movement to the higher level that will hold our attention. When an author decides to substitute one modality of substance for another, it is most often in order to give a formal value to his discourse. Thus, when Preminger, in *Bonjour Tristesse,* uses color and black and white, color is only for past events. At the end of *Joli Mai,* Marker speeds up the film, and while Yves Montand gives the month's balance sheet of births, deaths, disappearances, quarts of milk and wine consumed, and Citroën and Renault cars delivered, parallel images pile up of cars accelerating around the Arc de Triomphe and, in a subway station, a speed-up of passengers getting on and off the trains. The modality of substance has taken on semantic value. If the commentary were cut from the sequence, it would have no value except in its opposition to other modalities of the substance-image used in the film. Tied to the sound (substance and expression), its value moves from one level to the next. It is the same with certain comic strips, in which the various typefaces used for the words and cries of the characters are a function of the impatience, nervousness, or anger of the character: the degree of typeface corresponds to the vocal energy of the words or curses. Dennis Tedlock has systematically used this procedure for a "visualization" of the orally performed narrative poetry of the Zuni in *Finding the Center*.[8]

At the integrative level, then, a change of modality or of substance can be analyzed as simply repetitive addition, according to its function in the higher unit of the form.

2. FIGURES OF EXPRESSION-FORM: NARRATIVE DISCOURSE

2.0. General

Here we are studying figures of expression-form only insofar as that form integrates the content-form. In other words, it is the discourse / plot relation—in the sense explained above—that will be our concern. In certain techniques of visual representation, especially in film, the realist illusion is such that the presence of significant forms is hardly felt: we project the data of the signified in terms of the referent. This illusion is lessened in the literary story, but it remains in play in such a way that the story, emptied by the discourse and in principle limited by it, seems to remain exterior to the discourse (anterior in its origin, posterior in its term) and consequently seems to go beyond it and also to enclose it.

2.0.1. LITERARY DISCOURSE

It is nonetheless rare that literary discourse is so transparent as to filter the story naively and that the concepts it transmits to us are spontaneously visualized as objects. Most often it opposes its progress, its syntactic play, to the imaginary representation of the event. Thus, there are certainly two universes coming into being in its development: the universe of the story, where beings and objects move according to specific laws, and the linguistic universe, where syntactic norms govern the sentences and impose a certain order on these elements. Discourse can be subsumed to representation, can in fact efface itself, allowing the events themselves to rise or retain only certain elements useful for configuration: in five lines, Voltaire describes the war between the Bulgares and the Abares:

> First the cannons battered down about six thousand men on each side; then volleys of musket fire removed from the best of worlds about nine or ten thousand rascals who were cluttering up its surface. The bayonet was a sufficient reason for the demise of several thousand others.[9]

The novelist is free to stumble against objects or to insinuate himself between them; in turn, he is free to be, even within a single sentence, inside or outside his characters. Often careful to efface himself, even Flaubert intervenes, for example, whe he tells us what Charles was not thinking about: "As for Charles, he didn't ask himself why he enjoyed going to Les Bertaux."[10]

As limited as the conventions of Flaubert are, they reveal the ambiguities of discourse, which at times tells the story, at times tells itself, at times disappears to become a transparent reading of the events, at times comes forth to engage the reader in dialogue. Thus Fielding suspends the action in the liminary chapter of each book of *Tom Jones* to deliver various reflections and to engage in criticism. Even better, as a powerful and facetious master, he does not hesitate to let us know that he may be hiding something:

> Whether he was innocent or not will perhaps appear hereafter; but if the historic Muse hath entrusted me with any secrets, I will by no means be guilty of discovering them till she shall give me leave.*

2.0.2. THEATRICAL DISCOURSE

In the theater the author is absent, each scene being given to the characters, "whose unique presence removes the author to the background."[11] Authorial intervention does manifest itself, however, in the divisions that he imposes on the work. To consider but a single example, we note in Racine's *Britannicus* that the story is already in progress when the curtain rises (Nero has had Junia carried off) and that the story is still continuing when the curtain falls (an alliance has been formed between Agrippina and Burrhus, who will try to reason with the Emperor: "Let us go see what we can do" is the last reply).

It remains true that the actor-character is certainly the vehicle of the process of utterance. In principle, he is a unique relay. But, on the one hand, the actor can separate himself from the character and include this differentiation in the performance (which is the Brechtian distancing whereby the actor shows the character but remains different). On the other hand, he is the medium allowing the character to contact the public, and at that moment the illusory space of the action and the real space of the theater become confused.

2.0.3. FILM DISCOURSE

Film allows three possibilities for the process of utterance: montage; camera angle; titles or, since the appearance of talkies, the sound track. Montage imposes its own order, duration, or rhythm on the spectator. This organization of the angle of shots can suddenly reveal unawarenesses (events omitted) or integrate elements foreign to the plot in its development (Eisenstein's famous "metaphors"). The presence of the director is also shown by montage, indicating what is now shown (the camera within sight of the action but refusing to contemplate it) or in anticipation (in *Stagecoach*, where a panorama reveals the presence of Indians before the passengers in the stagecoach are aware of them). Finally, the titles, by means of which the narrator could address the spectator directly, gave way to the sound track, which, as soon as it includes commentary, doubles the visual discourse and, with the exception of interior

*[Bk. 2, chap. 6. *Trans.*]

monologues, presents two temporalities simultaneously. Sound, in fact, is felt to be a more recent past, a closer present, than the screen.

There are some rather infrequent effects by which the character reminds us of the presence of a recorder, addressing himself directly to the spectator (as in *Annie Hall,* where Woody Allen suddenly asks the audience to confirm his side in an argument).

2.0.4. NORMS AND DEVIATIONS

In this first part of the examination, we have grasped a certain number of deviations by comparison with a theoretical norm whose ideal is for discourse to be so transparent that the story would seem to flow by itself. In the modalities of their actual existence, literary, theatrical, and film stories are achieved only through a discourse that always has the ability to remind us of its own existence, forgoing the utterance of the story to express itself. We recognize here the rhetorical function in its fundamental effect: to draw attention to the message itself.

In practice, we must include in the norm a residual presence of the discourse expressing itself as such. The intervention of Flaubert or the omissions of Racine in no way disturb the development of the plot. Discourse utters itself, but as an internal reflection within the reading of the story. On the other hand, when an author-reader relationship is superimposed on the discourse-plot relationship, a deviation is felt. But its determination seems to come from an undercurrent of the metaboles of the interlocutors.

An extreme case of distancing between signifiers and signifieds is shown in certain modern novels where discourse is in opposition to the plot, where the author gives two or several versions of a scene. A play of possibilities is offered to the reader, no single scene given preference. The illusion of realism is still in effect, however, in this succession of possibilities; a plot is still visible through the discourse, but this plot is organized within the meanderings of the discourse organizing it. We have, then, the plot of the discourse's organization. No doubt this is an analogue of the figures of the multiple isotopy that we noticed above (chap. I, sec. 2.1.5). Degree zero remains indeterminate.

In the following pages, we shall try to classify the principal areas where figures can appear. Once again, each genre has its conventions and proper conditions, variable according to the schools, so that the norm will have several modalities. But it is always possible to arrange the genre schematically by reference to cognitive function. Scientific history as practiced by historians can serve as the reference, a kind of ideal model.

We start from a first given: plot, like discourse, is by necessity progressive; it begins and ends in diegetic time, as discourse begins and ends in the instance of uttering. Between the two empty spaces preceding and following it, plot unfolds in its time. On this first homology, which is chronology, other similarities can be found. The norm of the sentence is clarity; words are arranged in it in logical relationships, and in the same way, events of the plot also are arranged along a clearly causal line. Finally, since discourse is necessarily carried by a voice, anonymous or named, a coherent point of view is constituted for us, since the teller hides or affirms his presence as witness or even as subject of the adventure. There is one more need imposed on discourses of visual presentation and, in part, also on the novel. Discourse is, in fact, localized in the very space of the plot. The norm here will be that this localization not be felt, that discourse not be the screen on which the plot is seen.

From this we grasp places where deviation is possible: in relations of time, of chronological direction, of causal determination, of spatial localization, and of point of view.

2.1. Relations of Duration

In principle, we can ask that the duration of recounting be of a shorter period than that of the story being told. These two durations might coincide if the discourse were to reproduce strictly the temporal data of the story. This is true of dialogue, at least when it records the actual words exchanged. Let us now see how discourse shortens narrative duration in the three forms under consideration—theater, cinema, and novel.

In classical theater, where the process of utterance is not done by the author, but by the characters, compression of the story's duration by the duration of discourse is felt in the relations of act to act, scene to scene. The interpretation of the rule of the three unities was a suggestion that a day-long story could be reduced to a discourse duration of a few hours. Outside the silence between acts, the passages from one scene to the next, an abbreviation of duration is assumed even in the dialogue.

This abbreviation, understood as the norm, is first of all a part of the clarity of expression of thought: expression ties thought into an organized and coherent whole, disallowing a kind of realistic lengthening of its evasions, its turns on itself, its projections into the action. In Racine's theater, if ambiguity does exist, it does so in terms of the plot (does Nero accept a reconciliation with Britannicus or not?), not in terms of the discourse (Nero can question his acts, but not his words).

The abbreviation can be a relation of actions to characters: Phaedra neither eats, drinks, walks, nor sleeps; she is only speech. Moreover, the secondary characters have no interests proper and distinct from the action. Pyrrhus, no doubt, and especially Narcissus are taken up by the central action, but at no time does the instance of utterance broaden to include in its duration their problems and personal conflicts. It is in this way that there exists in the theater a discourse of plot that compresses time.

Except for alteration of substance, each shooting of a scene in film integrates the very duration of the fragment of plot grasped by the fragment of discourse. This coincidence of fragmentary durations can be extended to the whole work (*Cleo from Five to Seven,* by A. Varda). But more usually the editing of shots compresses the duration. In three shots I can pass from character A, starting his meal, to character B, who is watching him and speaking with him, and the return to A, who is finishing his meal. Each of the shots has respected the duration of the story, but from one to the other a part of the story has been eliminated.

All evidence indicates that the distance separating duration of discourse and duration of plot is even greater in literature. As we noted in section 2.0.1, two universes come together in literary discourse: the space of the plot is named in the description, indicated in dialogue; the time of the plot is suspended in description, imitated in dialogue. On the other hand, discourse that affirms its first duration in a narrator-reader relationship can assimilate dialogue, condense it in indirect style, lengthen it, whether by analysis (the reflection of the narrator turned toward the reader) or by investing the characters with an interior linguistic universe. We discover the equilibrium, the norm, in the meeting of Emma and Léon at the Croix-Rouge (*Madame Bovary*), where three hours are reduced to four pages. Our habits with narrative and literary conventions fortify this norm.

2.1.1. SUPPRESSION

The deviation, that is, suppression, is noticed when the novelist eliminates dialogue, concentrates the content of the words, or piles up events, as in this famous passage from *Sentimental Education:*

> He traveled.
> He knew the melancholy of packet-boats, the cold awakenings under a tent, the stupor of landscapes and ruins, and the bitterness of broken loves.
> He returned home.
> He mingled in society and had yet other loves.

2.1.2. ADDITION

A figure first appears when analysis reaches into interior monologue, where the time of telling stretches into a duration of miniscule parcels of time (the end of Joyce's *Ulysses*). The phenomenon becomes even clearer when, as Auerbach notes,[12] thanks to analysis, thanks to the flow of imagination, interior time confronts exterior time. In Virginia Woolf's *To the Lighthouse* the meditation of Mrs. Ramsay is inserted between two replies that in reality would have followed each other closely. The same is true when a tension arises between what is said and what is thought, or, to use the expression of Nathalie Sarraute, between conversation and hidden conversation.[13] There, in fact, the least exchange of words swells into a thousand explanations, a thousand ramifications.

The aside in theater, which conveys to the audience the intimate thoughts of the character, also lengthens duration. But there will be no figure except when it is used extensively. Such a use is already felt in *Cromwell,* where Victor Hugo gives the character two voices.[14] It is even clearer in *Our Town,* where Wilder systematically reverses the conventional relationship between the lengths of dialogues and asides.

Literature has found other deviations of addition on the plane of time: description and digression. If Lessing could praise Homer for describing Agamemnon's armor at the very moment when the king was donning it, of having seized the object in movement while describing it, it is in fact more usual for description to suspend narration to the point of stopping it, replacing it with another time span, the time span of the story. This phenomenon is evident in the long description found in the *nouveau roman,* especially in Robbe-Grillet or John Hawkes.

Digression is a more ambiguous phenomenon. Even if it is the act of the author and interrupts the continuity of the story only to turn the speech instance toward the reader, it still appears as a digression of the discourse:

> I think, replied my uncle Toby, taking his pipe from his mouth, and striking the head of it two or three times upon the nail of his left thumb, as he began his sentence,— I think, says he:—*but to enter rightly into my uncle Toby's sentiments upon this matter, you must be made to enter first a little into his character....* [Sterne, our emphasis]*

And then we must wait some thirty pages before finally learning that Uncle Toby thought that "it would not be amiss, brother, if we rung the bell." Uncle Toby is, no doubt, only a simple stand-in for the narrator, but this sudden acknowledgment of the narrator-reader relationship interrupting the narrator-story relationship can appear only as a distortion of time.

We know that the narrator is permitted to go from character to character. In Fielding's *Joseph Andrews,* Lady Booby and Mr. Didapper hear the story of Lennard and Paul read to them by Parson Adams's son. But he is forced to interrupt the story by his father's corrections—disgression, suspension of the story, but not ones that alter at all the continuity of the basic time span, a time span in which Lady Booby, Parson Adams, and his son take their place.

Finally, digression can constitute a figure of plot, in which case only the action is deferred, and time continues. In J.-L. Godard's *The Outsiders,* this will be a trip through the Louvre improvised by the heroes, who arrived too early at the place agreed on for their crime.

We recalled above the cinema's use of slow and rapid motion, noting that

*[Bk. 1, chap. 21, *Trans.*]

starting as modalities of substance, these procedures finally became modalities of discourse, one an addition, the other a suppression. Stopping the image has the same value as addition on the temporal plane, used with the most relevance in Kon Ichikawa's *Odd Obsession*. At the beginning of each sequence, the movements of a character are slowed, and everything happens as if the author were asking the audience, What if he now stopped, gave up his decision, denied the ineluctable?

2.1.3. SUPPRESSION-ADDITION

If subjective temporality is substituted in literature for wholly objective time, we can call it suppression-addition. In fact, we no longer have the idea of a simple addition of interior duration compared with the continuity of the narration, but of the displacement of one duration by another.

The first example may make us hesitate. In Ambrose Bierce's "The Occurrence at Owl Creek Bridge," a man is taken out on a bridge where he is to be hanged; the cord is put around his neck, the order for execution is given to the hangman, the condemned man suddenly plunges into the river, dodges the soldiers' bullets, gets to shore, runs through the woods to meet his wife, and at the moment he is about to take her into his arms, the reader is brought back to the man hanging from the bridge. This expansion of a few seconds, of some tenths of a second of his dying, into an imaginary time is given continuity. The author has run together one temporal duration with another, and it is only at the end of the story that we realize the substitution. Obaldia has done the same thing in his play *Genousie*.

If we hesitate to classify these cases as suppression-addition, it is because we are in a position to grasp *a posteriori* the moment when we move from one duration to the other and because the artifice of the author is in some way unveiled. But when we are given only fragmentary and uncertain information on objective duration, there is no doubt that this is substitution. The procedure is frequent and obvious in Faulkner's works and in Virginia Woolf's novels.

Film does not seem to use the figure of suppression-addition, at least not in its complete form. This is because the shift from clock time to subjective time is always clearly underlined either by alterations of the substance or by dissociation of sound and image. In Hitchcock's *The 39 Steps* the landlady discovers a body, then opens her mouth in a scream while the sound track responds with a train whistle. But film has more complex phenomena where addition and suppression, localized at easily discoverable points, add their effects in a hybrid figure.

Take the remarkable example in a film composed of stills, with one exception, Chris Marker's *The Pier*. At the end, the hero falls on the Orly Pier. The image retains only four moments of his fall. Thus we have reduction in comparison with the continuity of the story that it recounts, creating a phenomenon of addition.

2.1.4. PERMUTATIONS

Since we have dissociated duration as such from the events inscribed in it, permutations of a temporal order will be discussed in relation to chronology (below, sec. 2.2.4).

2.2. Acts and Chronology

The novel plot is traditionally presented as a copy of the historical story. In general, the imagined facts are supposed to pertain to the past and are related retrospectively. In other words, the opening of the recounting instance is in principle later than the beginning and even the end of the recounted story. An aesthetic ideal has been gradually imposed whereby the writer suppresses in himself his foreknowledge about the succession of events and finds an "open present," which he knows as a "closed past." Most often, however, the story will show signs, whether voluntarily or not, of this knowledge of the writer.

But chronology interests us especially in the relationship it establishes between the order of events and the order of their discovery by the reader. We often find in the novel those recountings of small pieces of the past when two characters tell each other what they did the night before. Or the author may introduce a new character and give a motive for his presence by sketching in his recent past. Such breaks in chronological direction hardly form figures, and we cannot consider as an important flashback the retrospective story of Charles's childhood after the initial scene of *Madame Bovary*.

2.2.1. SUPPRESSION

Chronology of the plot and of discourse move in the same direction. But an event can be hidden and will not constitute a figure if it is insignificant unless the author omits transition as well and creates in this way an effect in the discourse. In the following sequence, for example, nothing immediately indicates that between the fourth and fifth replies an episode has come to an end and Lieutenant Scheisskopf's wife has returned home. Heller has surprised the reader in this way, forcing him to correct, *a posteriori*, the unfolding of the action.

> "Darling we're going to have a baby again," she would say to Yossarian every month.
> "You're out of your goddam head," he would reply.
> "I mean it baby," she insisted.
> "So do I."
> "Darling, we're going to have a baby again," she would say to her husband.
> "I haven't the time," Lieutenant Scheisskopf would grumble petulantly.

When the omitted event has some importance, ellipsis can be of two modalities. In the first place, the event is defined by anticipation; in the second it is retroactively deduced.

The first modality is frequent at the close of the discourse: an event is announced that the author does not develop. When Camus finishes with Meurseault on the last page of *The Stranger,* the execution has not yet taken place.

The second modality is more frequent at the opening of the discourse: plunged *in medias res,* the reader or spectator uses induction, trying to understand causes from their consequences, to grasp the reasons for the presence of Agrippina at Nero's door by learning about the kidnapping of Junia (Racine, *Britannicus*).

The figure is more clearly marked when it comes in the course of the narrative. In *Redgauntlet* (Scott) the letters from Alan Fairford to Darsie Latimer, and from Darsie to Alan, fail to tell us that Darsie has been kidnapped. More recently, we find writers using the recounting instance itself as one means of revealing the hidden event. In *Aytré qui perd l'habitude* [Aytré who loses the habit], Paulhan uses the form of a diary kept by Aytré during a trip. From 27 December to 18 January there are only uninteresting notes. Nothing is written for 19 January. Then there is a different tone in the writing starting with the twentieth, when Aytré begins to talk about an inquiry into the assassination of a woman. The entries are longer, and personal considerations are added to the trivia. Aytré has "lost the habit," and we can guess that on 19 January he murdered Madam Chalinargues.[15] The opposition of the discourses—their respective lengths, contents, and styles—before and after the event, grasped first on the distributional plane of expression, overflows into the content or the plot.

2.2.2. ADDITION

If we accept that the actions of the plot handled by the discourse are hypothetically complete, simple addition is obviously not conceivable. Nonetheless, since a rule of discourse is to filter the facts and chronological indications, we could accept as cases of addition those instances where the author lingers over insignificant details and multiplies chronological indications. Take the following passage from *Ulysses:*

Mr. Bloom put his head out of the window.
—The grand canal, he said.
Gas works. Whooping cough they say it cures. Good job Milly never got it. Poor children! Doubles them up black and blue in convulsions. Shame really. Got off lightly with illness compared. Only measles. Flaxseed tea. Scarlatina influenza epidemics. Canvassing for death. Don't miss this chance. Dog's home over there. Poor old Athos! Be good to Athos, Leopold, is my last wish. Thy will be done. We

obey them in the grave. A dying scrawl. He took it to heart, pined away. Quiet brute. Old men's dogs usually are.

A raindrop spat on his hat. He drew back and saw an instant of shower spray dots over the grey flags. Apart. Curious. Like through a colander. I thought it would. My boots were creaking I remember now.

—The weather is changing, he said quietly.

When Bresson, in *Pickpocket* (or Antonioni in *Red Desert*), opens the film before the hero is in the camera field and closes it after the hero has already walked off camera, he is introducing into the sequence indications foreign to the action.

Strictly speaking, if discourse is unable to add an event to the plot, it can repeat the same event. Repetition may be simply a figure of plot when discourse reproduces faithfully what the fiction offers, but repetition belongs to discourse when, in the instance of recounting, it refers only to a single event of the plot. Medieval literature used this procedure often. In *The Life of Saint Alexis,* when the groom joins his wife in the bedroom on the day of the wedding, he tells her that he will not know her carnally. The following three stanzas handle the situation as follows: stanza 13 recapitulates the situation already introduced in 12 but carries the action further and in a different direction; stanza 14 repeats, concretely and in direct discourse, the statement made in stanza 13.[16]

2.2.3. SUPPRESSION-ADDITION

Alternation. Textual continuity permits only one large circumstance of narrating, even if different narrators are used in the course of development. Certainly we can imagine a page layout where the shift of narrator is indicated line by line or page by page (Faulkner). But as a general rule, the movement from one action to another simultaneous one is done by succession in the novel plot. The relationship is, in fact, complex. If I interrupt the point of contact between actions A and B by action X, there is suppression or retardation of point A/B, but there are also the relations A/X and X/B. Better yet, point B as a prolongation of A is never grasped as an immediate chronological succession to A. Temporal ellipsis with a duration about equal to X separates A from B. Substitution is, therefore, clear on the plane of acts and their linkage. This phenomenon is found in *Crack in the Mirror,* where Richard Fleischer juxtaposes difficulties that a young lawyer encounters in his practice and the lower-class life of a man who will be his client in a murder case. The two lines of development work along the same chronological axis, each event shown successively on its own line and parallel with an event on the neighboring line, the chief actors taking two roles.

Breaking Chronology. The same process is at work when chronology is broken. If memories and projects for the future thrust themselves into the same temporal development, this will be substitution rather than addition in that the development is supposed to be followed, while discourse has taken care of the past, the imagined, or the future. This fact is already striking in frame stories such as the *Decameron*. It is even more so when, as in Proust's work or in some films (*Hiroshima, Mon Amour*), it is in the free associations of reverie that memories arise and pass from actual concrete data to an imaginary time.

Film Metaphors. In Resnais's *Hiroshima, Mon Amour,* the first break in chronology takes place when the stretched-out body of a German soldier is substituted for the image of the Japanese man lying in bed with his hand open, images that are striking for their similarity. This is the justification for the intrusion of the memory or the mental image. On the other hand, the famous metaphors of Eisenstein (shots of slaughter houses interrupting the charging police in *Strike,* harpists who symbolize the mollifying speech of the Mensheviks in *October*) appear as authorial intrusions in the development of the plot and as internal relays for the discourse. In *October* the speech of Kornilov calling on the patriots, evoking God and country, is illustrated first by a series of images of divinities and second by showing, synecdochically, epaulettes and military medals. Here, Eisenstein omits the visual development Kornilov would have himself given to his words and substitutes for it a personal development that derides it.

2.2.4. PERMUTATION

Here again, permutation can take many forms, including inversion. We have called substitution the intrusion of non-chronological elements using the consciousness of a character. But as soon as chronological order is broken simply by the choice of the discourse and with concern for its organization, as happens especially in the presentation of a mosaic of biographical newspaper stories (from the death of Kennedy, there is a shift to his war experiences), we must consider this some kind of permutation.

It is also permutation when the passage of time is given referentially, not homologous with conventional time. If this is retrospective time, we can speak of permutation by inversion.

In film we can see divers gracefully return to the board, dismantled objects come together before our eyes, a tube of toothpast squeezed empty on a table suddenly pulling the ribbon of paste back inside, leaving the table clean. This situation is especially clear when inversion is given as the natural order of the narrative universe (*Die parallele Strasse* by Khittl or Borowczyk's *Renaissance*).

In the nineteenth century, Lewis Carroll had already written:

For instance, now . . . there's the King's Messenger. He's in prison now, being punished; and the trial doesn't even begin till next Wednesday; and of course the crime comes last of all. [*Through the Looking-Glass*]

Jean-Jacques Mayoux has mentioned the passage in *Finnegans Wake* where Shaun goes back through events just described from end to beginning.[17] In this case, as in the palindrome, time becomes circular, and beginning and end are tied together. We recall here Borges's dream of eternal return, the English film *Dead of Night,* or Queneau's *Le Chiendent,* where the first and last sentences match.[18]

The events of the plot are connected along a chain where each kernel is at the same time the result of the preceding one and the cause of the following one. Thus each event is grasped through its coordinations, which have a certain verisimilitude. A man is dead: it is a crime, a suicide, an accident, a mystery when we try to find the cause. There is a burial, a will and inheritors, family conflicts when we seek the consequences.

2.3. Train of Events and Causal Determinism

Causal lines (of discourse and of plot) are parallel to temporal lines, and certain accidents of temporal development (when the recounting circumstance leaves out an important event) obviously affect the causal line. Causal lines, parallel to the temporal ones, are also developed along the lines of point of view. Causes can be external (a landslide isolating a small group in the mountains) or internal (the hero decides how to act). The first kinds are created from the space of the plot; the second belong to interior space. The norm is found in an equilibrium: to name the intention-cause, to show the act-effect. This equilibrium between interior and exterior is seen especially well in stories of Henry James—"The Middle Years" or "Paste." Hence, in the first of these stories:

> He *liked* the feeling of the south so far as you could have it in the north, he *liked* the sandy cliffs and the clustered pines, he *liked* even the colourless sea. "Bourne-mouth as a health-resort" had sounded like a mere advertisement, but he *was thankful* now for the commonest conveniences. THE SOCIAL COUNTRY POSTMAN, PASSING THROUGH THE GARDEN, HAD JUST GIVEN HIM A SMALL PARCEL which he took out with him, leaving the hotel to the right and creeping to a bench HE HAD ALREADY HAUNTED, a safe recess in the cliff. It looked to the south, to the tinted walls of the Island, and was protected behind by the sloping shoulder of the down. He *was tired* enough when he reached it, and for a moment *was* disappointed; he *was* better of course, but better, after all, than what? (The capitals and italics are ours.)

2.3.1. SUPPRESSION

Suppression appears when the recounting circumstance diminishes interior space and understands the behavior of characters from the outside. This ellipsis was responsible for the novelty of Dashiell Hammett's novels when they first appeared. It forces the reader to move from acts to causes or motivations, from appearances to depth when we see the characters in all their opacity. We shall consider this procedure again when we discuss point of view.

Less frequently, exterior causes are eliminated. We can speak of total suppression when cause is admitted as unknown by the author. This is the case in stories of fantasy or mystery, such as Maupassant's *Le Horla* or Vonnegut's novels.

2.3.2. ADDITION

We have the figure of addition when the author isolates psychological analysis or introspection from the story (George Eliot) as one means of penetrating the intimate thoughts of the character and elucidating his inner reasons for acting. We find simple addition when, as in detective novels, the author multiplies explanatory hypotheses.

Repetitive addition, where a simple cause is explained in twenty different ways, is an easy comic technique, found in Molière's *Le Médecin malgré lui*.

2.3.3. SUPPRESSION-ADDITION

A false relationship of cause and effect is a technique in Flann O'Brien's novels. The stories begin with an event that seems to follow logically from what precedes it, but which, by the end of the reading, is seen to be completely foreign.

Through montage, Eisenstein, in *October,* also creates a relationship of cause and effect between two non-contiguous elements: an official in Petrograd jumps as if he were reacting to the distant bombardment of the trenches. This relationship, which is false if we accept that the space of the story, is, in fact, tied to the discourse and raises the idea that the official is making the decision to pursue the war and suffer the consequences.

2.3.4. PERMUTATION

In arranging a chain of causes and effects, there can be permutation that will be perceived as a figure only if there is disproportion between the last effect and the first cause. The lasting success of the folktale Type 2040, *The Climax of Horrors,* is due to the fact that we go back up the chain of causes, starting with a neutral fact and arriving at the initial catastrophe.*

Permutation by temporal inversion is doubled by causal inversion: the effects create the causes.

---

*[See Anti Aarne and Stith Thompson, *The Types of the Folktale,* 2d rev. ed. (Helsinki, 1961). A good English example, "News," can be found in Katherine M. Briggs, *A Dictionary of British Folktales,* pt. A, vol. 2 (Bloomington: Indiana University Press, 1970), pp. 199–200. The orignal here cites the success of the popular song "Tout va très bien, Madame la Marquise" with its antiphrastic title, another example of this narrative pattern. See Stith Thompson, *Motif-Index of Folk Literature,* rev. ed., 6 vols. (Bloomington: Indiana University Press, 1966), vol. 5, motif Z46. *Trans.*]

2.4. Representation of Space in Discourse

In the visual arts of theater and film, space is an immediate given, while setting can be subject to different maneuvers and manipulations. In the novel, verbal discourse strongly mediates the representation of physical space. Localization by discourse can go from the simple mention of the "theater" of action to the most detailed description of the decor, its objects, and its characters. In literary discourse, the physical world is made up only of approximations, general indications and fragmentary details—it is up to the reader to complete them imaginatively. It should be noted also that in some manner, representation of space is tied to the nature of the point of view, an aspect to be examined next.

2.4.1. SUPPRESSION

Wide-angle cinematography, so frequent in *La Passion de Jeanne d'Arc,* reduces space; but the novel also uses this procedure: the description of Charles's cap in *Madame Bovary* fills the scene, and the owner of the cap seems to have left the field of vision.

The angle chosen can be total, and in the 1914 Italian short *Amour pédestre* the camera remains relentlessly fixed on the legs and feet of the "hero." The action continues and remains clear as we see the young fellow on the heels of a fashionable woman, playing "footsies" with her in a streetcar, and slipping a note asking for a rendezvous into her shoe.

2.4.2. ADDITION

The opposite of this reductive figure, where the part leads to the whole, is the operation of addition, where the whole includes the part. Buster Keaton's films frequently use inclusive shots to let the spectator see the spatial coordination of the elements at play. In *The Navigator,* Keaton and his fiancée are the only passengers on a steamship, and neither one is aware that the other is aboard. Each of them guesses, however, that he is not alone and starts searching for the other passenger. Several shots of the entire boat show them simultaneously, each following a different path around the ship.

2.4.3. SUPPRESSION-ADDITION

Suppression-addition most often gives rise to ambiguity. In *The Idle Class,* Chaplin is reading a letter from his wife asking for a separation. He sighs and turns around; his back is shaking as if he were sobbing. But when he turns around, we see that, with a gleeful eye, he is shaking a cocktail. This technique works on space and time simultaneously, on causes and appearances. Three moments are, in fact, shown here. From the first of them, we deduce the signification of the second, because we believe that a man abandoned by his wife will feel the hurt. But the third moment throws the meaning of the second one into doubt; it suppresses it as erroneous and adds another meaning. The technique derives above all from the reciprocal localization of the camera and the character. But there is a truly comic effect only if an opposition arises between appearance and reality. Therefore, such a suppression-addition will often be negative. (The final signification is antiphrasis: certainly, he's in pain, some real pain.)

Another form of suppression-addition is the refusal of discourse to report the action. These spatial ellipses are frequent in Lubitsch's comedies and derive no doubt from the theater, perhaps for reasons of decorum: refusal to show violent scenes (the duel in *Le Cid*) or intimate acts. The central act of Corneille's *Horace* is based on the relationships between the place shown (the house of the Horatii) and the exterior places where the action takes place (the arena).

In the novel, we can cite some passages from Diderot's *Jacques le fataliste et son maître*, where the narrator has to guess the actions of the characters from the sounds overheard. Then there is the famous carriage scene in *Madame Bovary*, in which we follow the carriage through the streets of Rouen, only hearing the voice of Léon and seeing the bare hand of Emma as indications of their presence and their acts.

2.5. Point of View

The concept of point of view has played a large role in literary theory and practice in English-speaking countries since Henry James. Just as the painter gives us things to see "in perspective," the novelist also reveals them from a certain angle of view, which the rhetoric of narrative discourse must take into account. Along with T. Todorov, we say that point of view designates "the way that events are perceived by the narrator, and consequently by the eventual reader also."[19] The author explains his definition more precisely by separating two fundamental aspects in the idea of point of view: the more or less marked presence of the narrator in discourse and his closer or more distanced relationship with the characters and their consciousness.

Where can degree zero of point of view now be situated? Two positions look possible, but they are almost contradictory. The first would be a kind of scientific ideal of point of view. As objective chronicler, the narrator would assemble and order events without showing himself, allowing meaning to emerge by itself. The second would, on the contrary, advance the rights of imagination, the rights of the creator as sovereign master in his own creation. Since the whole work is his conception, the novelist knows everything about it, and he is thus allowed to share this knowledge at will by sharing (and allowing us to share) the secrets of every character, eventually anticipating the action, proffering judgments, and putting himself into his own discourse.

Neither of these extreme and contradictory opinions can, in fact, satisfy us as being degree zero for the good reason that the modern novel has fixed on as

Table 17.   Figures of Point of View

	Representation of the Narrator	Relationship between Narrator and Characters
Suppression	Objective narration	View from outside
Addition	Intervening narration	Omniscient view
Suppression-addition	First-person discourse	View "along with," diary, letter, interior monologue
Permutation	—	Mixed points of view

its norm a transparent point of view, which is achieved by a narrative attitude situated halfway between the two poles distinguished by Todorov. This is Zola's or Flaubert's manner. The narrator is discreet without absenting himself; he can be noticed only obliquely in the consciousness of his characters and of his preferred hero. By this single means, omnipresence and omniscience of the narrator as well as objective and external vision have become at this point deviations in the perception of the modern reader.

Once this comprehensive norm is established, it is valuable to study its manifestations, for experience of the novel has taught us that there are hardly any examples of point of view that, in fact, follow a single path sustained by absolute coherence. But if we want to avoid going too far astray, we must work in the most schematic manner, staying within the broad lines of development. Using, therefore, the two distinctive features noted above, we construct a table of the broad classes of alterations of point of view (table 17).

2.5.1. SUPPRESSION

One of the conquests of the novel during the past hundred years has been realistic narration in the third person where the narrator manifests objectivity by not revealing his presence. A Roger Vailland avoids comments from outside, evaluative judgments, and so on: he reports facts, words, and thoughts and allows the characters to judge each other. The case is different and somewhat freer when the narrator is forbidden to enter the thoughts of the novelistic characters; in the American novel, Hemingway and Hammett have used to perfection this behavioristic style, which relies only on gestures, attitudes, and physical acts. In this sense, the whole theater (and the novel in dialogue) is one vast figure of suppression. Its convention is to say that only gestures and speech can be reconstructed, leaving aside, on theoretical principle, the vast field of the inner life of the characters.

2.5.2. ADDITION

Certain authorial interventions do not lack humor, and give the effect of emphasizing the fictive life of their characters. Thus, in *Max Havelaar*, Multatuli moves his characters aside for a moment in the following passage:

Enough, my good Stern! I, Multatuli, take up the pen; you have not been called upon to write Havalaar's biography. I brought you to life. . . . I brought you from Hamburg. . . . I taught you to write passable Dutch. . . . I let you kiss Louise Rosemeyer, the sugar-maker. . . . That's enough, Stern, you can go. . . .

Such easy lack of constraint is not unfitting, but when a popular novelist such as Marie Corelli or Horatio Alger lets it show too obviously that he holds the strings with the remark "we can now return to our hero to see if he is going to get out of that scrape," the writer's intrusion becomes irritating or ridiculous. We know that even Balzac does not escape this same ridicule with his numerous and varied intrusions. Balzac, moreover, is a paragon of the omniscient author. His point of view embraces all the minds in the novel, all intentions, all motives, always and everywhere. Polyvalent point of view, the supreme figure of addition.

2.5.3. SUPPRESSION-ADDITION

Todorov also writes: "The true narrator, the uttering subject of a text where one character says 'I' is all the more disguised. The first-person story does not make the image of its narrator explicit, but makes it even more implicit."[20] Seen in this way, the disguise of a first-person novel is the perfect example of substitution. Faced with his characters, the narrator is in a double—an ambiguous—relationship. Intimacy is pushed to a maximum on the one hand, since the narrator is as close to the characters as possible. Even though Stendhal uses third-person narration, we feel him "glued" to his Fabrice at the Battle of Waterloo. But at the same time, he gives up his place, substituting another logic for his logic, another discourse for his discourse, using the diary, the letter, or interior monologue.

2.5.4. PERMUTATION

As just indicated, since substitution can involve competing points of view (*I* and *she,* several *I*'s, narrator and character, several characters), the play of these "rivalries" can be inscribed on a syntagmatic axis with typical permutations: A can see B in one letter, and in the next, B lets us see A. The narrative giving several versions of a single action, particularly a crime, pushes this procedure to the limit. Examples are not only the detective novel but also psychological stories. In the novella "In a Grove," by Akutagawa, the story on which Kurosawa based his film *Rashomon,* a bandit comes across a couple in the forest, ties the man to a tree, and rapes his wife. These are the common features in the respective recountings of wife, bandit, and a "ghost" of the dead man. But on the question of the causes of death, the testimonies are in conflict: the bandit defends his honor saying that he killed the man at the end of an honorable duel; the woman admits that she killed her husband so that he not survive the shame; the dead man claims that he killed himself. Who is to be believed? The story says nothing, and the butcher who discovered the body is of no help either.

We note that this last example could be reinterpreted from another point of view, not mentioned until now. Here the distinctive feature would be the more or less complete kind of information. Has the author told us everything in its proper time? Stendhal has been criticized for having hidden Olivier's impotence in *Armance*, even though we are constantly close to the thoughts of the character. Others are criticized for telling too soon, revealing prematurely the outcome of a conflict. But this third type is mentioned only by virtue of an example.

3. FIGURES OF CONTENT-FORM: THE PLOT

3.0. General

To Roland Barthes[21] we owe a general approach to types of plot units. He has aligned in opposing positions cardinal or nuclear functions, indices, catalyzers, and informants. The first pertain to the action or the doing (the purchase of a revolver has as a correlative the revolver's being put to use) and are developed in a process with three necessary phases: an opening where there arises the possibility of a particular conduct to the followed or an event foreseen; a realization where this potential will take form; a closing where some result is achieved.[22] On the other hand, the indices indicate a "functionality of being" and aim at describing or defining objects or characters. Catalyzers appear as descriptive extensions that take place in the development of the cardinal functions. Informants allow us to place the action in time and space. These distinctions will serve as the base of our expositions. We shall not, however, differentiate catalyzers from nuclei, because together they form a single unit. On the other hand, if the characters can be defined according to a system of indices, they are aligned above all in the action and its development as agents, or rather, to use the current term, as actants. Among the informants, finally, we retain only three elements: places, objects, and deeds. Each time, we shall attempt to define the theoretical norm and the deviation it can undergo. We follow the order outlined below:

1. Nuclei
2. Characters and indices
3. Informants
4. Actants and the relationship of characters with actants

3.1. Nuclei

Two nuclei may follow each other. This succession will be by loop or by staircase, to use Shklovsky's expression,[23] according to which closure exhausts all possibility of action or, on the other hand, occasions the simul-

taneous opening of the following nucleus. The death of a character can definitely close the conflict of which it was a part—this is the loop—or, even if it
is the end of one action, it may open a new conflict between the legatees, the
successors—this is a staircase. One nucleus can be contained in the development of another, and a general frame (principal nucleus, in comparison with
internal nuclei) is always possible. Two nuclei, finally, can alternate their
different phases in the chronology of the plot.[24]

3.1.1. SUPPRESSION AND 3.1.2. ADDITION

It is probable that figures of addition and suppression are first to be counted
among the nuclei. Certainly, no norm exists as to how many of these there are
to be; the author determines this. Nonetheless, in narratives with temporal
reference, a norm of verisimilitude comes into play, tied to socio-cultural
customs. The quarrel of *Le Cid* was no doubt inspired by a question of
decorum ("An honorable young woman does not marry the murderer of her
father"),[25] but it is extended because of the fact that the duel and the engage-
ment happened the same day (and we omit Rodrigue's other exploits that
day).

Perhaps in a comparative study of the evolution of a genre—the Western,
the detective novel, the melodrama—we could uncover phenomena of addition and suppression (precipitation of events, development of slack time) not
only on the plane of discourse (play of ellipses and extensions) but also on the
plane of plot. But such a study would be diachronic and thus would not suit
the present work.

In the frame of a single plot, however, effects of this order can intervene.
Sudden urgencies will follow the calm succession of days; action will follow
hesitation; calm and Sunday rest will follow a busy week. We find an opposition here between narrative nuclei and descriptive ones. The introduction of a
descriptive nucleus in a narrative development certainly constitutes a figure of
addition. Must we add that most often discourse, as socio-cultural imperative,
will use such figures economically and will not be likely to show us at length
James Bond's leisure during an English weekend? For the discourse, his
active life cannot admit of such slack times.

Within the limits of the nucleus, finally, the development of catalysis can
be expanded or restricted—insofar as it pertains to the universe of the story, it
is posed in terms of referential time. *A priori,* there is no norm: the telephone
rings, and according to how I choose to act, I can jump to get it or calmly
cross the room, lighting a cigarette before picking up the receiver. The plot
itself will set its own rules by example, will create its own norms—long or
short catalyzers or both together, according to the psychological qualities of
the character presented. Deviations are to be grasped as they relate to a norm
previously established in the story itself. Let us take a simple example. In the
film *Strangers on a Train,* Guy plays a tennis match. As a principal nucleus,
the match is subdivided into internal nuclei, the sets. The first ones are quickly

won by Guy, while the third one is stretched out and ends with his opponent winning. We thus have one of the dynamics of the plot, and it makes little difference in our analysis that it is countered by the dynamic of Hitchcock's discourse, which gives the first two sets in their continuity and shortens the third by a series of ellipses.

Additions can be repetitive—the same situation, the same nucleus, can be repeated in the plot. Three times without result Olivier tries to convince Roland to blow his oliphant (*Song of Roland*). For three days the *Pequod* chases Moby Dick.

3.1.3. SUPPRESSION-ADDITION

We can consider here the trick of disappearing repetition (such as the Quaker Oats box with the picture of a mother holding a Quaker Oats box with the picture of a mother holding a Quaker Oats box with the picture of a mother, ad infinitum). We know the history of this expression (*mise en abyme*), proposed by Gide in "*The Counterfeiter's" Journal* and used again by Claudel to describe Rembrandt's *Nightwatch*.[26] We shall examine the problem again here. Gide was thinking first in terms of the blazon, since the word *abyme* once meant the center of a shield when this itself represented another shield. In a clearer manner, Ukranian *matrioshka** produce themselves; and then closer to us, Benjamin Rabier's cheese boxes (*Laughing Cow*) repeat their own design as earrings. In fact, the elements are repeated there in a perspective leading to infinity. Gide was interested in another process that concerned functions of the characters: the action of the narrator became the action of a character; the writer Gide was portrayed by the writer Edouard. In this way, a painter can show Saint Luke painting the Virgin, or a comedian can become an actor in a play within a play, as in Peter Weiss's *Persecution and Assassination of Jean-Paul Marat Produced by a Theater Group at the Asylum of Charenton under the Direction of Monsieur de Sade*. The link here is internal and in principle does not differ from the narrative link introduced by the *Decameron*. More interesting is the opposite case, when the character reflects the activity of the reader or spectator. This is the case in the play within a play in *Hamlet*, or in the opening scene of *Play It Again, Sam*, where Woody Allen is contemplating Bogart in *Casablanca*.

This repetition to infinity will hold our attention only to the extent that it shows itself to be a microcosm of the plot itself; that is, when the elements it brings into play reflect the actual elements of the action.

It can intervene at the beginning and contain in a fatalistic sign that which succeeding nuclei will develop. Such is the prediction of the witches in *Macbeth*, as are also the three interventions of destiny in *Oedipus*.

Repetition at the end of the action often can have a negative value. At the

*[Hollow wooden dolls with smaller replicas inside. *Trans.*]

end of *Sentimental Education* Frédéric evokes a day of his youth when, with a friend, he went to a bordello, from which he immediately fled, adding: "That was the best we ever had." We discover here in the frustration of these high-school boys a reflection of the frustration of Frédéric in his adventure with Madame Arnoux and also an analysis of the significance of this adventure.

Ricardou has shown how repetition to infinity can be disputed by the story. It is, in fact, because Oedipus lacks clairvoyance that he allows himself to be questioned by the Sphinx. But in "The Fall of House of Usher," the narrator is put on guard by strange coincidences between events he has witnessed and events in the book he is reading, and he flees in time from the house because "he already knows the end of the story."[27]

When repetition contradicts the significance of the story, even if this is only partial, it appears as a negative addition-suppression.

3.2. Characters and Indices

3.2.0. GENERAL

Barthes has recalled how some critics avoid giving a status to characters.[28] There is no question, however, that the story is presented to the reader through characters and their actions. We would like to understand here, on the one hand, how they form a system and, on the other, how this system is itself absorbed into the play of functions.

In our progress through the story, we catalog the characters. This may be done explicitly or implicitly. In the first case, they are named in the text ("He was a good fellow"); in the second, they are known through the action. In both cases, the cataloging may be of a being, of an accident, of a becoming. Their definition can be internal to the character (will he be good? will he be bad?) or external, as seen in the relationship between characters. Internal or external, this definition will hold through the story and is true at the level of each nucleus, in relations between nuclei, and at the terminal level of the whole.

At the end of the story, we may define, in a retrospective moment, the cataloged constellation maintained by the discourse. Each moment, each fragment, has sent us to the whole, which it has defined but from which it has received afterwards a surplus of signification. In *Britannicus*, for example, we have seen Nero bow before Agrippina, before Burrhus, before Narcissus, actions from which we can derive a clear internal definition of his weaknesses when he is faced by others (in contrast with his possible personal energy). In the same way, we have noted the attitudes of Burrhus and Narcissus as counselors to Nero, which is another external definition. The indices are numerous: we find them in physical appearance and character, in dress and language. Apprehending the norm can be done only intuitively, and it will be more a result of the deviations than something given in the beginning.

3.2.1. SUPPRESSION

Limitation or even absence of the indices can be an effect of discourse (when the narrator describes the characters according to his wishes). Especially in detective novels, it will happen that a character is grasped "as aspect," that is, as he is seen by others. In Dhôtel's novel, we know nothing about *L'Homme aux gants verts* [The man with the green gloves] except that he drives a noisy motorcycle and wears his famous gloves. Hammett's *The Thin Man* works on the same principle.

3.2.2. ADDITION

There is addition as soon as indices are multiplied, but it becomes even more obvious when it is supported by an external operation in which two characters are involved. This is the case with those famous couples Don Juan and Sganarelle, Don Quixote and Sancho Panza, Laurel and Hardy. In these cases, the oppositions enrich each other—characters and behavior, appearance and props reinforcing each other. The same reasoning holds true for them as for antithesis: they are repetitive additions.

Multiplying manifestations of the same indices also constitutes deviation by addition. Paired characters (master and servant, lady and confidante) also reinforce each other by addition, but directly, not by antithesis.

3.2.3. SUPPRESSION-ADDITION

Suppression-addition is to be found at different levels. It is the contrast between appearance and reality, as when elegant dress disguises vulgarity of sentiments. In *Stagecoach,* Mister Peacock is a whiskey salesman with the exterior of a clergyman; in *Zéro de conduite,* the headmaster of a boarding school is a dwarf. Such deviations run against the norm of coherency. Such contradictory indices, therefore, play the role of a plot oxymoron, that is, of a negative suppression-addition.

The figure may also be shown by superposition of contradictory indices simultaneously. Rabelais has given us poor Gargantua in the terrible perplexity of not knowing whether to weep over the death of his wife Badebec or to rejoice at the birth of his son.

Finally, they are seen in the relationship of two characters with similar functions. In *Madame Bovary,* Rodolphe and Léon have the same function in reference to Emma but are different characters. Thibaudet has carefully indicated their similarities and differences. Similarities: "In the cab, as in the forest, both men are only the male under the glass of an entomologist." Differences: "By his soul, Léon became the opposite of Rodolphe, the dominated male" and "when Homais, during the visit to Rouen, corners him, takes him from Emma, he lets this happen; compare the ease with which Rodolphe scatters bores at the meeting of the agricultural committee.''[29]

3.3. Informants

3.3.1. PLACES

The norm would say that places are to be neutral, that they are but simple informants that inscribe the story in the diegetic universe. But while, on the one hand, certain buildings, certain rooms have a determined cultural and social function (church, kitchen, and so on) that can be used by the plot, on the other hand, narrative plays frequently on the oppositions between different places where the action develops—between closed places (rooms, offices) and open places (streets, rivers, plains). This opposition will certainly be more apparent in arts using visual representation, since they speak to us in terms of space, but it exists also in the novel. A synthesis is achieved at the end of the story where the retreat and the road alternate in succession (in the latter, in predominance of travel and route; in the former, in the primary importance of recollection and waiting).

Outside this total relationship, another connection can be developed between the closed space and the open space simultaneously. Alfred Hitchcock's *Rear Window* takes place entirely in one apartment, but by changes in the light coming through the large window, the director has maintained the felt presence of the wider world; and from this, a secret connection between the action and space has been established.

3.3.1.1. Suppression and 3.3.1.2. Addition.   Space, then, ceases to be indifferent. When its tonality prolongs action, we speak of addition; when, on the other hand, its independence opposes action, we have suppression. The idea of strict correspondence between intimacy of feeling and the decor feeding it has certainly been used since the eighteenth century. It is found in Rousseau's *The Reveries of a Solitary Walker* as well as in the meditation on despair that an engraving by Dürer inspired in James Thomson. It is continued in the affinities Keats discovered between a summer night and his death wish or in the murky London fog that surrounds the High Court of Chancery, the Court itself, and the Lord High Chancellor (*Bleak House*). Each time, decor reflects the feelings of the characters.

Flaubert, on the other hand, although in a first draft he had imagined the burial of Emma under a rainy sky, finally chose to write it as taking place in the spring. The sentences emphasize this opposition: "All kinds of joyous sounds filled the air."[30]

Such examples are not hard to find in film. Reflection: the white poplar in the Po Valley, where Antonioni's hero is wandering (*The Cry*); opposition: bombing under the sun in June 1940 in *Forbidden Games*.

3.3.1.3. Suppression-Addition. Suppression-addition does not exist in the story. Spatial effects are not prone to any substitution. Nonetheless, relationships established between two or more scenes can show the complex play of similarity and opposition. In *Madame Bovary,* if the Léon episode corresponds to the Rodolphe episode, the places where they happen are opposite ones: the former takes place in bedrooms, the latter in open air. Underlining this difference, Jean Rousset discovers also a contrasting play between the opened windows during Emma's wait and the closed ones during her happiness, both those of the cab and those of the bedroom in Rouen.[31]

3.3.2.0. Objects. Objects have a primary function in the plot: the function determined in reality by their creation. They can fill two other functions: decorative if they simply fill in the action and place it in diegetic space; dramatic if they are used as agents.

3.3.2.1. Suppression and 3.3.2.2. Addition. The first opposition derives from their number. A Dreyer and a Bresson reduce furniture to a useful minimum. Orson Wells or Max Ophüls, on the other hand, overload their decor with thousands of objects. Ionesco also has often played with proliferation of objects, especially in *The New Tenant,* where the entire scene is filled by the movers searching for an unlikely exit.

The second opposition derives from the relationship of object to action, to character, or to his feelings. At times the object will be a reflection; at others it will be a screen.

Reflection can be understood as presence or as absence. As presence, it is the famous cap of Charles Bovary or the room prepared for the wedding (*Madame Bovary*). As absence, it is letters, portraits, souvenirs, Madame de Sévigné's tree that recalls her daughter.[32]

The object will be screen when it refuses its primary function. This is the door that is closed firmly, striking violently the rejected fiancé in Henry James's *Washington Square.*

3.3.2.3. Suppression-Addition. We first find suppression-addition when objects are turned aside from their expected functions, another function replacing the first one. A kitchen knife, in Hitchcock's *Sabotage,* and a paper cutter, in Renoir's *La Chienne,* become criminal objects. This substitution of functions is clearly marked in humorous films or stories. In Chaplin's *The Pawnbroker,* Charlie taps his alarm clock as though he were a doctor and then opens it as if it were a can of sardines. Actions and objects lose their meanings. In Richard Lester's *The Knack,* a bed becomes a means of locomotion.

Next, this figure is evident in the variations and metamorphoses of an object. Barthes has described in this way the metaphor of the eye in Bataille's novel *Story of the Eye,* where starting from invariant elements (whiteness and roundness), we are led through a number of objects: eye, egg, bull's testicles, each one engendering the next.[33]

Finally, the relationship of different objects through similar scenes of the same story reveals a play of addition-suppression. In Mérimeé's *Mateo Falcone,* the two seduction scenes of the young Fortunato both start from an object: a five-franc piece, a watch.

3.3.3. ACTIONS

The status of actions is ambiguous. If they can be called indices because they define the qualities of a character, they are nonetheless coordinated and tied to objects. Hence the necessity of examining them as informants.

3.3.3.1. Suppression and 3.3.3.2. Addition. Here we find both the oppositions pointed out in the examination of objects: from multiplicity to reduction and from reflection to screen. But these two oppositions work together. Nothing betrays Mateo Falcone's emotion while he is killing the child. Every manifestation is suppressed, and simultaneously this suppression is a screen of profundity. On the other hand, what the mother of Alexis manifests when faced with the cadaver of her child (*Life of Saint Alexis*) is multiplied, each manifestation reflecting her sorrows.

3.3.3.3. Suppression-Addition. We have already noted how Chaplin turns objects and actions aside from their expected significance. Another example is the meal scene in *The Gold Rush,* in which Charlie rolls a shoelace around his fork as though it were spaghetti and carefully sucks the nails of his boiled shoes as if sucking on bones. A more serious situation is the death of Donald Crisp, struck down by a pistol shot, in *Broken Blossoms.* At the point of collapsing, he stretches out his hand to his enemy as if demanding that he wait; then, taking a boxing stance, he falls to the ground as though struck by an uppercut. For the dying man has been substituted the boxer collapsing on the mat.

3.4. Actants and Their Relationship to the Characters

Outside the elements indicating his status, the character is first of all a participant in his action. He takes on a clearly determined function in the frame of the narrative nucleus. We owe to Propp, Souriau, and Greimas the reduction of the multiple combinations that narrative uses with several clearly defined functions. There are six for Souriau and Greimas.[34] For Souriau:

(1) Directed thematic force. This can be passion: the love of Nero for Junia.
(2) The receiver of the desired good, of the directing value: Junia for Nero.
(3) The potential receiver of this value: Britannicus.
(4) The opposer: Britannicus.
(5) The attributing arbiter of good: Agrippina, Nero.
(6) The rescue—doubling of the preceding forces: Agrippina and Burrhus as opposers, Narcissus as abettor of the directed thematic force.

Greimas has tried to articulate Souriau's table into categories and thus opposes subject to object (1 and 2), receiver to sender (3 and 5), helper to adversary (6 and 4 + 6).

The model proposed by Greimas is of interest for its reduction of functions to binary oppositions. As in the case of interlocutors, suppression-addition within paired opposites is called commutation. The norm for actants (considering either of the related models above) has, nonetheless, a particular character, since it demands the separate presence of the six functions: an actant/a character. Deviations will appear either as a doubling of functions (addition of characters) or as fusion of several functions in the same character (suppression of characters). In the last case, we shall have to determine whether the united functions are incompatible (union of a pair of opposites) or simply foreign to each other. We see, therefore, that a rhetoric of actants will have bearing especially on the relation of characters to the actants they embody.

The play of the six functions is perceived as a shifting constellation. In fact, even if the discourse narrows the story to one point of view, we can expect that each character will be considered as holding the central position, and we would then orient the other characters differently. Thus, we could arrange different tables where the same functions could be operating, starting with Britannicus and his love for Junia or starting with Agrippina and her will to power. This essential mobility of the constellation, whereby within a single action each character is differentiated by his unique point of view, offers also a temporal mobility, where relationships also can shift for each character. An opponent can offer help; a friend can become a rival.

3.4.1. Suppression

These six functions will be reduced in a story using only two characters: the young lover, as the directed thematic force, assumes his own fight (he is his own helper), and from the beginning he can be his own potential receiver; the beloved woman will be in turn the desired good, the obstacle, and the arbiter. We are supposing in this example that the chosen point of view of the discourse is the lover's, for in this case the suppression will compound functions that are compatible between them and the contradictions that the functions of desired good and obstacle imply. The functions of obstacle and arbiter are then grasped from an exterior point of view.

The situation will be different when the superposition of functions gives rise to antagonisms. Then, in fact, as each additional function appears, it will neutralize the first one. Hitchcock often uses this mechanism. In *I Confess* the sacristan Otto Keller, disguised as a priest, has killed a professional singer and has then confessed his crime. For certain reasons, the priest who has confessed him finds himself accused of the murder. For the confessor, the good to be obtained is his acquittal; the necessary help, his own word; the arbiter, himself. But it is he who is also the obstacle, since his own word is tied to the inviolable secrecy of the confessional. One added function has neutralized the first one. Even more complex is the role of Bannister in the trial scene in *The*

Lady from Shanghai, by Orson Welles. In fact, the rival of Michael, who is his wife's lover, Bannister then becomes the lawyer—uniting in this way the functions of opposer and rescuer. He is then called as a witness, adding the function of arbiter to the two above.

The model of actants given above will not need to be realized in its totality in every story, for in reality many stories do not incorporate all the actants as separate characters. When a character does fulfill the functions of more than a single actant, the resulting roles are paradoxical and contradictory.

3.4.2. ADDITION

A deviation of addition can appear as simultaneity, as in cases where two parallel actions develop similarities at the same time. In Molière's *The Would-Be Gentleman,* Cléonte, the lover of Jourdain's daughter Lucile, and his valet Covielle, lover of Lucile's servant Nicole, are both led astray by the women they love. The narrator emphasizes their similar situations by giving their complaints as pairs of responses, using syntactical similarities and opposed semantic registers.

> Cl: Did you ever, Covielle, see the like of this ungrateful Lucile?
> Cov: Or you, sir, of this wicked Nicole?
> Cl: *After all* I have done for her, the sighs—the devotion that I have paid to her charms.
> Cov: *After all* my constant attentions, all the service I've done in the kitchen.
> Cl: *All* the tears I've wept at her feet!
> Cov: *All* the buckets of water I've drawn for her!
> Cl: *Such* love that I've shown here—loving her more than myself.
> Cov: *Such* heat I've suffered—taking her place at the roasting spit.
> Cl: *She* treats *me with* scorn!
> Cov: *She* turns her back on *me with* impudence!
> Cl: *It is such* faithlessness as to call down the greatest punishments.
> Cov: *It is such* treachery as calls for a thousand lashes.

Here the two constellations, moving in the same direction, work separately as well as simultaneously. Since they are parallel, they cannot be contradictory. In Salacrou's *When the Music Stops,** also, there are two parallel constructions, but each reverses the meaning of the other. A husband, on the very day he discovers that his wife has left him, gives shelter to his best friend and the friend's mistress, who has left her husband. Thus, the parallel situation leaves each person face-to-face with his or her opposer.

3.4.3. SUPPRESSION-ADDITION

In suppression-addition, we are faced with a reversal of functions. The reversal is most often accompanied by a change of the indices or by an internal broadening of point of view (that is, a change in point of view not done by the narrator or narration, but which becomes operative in the thoughts or acts of a

---

*[*Histoire de rire,* also translated as "No Laughing Matter." *Trans.*]

character). The entire work of Fritz Lang, from *M* to *Beyond a Shadow of a Doubt*, is marked by this turnabout of things whereby the innocent is found guilty, the guilty innocent. The good desired by the condemned person is the victim he is stalking. The good desired by society is the condemned person whom society is stalking. Most important is that the condemned one himself expresses the circularity of the mechanism. This mechanism frequently appears in scenes that reflect each other, depend on one another. In fact, two processes have come together: the first is similarity, the second opposition. In Sternberg's *The Scarlet Empress,* young Catherine is stolen from her family by the Czar's emissary, later becoming the emissary's mistress. Two subsequent scenes reflect each other. In the first, Empress Elizabeth is in her room and asks Catherine to leave, but to unlock the secret door by which her lover will enter. The lover is the same emissary. In the second scene, Catherine, now empress, orders the emissary (who still desires her) to leave, but to show in her new lover. The similarities are clear: the two scenes take place in the same room, the actions are similar—A asks B to let C enter. Two of the characters present are the same, but their positions have changed: Catherine has moved from B to A, and the emissary from C to B. This suffices for their positions. On the plane of functions, and since both scenes are given from Catherine's point of view, the situation is different: in the first scene, while the good she would like to obtain is the emissary, she must become the helper of an opposer; in the second scene, she forces an opposer to become her helper to attain her good. From the first to the second scene, the indices have changed: from niece of the empress, Catherine has become empress; and the emissary has moved from lover of the first to aspirer for the second. We have spent time with this example because it shows for our analysis the difficulty of integrating both orders, that is, the relationships of the nuclei and of the functions. There is repetitive addition in the nuclei and suppression-addition in the functions.

Such a meeting of operations is not, however, proper for figures of plot. All metaboles can be described *in abstracto* with some precision—as we hope we have shown in the course of this work—but expressive realities of language, like all realities, are not always perfectly rational.

Afterword
Rhetorical Mirrors:
Seven Years of Reflection

The rhetoric of titles—just like that of subtitles recently sketched by Ginsberg[1]—will be of concern here only as a means of beginning the discussion, and first of all, to explain the title of the present article. We would like here simply to respond to some of the reactions and polemics raised by our *A General Rhetoric* of 1970[2] (hereinafter cited as *GR*) as well as take up certain problems that have appeared with the awakening of "the lady of the mirrors." Moreover, the following pages are concerned with only two among the various studies our "treatise," or "manual," provoked some seven years ago. Under the warm and metaphorical title *La Métaphore vive,* * Paul Ricoeur, on the one hand, and under the soberly denotative title "Synecdoques et Métonymies," Nicolas Ruwet,[3] on the other hand, asked themselves—with different results—about the mechanisms implied by certain "figures of style" inherited from the rhetorical tradition and redefined by Group μ and others.[4] Before answering some of the objections formulated by these two authors against the concepts brought out in *GR* or rectifying certain misunderstandings they have about it, let us comment briefly on the actual title that graced that work of 1970. If its collective author had been faithful to one of the theses advanced there, no doubt he would have chosen a less ambitious name and especially one more fitting the content (intertext, via Robert: "The titles of books are often bald-faced imposters" [Balzac]). In all strictness, it would have been less hyperbolic and less synecdochic to give that book the title *A Theory of the Figures of Discourse*. Perhaps degree zero might even have been something like "Essay on Some Categories of the Figures of Language." But in natural languages it seems next to impossible to avoid all contamination of meta-language by procedures of language-object; that is, when it occurs, to speak of figures without producing some, more or less

From *Poétique* 29 (1977): 1-19. Jacques Dubois, Francis Edeline, Jean-Marie Klinkenberg, and Philippe Minguet authored this piece.

*[Translated as *The Rule of Metaphor*. See below, n. 33. *Trans.*]

fortuitously. A certain "theoretician" hellbent on denouncing the pseudo-scientificity of rhetoricians can do this, it seems, only with a large battery of comparisons and allegories: rhetoric would thus have "civil" as well as "military" frontiers, and "as organic as skin," it would be a "register of surveys" or "cartography". . . .[5]

In spite of efforts to limit as much as possible the employment of figures in the discourse describing and analyzing them, our essay merrily sinned on this point. Since there can be no question of rectifying here a situation whose consequences are probably not dramatic, we shall be happy to admit in what way this title—*A General Rhetoric*—is acceptably rhetorical. These admissions will, no doubt, be all the more necessary since some of those in the literary field—in France especially—regularly forget that persuasive discourse was the principal objective of ancient rhetoric, so that, for example, the neo-rhetoric of a philosopher such as Perelman had good reason twenty years ago for using this label to evoke a theory of *argumentation* (this term being used in opposition to *demonstration*).[6]

Let us repeat that, at first sight at least, such an enterprise, which is in conformity with the most ancient traditions, has only a small connection with what Group μ or Jacques Durand is doing, except that the theoretician of argumentative discourse necessarily comes up against procedures of style, understood as *means* of persuasion, which are commonly called "figures" and which also characterize discourse whose principal goal is not necessarily to gain the consent of the hearers. Bluntly, our rhetoric would seem rather to arise from literary theory in that it is first of all concerned with what is called the "poetic" function of language. From the polemic point of view, the neo-rhetoric of 1970 has effectively defined itself as against the insolvency of stylistics exactly as the other neo-rhetoric had expected to rehabilitate what logical empiricism was neglecting. Taking up the positivist challenge according to which every value judgment is irrational, the theory of argumentation examines the relative rationality of discourse that does not follow the strict rules of induction and deduction. Modern stylistics, in the same way—less insofar as it followed the work of Bally rather than the "stylistic criticism" deriving from Croce—has generally scorned the study of stylistic procedures more or less codified by rhetoricians of the past, in which it saw only idle naming and useless nomenclature. To the extent that literary analysis has not yet rid itself of the ubiquitous password "image" or remains content with simply "metaphor" to designate just about any figure whatsoever, this interlude is not completely dead today.

In any case, we have never claimed to offer the public a treatise on rhetoric. Those who have assigned us this ambition are the first to know that there would have to be more than six of us to cover the field of problems that have been lumped under the term "rhetoric" in the course of several centuries and in different cultures. It is even of little importance that the matter treated in *GR* corresponds largely to what was once known under the term *elocutio*. That the rhetorical corpus with its multiple strata—transhistorical and panethnic—could not be today the object of an individual approach is rather clear. It remains for us to justify—to whatever extent that can be done—the decision to entitle ''rhetoric'' an essay that is limited simply to figures. As we admitted in the beginning, this justification could be only partial—or ''rhetorical,'' in the common meaning of the word. It is only by using figured language that the part can be used to name the whole. But it is the fate of certain figures to be no longer recognized as such because they have become banal. We are hardly claiming that it has become quite current to designate as ''rhetoric'' a study of figures. But it is a fact in our time that the reduction in question is sufficiently established so that, after all, there is not so much reason to regret the generalizing synecdoche by which we announed *GR*.[7]

Now we must come back to what we said above about the ''literary'' orientation of a rhetoric of figures. This qualification can be maintained only on the condition of referring here, as Jakobson has done, to a function of language and not to a category of selected products. Just as the art of the *orator* systematizes a type of reasoning that all individuals practice in daily life—that which makes up internal deliberation—so the art of the writer, as Valéry saw clearly, ''is only a development of certain properties of language.'' It is true that the majority of our examples are, in fact, taken from more or less famous writers. *GR*'s offering as illustrations short extracts from the press, slang phrases, or advertising slogans in no fashion harms, as some have claimed, the idea of literary language as it is opposed to the idea of a degree-zero language.[8] This expression, which was once fashionable, is certainly not beyond criticism. Whatever the speech examples adopted, all of which have their problems, the essential thing is to understand that all speech acts can be ranged between two poles, that there are two fundamental and contradictory tendencies at the origin of messages.[9] Everyone would agree that it is preferable not to call ''poetic'' the function so named by Jakobson.[10] Even if it is correct that poetry, in the modern sense of the word, assumes rhetoric as a necessary condition, the figure itself is not sufficient to produce the effect of meaning that the reader seeks in lyric poems. The question of *ethos*, simply sketched out in *GR*, could legitimately be put off, since the concern at hand was the formulation of a model of figures as empty structures.

Was it necessary also to put off the generalization promised in the title, which, contrary to what was insinuated, clearly did not imply a dogmatic claim to universality? Some have recently taken the term *rhetoric* up again to designate the theory of utterances of which the theory of figures would be only a part (''linguistics is concerned with sentences, rhetoric with utterances'').[11] For us, it is certainly a question of ''going beyond'' the sentence, not only in Part Two, where units of another order are considered, but also in Part One, which is not exclusively a tributary of linguistics. Some have seen this manner of approaching problems of narrative as one of the newest discoveries of the work, but its principal merit has certainly been the claim that deep structures of the figure emerge clearly at the semiotic level.

Whatever the distinction is between linguistics and semiotics, it is certain that rhetoric in its new guise confronts the first, linguistics. Rapports between the two were necessary and necessarily tendentious—necessary in that rhetoric, defined as the means of expression used in a work, was to profit from the study of the most important means of expression; tendentious in that since linguistics had to select a primary object from among all the phenomena tied to language and its practice, it chose first to call itself, starting from the indispensable dichotomy language-speech (*langue-parole*), the science of codes. Must we seek elsewhere the source of the parentage clearly felt between rhetoric and certain new branches of linguistics (such as textual linguistics and pragmatics)? Must we search also for the misunderstanding separating rhetoricians from certain linguists?

The clearest expression of this misunderstanding is certainly to be found in the article "Synecdoques et Métonymies," by Nicolas Ruwet. This article is a criticism of certain points in *GR*, an important criticism because it is in good measure epistemological and methodological. Without asking himself about the internal coherence of the system of which he sees only certain elements, Ruwet holds that the taxonomy of tropes such as *GR* proposed is not able to constitute a predictive theory, especially because it does not allow a rigorous distinction between figured and non-figured language.

His demonstration concerns essentially the mechanisms and the status of synecdoche. This is for us the fundamental figure of the system of tropes.[12] One can, in fact, envisage a *deep tropic matrix,* which could be entered, on the one hand, by the pair of simple operations of addition and suppression and, on the other, by the two modes of semantic decomposition, which are, respectively, the referential mode (or mode Π: there is an equivalence between the proposition "x is a tree" and the *product* "x has leaves" *and* "x has roots" *and* "x has a trunk," and so on) and the conceptual mode (or mode Σ: there is an equivalence between the proposition "x is a tree" and the *sum* of the propositions "x is a poplar" *or* "x is an oak," and so on).[13] This matrix engenders four basic tropes: conceptual generalizing synecdoche (or Sg Σ—semes are suppressed), referential particularizing synecdoche (or Sp Π—parts of objects here are suppressed), Sp Σ, and Sg Π (semes and parts, respectively, added):

	Π	Σ
A	Sg Π	Sp Σ
S	Sp Π	Sg Σ

Produced by this deep matrix, metaphor and metonymy appear as complex tropes: metaphor couples two complementary synecdoches, functioning in inverse manner and determining an intersection between a given degree and constructed degrees (the intersection being at the same time synecdoche of the one degree and of the others). The relationship between the two terms and metonymy is effected via an ensemble that contains both, theoretically in mode Π or mode Σ, an ensemble of which both are the synecdoche.

We return to Ruwet, whose reasoning follows a very simple plan. First, he is intent on proving that tropic character is absent from a large number of the examples used by us or given by the rhetorical tradition, which it is best to relegate to the theory of "normal" language. Second, in the remaining cases there would be no reason for distinguishing synecdoche from metonymy. At this stage we again find the famous polarity: "the exemplary figural pair, the irreplaceable china dogs of our... modern rhetoric: Metaphor and Metonymy."[14] But there is more: some metonymies are also justifiable by the first reasoning and ought, therefore, to disappear from rhetoric. Finally (even though this is not explicitly said), would not all the remaining tropes be avatars of the famous metaphor?

We can lay aside the criticism of this "metaphorocentrism," to which Genette has done justice,[15] and look more closely at the linguist's demonstration. First, the removal of tropes (synecdoche and next metonymy). This is done under the cover of three kinds of arguments or maneuvers: synecdoche is nonexistent when the example used is either "bizarre," or "banal," or "explicable."

"Bizarre," "absurd," "contradictory," "the results of a bad joke" are common terms from Ruwet's pen that cannot prevent confusion between rhetoric and poetry. We need not consider the fact that these are judgments brought in the name of a particularly restricted taste, one that certainly falsifies the analysis: all who read Baudelaire know that "the beautiful is always bizarre." Rather, we are surprised that these "bizarre" utterances are to be excluded from rhetoric. Could this not be a result of the difficulties a generative syntactician with a vow of strict obedience finds in conceiving—not to speak of explaining—utterances that do not come out of "standard language" arbitrarily idealized? (The proof of this is that concepts like agrammaticality and degrees of grammaticality have hardly progressed in recent years.) This refusal involves serious confusions, like the one consisting in mixing facts of ethos and facts of the nuclear level (see *GR*, chap. VI): if a "bizarre" statement results from the replacement of *poop* by *sail* in the utterance "The poop moving out to sea leaves the shore behind," it is simply because a new trope is substituted for an old one, one that could in fact be considered standard language. But what is especially serious is not to notice that the rules—all of which we do not claim to have made explicit in *GR*—allow us to predict precisely the "figuredness": the "absurd" or the "contradictory" are certainly indices of the action of these operations.

Rather than finding this "bizarre," we find it "banal." For Ruwet, there is no figure in "Nelson saw a sail on the horizon": Nelson does, after all, see a sail on the horizon. But must we recall that different referents can be associated with this sentence and that among the possible interpretations is certainly "Nelson sees a *ship*"? Now contrary to what Ruwet says, the probable context of the sentence (a life of Nelson) and general knowledge certainly impose this last interpretation (it is certainly warships that Nelson is waiting for or fears; sails, as such, French or not, the admiral hardly cares about). A large number of analyses where the "claimed synecdoches" are contested are of this nature, and their basic sense is Crocean idealism, which holds that "the figure is true" and there is therefore nothing rhetorical. In the circumstance, this idealism is sustained by a somewhat limited realist prejudice (on which we shall have more to say later).

The third case in which the trope can be denied is when it is "explicable." Ruwet makes this comment about the example "A hand lit a cigarette," a catachrestic synecdoche that is hardly felt (in this way our caviller gives himself an easy ride; other examples were more troublesome for him). This utterance, as he sees it, does not contain a figure, because it is an application of Fillmore's theory of cases (which, however, the linguist challenges): since the agent is absent, the instrument can be subject. Such utterances would, therefore, be predictable starting from rules derived from the grammar of a language "or perhaps from general linguistic theory" (but is it not doubtful, we say in passing, for case theory?) and would not derive from a rhetorical operation. However, it will be noted that the analysis that for us simply shows that case theory explains the production of certain tropes is not, in fact, applicable without distinction to all rhetorically comparable examples (such as "loud voices were quarreling" or "he saw a sail"). Would this not prove that case theory is too coarse a grammatical theory, since it allows such rhetorical utterances to escape? (In fact, how does the rule of absence of agent function?) What is posed here, therefore, is the relationship between rhetoric and the science of the meaning of utterances, a theme underlying this whole discussion. Before going into that, we note again that "explicability" also allows Ruwet to decree the nonexistence of a number of metonymies, not just synecdoches. Commenting on the example "I have just read Balzac," he writes, "The verb 'read' imposes by its semantic representation a very restrictive interpretation of its object: the class of objects able to be read is limited to things written"; so that the act derives from a general theory of the interpretation of utterances and not from a theory of figured effects. It would be difficult for Ruwet to give a better resumé of what was written in *GR* (and which we are developing again elsewhere): that the trope is always perceived after an impertinence is noted! But to return to our explanation—a linguistic one—of the reduction of this impertinence, does it hinder the copresence in a reading of a perceived degree (Balzac) and of a conceived degree (the work of Balzac) from producing "figured effects"? We are putting our finger here on the logical fault at the base of this reasoning. Contrary to what our critic is suggesting, the theory of "figured effects" is not in a relationship of reciprocal exclusion with the interpretation of utterances. At the very least, the theory of figured effects is a part of the theory of utterances.

We are now in a position to consider two maneuvers that the linguist can use to bring all of *elocutio* to the metaphor-metonymy opposition (which alone—the affirmation remaining implicit—does, in fact, rest on a linguistic foundation). The aim of the first is to unite "claimed synecdoches" with metonymy; the second is to affirm the primacy of metaphor.

Take the utterance "There is smoke on the horizon," from which can be inferred, as above, the consequence "There is a ship on the horizon." If the context is such that we can perceive these two propositions not as antecedent and consequence but as equivalents (in other words, if the context indicates that we are dealing with a trope), one ought to call it metonymy; for as Ruwet contends, "no one would be willing to say that smoke is part of a steamship in the same way that a sail is part of a sailing vessel." Once again we find ourselves stuck in that naive realism that assures us that, in fact, smoke is not "a part" of a ship; naive realism because it must be noticed that rhetoric does not start with observable realities, but with representations of these realities. According to codes of representation, smoke is no doubt an element of recognition of the object boat (ask a child to draw a steamship and observe that in all cases if he omits necessary details in the "hyperrealist" boat, he never omits the indispensable feather of smoke!). The primacy of this ideological analysis has been fully studied in iconographic semiotics (even if works registered under this flag have not taken all the aid available from *Gestaltpsychologie*[16]), but a certain linguistic tradition is still mulish about this kind of consideration. In spite of a lively discussion since the famous Sapir-Whorf hypothesis, large sectors of linguistics, even the most modern groups, live with the evidently implicit idea that pieces of language correspond with pieces of the real; an illusion (or stupidity) that we are happy to say is not general. A Lakoff, for example, has systematized a "semantics of possible worlds," including the pragmatic study of the referent; these "possible worlds" are not ontological reality, but are constituted by the beliefs of the speaker. Do we need to add that this is the perspective of the rhetorician?[17]

To suggest that every figure can be brought under the rubric metaphor, Ruwet uses the following example, which he explains as a memory of his service in the Belgian Army: "I have a meeting this evening with a piece of ass," an expression to be interpreted, when coming from the mouth of a rather vulgar lieutenant, to mean "I have a meeting with a woman." Ruwet's reader and Ruwet himself think immediately of an undoubted case of synecdoche (part for the whole). The eminent linguist catches himself, however, and concludes once again with metaphor, since in the circumstance it was a question of identifying the woman by the ass. Anatomically, this example calls for a confrontation with another example, cited later on the page by Ruwet: "what a prick-head (*couillon*) that guy is!"[18] We note in passing that this example of his corpus is called an expression found in "Belgian French" and that its Parisian analogue would be "what a cunt-face (*con*) that fellow is."[19]

Ass, *cunt*, or *prick*—we ought in any case not to confuse distinct *mechanisms* because of a resemblance of *effects*. However, we cannot deny that there are common features in the functioning of metaphor and of synecdoche. How could it be otherwise? Both are tropes, and metaphor is the product of synecdoches. More importantly, all tropes carry an attribution to the referent at the conceived degree ("woman") of properties pertaining to the referent at the perceived degree ("ass"). We can go further into the case. It is very possible that the decoding of *ass* is, *de facto*, of a metaphoric character. No more nor less, however, than the *"prick-imbecile"* of our little Belgian neighbors. Guiraud again: *"Pricks* are certainly actors, as the coherence of the system demands, but somewhat comic and futile actors that vainly circle around the champion like a fly around a sow."[20] This gloss certainly suggests that the structure of the empty metabole is one thing and that the *ethos* of the achieved figure is quite another. Once again, working on "utterances" deprived of their pragmatic dimension is a pedagogical commodity, nothing more. However, as we have seen above in the example of the sail/boat, it is necessary to refer to the biography of Nelson, and so on.

Therefore, we can concede, without weakening the theses upheld in *GR*, that a particular decoder in a particular context has the choice of several routes. This relative indeterminancy, already mentioned in *GR* (chap. 4 *in fine*)—one obviously paralleling that of the decoder—in no way weakens the coherence of the *system* of tropes. We have continued the study of interactions between conceived and perceived degrees of the figure subsequent to our theory in *GR*.[21] What we note is that Ruwet and other linguists like him are incapable of conceiving the trope as other than an "abridged comparison" (which has always been the definition—a false one, as Goslar reminds us—of metaphor; but this definition does perhaps satisfy the syntactician, who is quick to explain semantic phenomena by facts of ellipsis). The following reasoning shows that this is begging the question: "If it is true . . . that (in general) there is a figure only if at the same time there is suppression of something and addition of something else, [synecdoche] would not derive from a theory of figures."[22] Here we have a definition of tropes by suppression-addition (the operation that produces metaphor and metonymy). But if there is a trope only when there is suppression-addition, it is clear either that there are no synecdoches (tropes by simple addition *or* suppression) or that we are working under an illusion and that the examples we are giving as synecdoches are either metaphors or metonymies.

By these piecemeal explanations (piecemeal in that they are not parts of a unique theoretical field),[23] it is as easy to reduce the field of rhetoric as it is an ass's skin: at times tropes are "normal language," at other times the effect of ellipsis or the product of a reduction of redundancy (which is indicated in *GR*). At times they belong to the application of case theory; at other times they are negligible oddities. If we look closely, all maneuvers—surely heterogeneous—used to restrict the field of rhetoric in this way have in common two points outside their polemical aspect: the elimination of the context and the refusal to take into consideration the rules proper to rhetorical discourse—points clearly related.

By selecting certain contexts according to the needs of the argument, or more precisely, by supposing the copresence of the utterance and its most probable context (a very "linguistic" maneuver), the figurality of an example such as "He saw a sail" can be eliminated. Certainly such a sentence contains a trope only when the context makes it obligatory to read "He saw a boat." Fundamentally this maneuver is the same as eliminating those aspects of the context that make the rhetorical reading obligatory. Purely and simply, it is by eliminating this context that the figurality of an utterance such as "The animal flew" is eliminated. (There is obviously no trope without a context indicating that we are dealing with a tiger: "The tiger was creeping forward. The animal flew for the throat of the unfortunate boozer. . . .") Giving utterances out of context, Ruwet has no difficulty writing: "They say that a term that normally designates a part of a certain object (proper meaning) can be used to designate the object itself (figured meaning). But, this being said, nothing has been said. Almost anything can be considered as part of some larger structure"[24] (a true sentence for Π decompositions, but applicable also for Σ decomposition). This argument, which rings true for common sense, is true only outside an actualization of these terms. Take the text "The driver of the car saw an animal. It was a tiger." Obviously we do not see synecdoche here: the utterance "It was an animal" can leave the reader waiting for the name of the animal class, a specification given by the occurrence of *tiger*. There is a trope only when there is superposition of two semantic representations, one induced by an utterance of the sort "He drank x," the other by an utterance containing a term not having the classemes expected for x (liquid), for example: "Bibi Fricotin is drinking the obstacle." The rhetorical reading is, therefore, double, both horizontal and vertical. To suppress the context is the same as suppressing the second dimension and therefore the trope.[25]

Another example pushed to absurdity to deny the figurality of synecdoche: the linguist will fabricate examples like "Three hundred cuirasses made a wall around Napoleon with their bodies" or "The hand took a cigarette and lighted it with the left hand"—utterances that ought to be possible, we are told, if it is true that synecdoche exists and if, in these examples, *cuirass* were an equivalent of *cuirassier,* and *hand* of *man.* But you see that this is a caricature. On the one hand, it has been known for some time that tropes are not produced purely and simply by relations of equivalency. This is one of the reasons why one can be distrustful of terminology like "proper" and "figured" or "tenor" and "vehicle." It is useless here to repeat Breton's sentence, which has no demonstrative value but has the merit of stating this truth energetically.[26] On the other hand, the syntactician refuses to see that certain internal rules of tropic discourse exist, rules for which the study of the extended metaphor furnished a first approach.[27] In the present case, we could invoke a rule (quite optional, it is true) prescribing classemic compatibility not only between the conceived signified and the isotopy of the context but also between this context and the indicated signified (the cuirasses have no bodies, and the hands no hands).

All this clearly illuminates the issues around which neo-rhetoricians and some linguists oppose one another, issues clearly perceived by our critic: "A theory of interpretation of utterances ought to have several facets, allowing for complex relationships: (a) a semantic theory of interpretation of sentences; (b) a theory of references; (c) a theory of the acts of language; (d) a theory of the effects of context, discourse, and situation; (e) an encyclopedia taking into account knowledge of the world and beliefs of speaking subjects. If the semantic theory (a) is obviously within the realm of linguistics, the role of linguistics in (b) and (d) is not clear; the encyclopedia (e) clearly is not a branch of linguistics."[28] We register our agreement with the first remark and the following five points; and we ought even to add that it seems good that rhetoric be a part of or the equivalent of this theory of interpretation of utterances. We do not believe that our fellow citizen can complain about us on that point. But it is true that his remarks in no way loosen the truly complex links between everything that today is lodged under the sign of rhetoric and this theory of the interpretation of utterances as it can be considered; his remarks are intended to show that if the construction of such a theory should appear to be possible, our own taxonomy would have no place in it, for the reasons stated above (non-discrimination of figured usages, and so on). But each of our answers has brought out, quite succinctly, that the debate was not, in fact, where our critic claimed it to be. What we see is instead a veritable refusal to envisage components (b) and (e) of this theory and perhaps even component (a)! Whether the debates that are shaking linguistics at present lead to the recognition of the linguistic character of each of these components has perhaps little importance finally for the rhetorician. If they are not linguistic, he will then say that rhetoric includes certain linguistic disciplines; if they are, he will admit that rhetoric is identified with a very broad linguistics. Ruwet has already cut through the linguistics debate, not by decreeing *a priori* that components (b) and (e) are not of a linguistic nature, but rather by refusing to take them into account in a problematic situation of rhetoric where their intervention is obligatory. These two attitudes generally contradict all linguistics being done at present: pragmatics, textual linguistics, generative semantics. Are not the generative semanticists affirming the necessity of integrating with their own models this encyclopedia forever debarred by Ruwet?[29]

It is clear that our essay of 1970 could not make use of the most recent discoveries since made in these new directions. But today's reader can see that *GR* was already working in the then feeble current that aimed at constructing a general theory of the interpretation of utterances. The reformulation of the theory of tropes, to be found in *Rhétorique de la poésie,* brings rhetoric even further into the current, we believe. But starting with *GR,* themes indicating the role the encyclopedia plays in rhetoric were already present. We shall take only the example of the two decompositions, referential (Π) and conceptual (Σ), a distinction that could have helped our critic solve certain questions he has asked (such as "Why can we say 'a fleet of a hundred sails' but not 'the sail [for *ship*] has sunk'?" The answer can be found easily in the pages of *GR* devoted to "essential semes"[30] or in another of our works[31]). For us, however, it is not a question of putting all the components of the theory of interpretation of utterances "on the same footing," as for example a theory of reference and a theory of conceptual representations. In *GR* it is rather a question of showing the interaction of these components in a rhetorical theory and, in doing this, to contribute to the building of a linguistics that is not limited to the simple description of a code as much as to the elaboration of a stylistics that takes into account all the facets of the certainly complex phenomena that are tropes.[32]

A work that sets some foundations for such a theory risks attracting the attention of philosophers attached to the hermeneutic school. Thus, Paul Ricoeur, in his recent work *The Rule of Metaphor,*[33] studies metaphor in its principal aspects and devotes several penetrating pages to the fundamentals of *GR.*

His first objective is to determine the relationships between poetic rhetoric and the ontology that is implicit in the metaphoric utterance. The first can be analyzed at the frontiers of semantics, while the second "takes up" the theses of linguistics essential to a philosophy that will, however, remain a discourse distinct from rhetoric. What interests Ricoeur above all in this perspective is a hermeneutics that concerns the *reference* of metaphor and, more particularly, its "power to redescribe reality," its "heuristic power." We will leave aside the concept of "tensional" truth and will look at here only his reservations about the new rhetoric.

We quickly understand that Ricoeur is intent on refuting the conception that the neo-rhetoricians (Genette, Cohen, Le Guern, and Group μ)[34] might have of the "metaphor-word." He cannot admit that this figure might be limited to a substitution of words or a change in the meaning of a word, for this would be at the same time imprisoning rhetoric of tropes in the field of semantics, which is interested in the meaning of units of the code. For the philosopher, it is also—and especially—a problem of signification, therefore implying reference, and such a problem can be approached only at the level of the sentence or, more generally, at the level of the utterance. He favors, therefore, a conception of the "metaphor statement," where different units interact, some metaphoric, others not. Such an utterance is auto-destructive (that is, incapable of making sense), and the reduction of the deviation that follows reestablishes meaning at the level of the sentence and not of the word. The theoretical justification of such a position is to be found in Benveniste, who differentiates semiotic units (or signs) and semantic units (or sentences): true meaning appears only at the second level.

Those who have read the preceding pages know that this point of view calls for commentary rather than for refutation. We have, in fact, explained at length in GR how the perception of a deviation is tied to a contrast between a "mark" and a "base": these two concepts form an indissoluble pair, and each functions only in virtue of the other. Therefore, it is clear (from the point of view of the decoder) that the mark appears only as an integral part of the base.

Ricoeur has shown the importance of the utterance for metaphor by placing himself at the point of view of the encoder, not the point of view we generally took. It is, in fact, at the level of utterance that a general theory of tropes ought to be constructed.[35] But interested uniquely by metaphor and the figures attached to it (fable, parable, allegory, and so on), the critic cannot hesitate long at the care rhetoricians take to reincorporate figures like metaplasms and metataxes into a unique model. A very general scheme can appear, however, only from the comparison of the different classes, that which we call the *schema of three levels*.

Every figure, in fact, brings together three contiguous levels in the sequence of decompositions. We call these three levels—going from the simple to the complex—*creator, carrier,* and *revealer*. The carrier level is the one carrying the figure (for example, the word for a lexematic metaphor). The figure is constituted, however, by operations on units of decomposition such that they appear at the immediately lower level (for example, a suppression-addition of semes for metaphor). The figured unit remains, nonetheless, a unit; and to be discovered, its figured character requires intervention from the immediately higher level (for example, the non-isotopic sentence for metaphor). We have chosen metaphor purposely to illustrate our remarks, but we shall see that for the study of other figures, other triads of levels are required.

Figures by Suppression-Addition

Level \ Class of Metabole and Example	Metaplasm (pun)	Metataxes (syllepsis)	Metasememe (lexematic metaphor)	Metalogism (allegory)
Creator	feature	grammatical class	seme	word
Carrier	phoneme	syntagm(s)	word	propositional sequence
Revealer	word	grammatical sequence	utterance	designation*

*Relation of utterance to referent

If Paul Ricoeur's arguments hold up, it is because, as we have said, he is interested only in metaphor. Metaphor in reality is powerless to render an account of figures like metaplasms, which in no way call for a sentence to be coded. What is needed there is a context in the broad sense (the context that certain linguists tend not to take into account, as we have seen); and in this sense, the moneme is the context of the phoneme. At the other end of the scale, Ricoeur implicitly shows us right when he remarks, apropos of a metalogism (allegory), "Hence, the tension is not, then, in the proposition but in the context"[36] (here extralinguistic). We grant willingly, however, that certain formulations where the complete utterance is given as an "extrinsic condition" of the figure seem to attenuate the importance that must, in fact, be given to this condition.

In connection with the preceding, it is important to emphasize a fundamental aspect of the decoding attitude. Paul Ricoeur sees clearly that we consider degree zero infralinguistic and, for the reduction of certain figures, emphasize that this implies on the part of readers a position at the same time conscious and unconscious. This is certainly our point of view. The autodestructive character of figured utterances closes every *linguistic* issue for the problem of their decoding, while the very perception of the impertinence unleashes immediately a different psychological attitude, a *metalinguistic* attitude. One essential effect of the figure is to distance us from the code, putting us in a position from which we can consider logical and grammatical rules. Certainly, the reader of poetry, the person who looks at a placard, hears a slogan, is not a linguist. He has, however, at least a linguistic competence that allows him to proceed intuitively to semic analyses. What Ricoeur calls a "dynamic tension" is in fact the trigger of this metalinguistic attitude, and after this process, the figure appears clearly as an "analyzer" of the language, like an erratic block, which must be broken before it can be reintegrated into the system. And as no less essential a component of the figure, the system resulting from this breaking is modified. In this way perhaps we get a precise notion of what Todorov nicely but metaphorically called the opacity of figured discourse.[37] What remains to be determined is the status of what is in this way revealed "somewhere" in a triangle, whose sides would be the referent, the linguistic code, and this same code dislocated in the metalinguistic moment of rhetorical reduction.

There is a final and subtle objection. Ricoeur sums up our analysis of the reduction of metaphors starting with the concepts of "base" and "invariant." He notes that the base, which is of a syntagmatic nature, "remains unmodified," since it serves as a kind of foil allowing the figure to be perceived. On the other hand, the invariant by definition does not change. And he concludes, "This amounts to saying that no information comes through the figure."[38]

It is perhaps too easy to refer to the positive function of *ethos,* the specific aesthetic effect of each figure. Certainly the concept of "connotation," whose content is not easily defined, hardly allows anything but a reintroduction, seemingly with strictness, of the old methods of textual analysis (the word *blue* evokes, and so on). Rather we ought to ask ourselves in a positive way about what could be "the information from the figure." Information theory is not very helpful to us, for if it defines the measure of information as a number of binary choices, it also has recourse to the concept of originality, that is, unpredictability. The problem here, as everyone knows, is that a blind application of this criterion comes up against the paradox that the message most rich in information, therefore the least predictable and hence the most original, is identical with indecipherable "white noise." On the contrary, it appears more and more that the crux of the problem lies in the banal-original dialectic, in which we recognize with no trouble a travesty of the pair degree zero-deviation and of the pair base-mark.

In the sense of information theory and actually in virtue of its mode of presentation, the figure is not predictable and is therefore a carrier of information (except in the extreme case of the "natural" epithet or tautology and, more generally, of metaphors by repetitive addition). Just considering metaphor, central to Ricoeur's preoccupations, we discern two components:

a) The *predicative* component, call it invariant if you wish, or the conceived degree. It binds the figure to some factual or even scientific discourse to the extent that science consists in formulating general relationships between objects of the world. It insists on the classificatory character of metaphor.

b) The *figural* component, which consists in "the attribution to the union of two collections of semes properties that strictly have value only at their intersections." At this point rhetorical practice clearly deviates from positive science and even opposes it to the extent that rhetoric abolishes distinctions posed by science. It is in this very general character that we can find the explanation for the euphoric character of rhetoric. In poetry, for example, our relationship with the world is proclaimed, and the reader can find there the comfort of an anchorage in the universe. But it goes without saying that the relationship in question is only posed, not proved, that the information carried is not scientific but mythic, and that all the fragility of the superstructure is based on the voluntary confusion between intersection and union.

Our manner of analysis, although indicating where the information on figures is to be found, partially destroys it at the same time, showing its emptiness. While respecting and explaining the euphoria to which it leads, it demythifies its content. It is no more possible to construct a philosophy by "reconsidering" themes proposed by metaphors than it is possible to do this by aligning rhetorical slogans.

This logically leads us to answering criticisms addressed to the epistemological foundations of *GR*. There was no way of avoiding criticisms that the work was a collection of ideological operations, with the obscurantism that results from this. This was because the actual object of our analyses, at the moment we were trying to grasp them, was still largely the product of nonscientific practice devoted to studies of a bent that was moral, pedagogical, and so on; and any attempt such as we made to seek a truly theoretical status could not at the outset eliminate all the peripheral aspects that this discipline brought with it from a cloudy and compromising past. It is unlikely that rhetoric will be put back on its feet in a day's time, and it takes more than a simple gesture to get rid of the idealistic aspects in the processes of rhetoricians. It has been, therefore, a rather simple matter to radicalize criticism, as Pierre Kuentz has done by reducing the matters of neo-rhetoric to some nice taxonomic mania.[39] In this field, surveying things from high above and calling for faultless theoretical positions is, in fact, to put the work off for another time.

It is not a question here of advocating epistemological laxity, but really of distinguishing it from a heuristic process. What, for instance, is Pierre Kuentz doing when, opening the trial, he accuses neo-rhetoricians of an implicit practice of the positivism (which is basically essentialism) of science, of language, of text, of literature, and especially of structure itself? At his own pleasure, he has reduced the process to a caricatured schema. At the same time, he refuses to take into account a common methodological necessity according to which occurs a certain "realism of structure," through which general analysis must pass before coming to a theory of praxis or to the conditions of production that Kuentz calls for. It is in this way that our efforts have been directed almost exclusively to the establishment of a system of objective relationships as a description of the rhetorical object. It achieved a certain number of results, principally bearing on rules for the formation of figures. It is certainly possible that the prevailing character of the process had the result of hypostasizing these rules and the resulting figures. But this was but a necessary moment, just as it was also necessary to divide the linguistic "matter" into several aspects. Concerning this point, we tried to grasp here a kind of liquidation of the signifier, even of language itself, to the benefit of the concepts themselves. It is a refusal to understand that this is a useful methodological arrangement, one that in no way excludes relations from one level to the other. The accusation is all the more surprising since *GR* grants unprecedented place to operations on the signifier, operations producing metaplasms and metataxes along with their semantic effects.

Accusing us of essentialist positivism, as we expected, has had as first target the concept of degree zero and deviation. According to Kuentz, anyone thinking of rhetoric as a science of deviation—it would be better to say a science of deviation*s*—is starting already from an "absolute origin." Every analysis in our first chapter, however, is aimed at making the notion of deviation relative to the notion of degree zero and showing even that the more operative it is, the more it is relative. No longer given as tangible and fixed realities, zero and figured (or perceived and conceived) degrees are defined there in terms of relationship, symmetrical and variable, and at the same time as points of flight. However, it is from this perspective that the reference to scientific language must be understood.[40] This language is spoken of as the actualization of a tendency of discourse to seek univocity. It can be said, however, that this language is neither neutral nor free of figures, but, at the same time, has as its goal, among other things, isotopic continuity. Such a reference, with all its fictiveness, is not operative except with the condition of closing the rhetorical field and putting it into a situation of turning on itself. But isn't all this the contrary of an ideological maneuver and, in fact, the very principle of theoretical model building and the condition of an analysis of the constant mechanisms regulating figures? We cannot see how it could be done in another way, except perhaps by understanding the closure as provisional and foreseeing in the future "the reintegration [of rhetoric] in other apparatuses of communication."[41]

What is to be said about an accusation that is formulated in the name of epistemological exigency, one that takes the text as given by nature, and literature as a manifestation of that very essence that the literary function implies? Kuentz claims that rhetoric can hardly be differentiated from stylistics, since both are concerned with disengaging the "properties" of the literary text. To answer this surprising connection, it is enough to recall two or three positions clarified here. The first is that rhetoric, as we understand it, could not be confused with poetics; and that even if it is traditional to recognize its principal effects in literary discourse, our examples show it operating in other discourses—in all, in fact, when taken to the extreme. It is only in a more recent work that we have taken into consideration the problem of poetic (and not literary) specificity as completely different. In the second position, the rhetorical project seeks to establish stable structures defining certain uses of language. The third one says that recognition and analysis of these structures, which are in some way transhistoric, in no way exclude a sociology of discourses, bringing together formation and transformation of these objects in historic situations. But, whether it is a question of sociology or of a theory of utterances, it seems that these structures cannot avoid using notions such as metaphor or synecdoche. Those who are concerned with connecting figural practices, exorcism, taboo or fetishism ought to continue to describe the lingusitic construction of the trope. . . . Metaphor is not, perhaps, eternal, but we must note that today Jakobson, Eco, Barthes, Lacan must continue to analyze it on what are still called Aristotelian bases.

Pierre Kuentz is also surprised by the fact that the stylisticians say little concerning *GR*. He admits that this is because the work "makes a certain kind of camouflage impossible" and that it "makes inevitable a theoretical revision that surely runs the risk of exposing the fragility of the very notion of literature."[42] We can accept the prophecy of such a revision. In our break with a certain conception of style, attached empirically to expressivity and to effects (see our chapter on *ethos*), the new rhetoric chooses to be part of the current movement of scientific discourse analysis. It is, therefore, not to be confused with the stylistics that chooses to know only the particular. This single point ought to be sufficient to counter any assimilation. Therefore, this same critic has brought into question the very thing that most clearly separates rhetoric from stylistics, that is, the establishment of a taxonomic model. He recognizes in our work a will to order and autonomization that is upsetting for him, as well as very ideological. But it is not enough to be ironic about the mania for classification nor to recall for us the static hypothesis of Linnaeus as a means of disqualifying a structural work that uses tabular arrangements as a methodological necessity, starting with the principle that one must first differentiate components and next combine them. The autonomy given the rhetorical field is, in fact, more apparent than real, since the taxonomy proposed aims less at building a closed system than at making clear the possibilities of creation and generalization, starting with some basic operations. Contrary to what Kuentz suggests by using examples that have little to do with *GR*, if it is possible to propose for each figure a precise definition, it is also possible that particular successes will be the objects of contradictory analyses in terms of function of the context and the understanding of the decoder. And this is the way to clarify the fact that rhetorical theory does not reduce context to a neutral or innocent term: on the contrary, the figural process includes every utterance, and the didactic process of using citations in no way circumscribes the matter.

But on this point as on others, the controversy could certainly rebound. The preceding remarks surely do not exhaust the vast number of questions that a science of discourse cannot fail to raise. The most important ones are not perhaps those which, raised by chance, have been imposed upon us by the discussions during recent debates.

Notes

INTRODUCTION

1. Paul Valéry, "Questions de poésie," in *Oeuvres complètes,* ed. Jean Hytier (Paris: Gallimard, 1957), vol. 1, p. 1289; first published in 1935.

2. Jean Paulhan, "Les Figures ou la rhétorique décryptée," in *Cahiers du Sud,* no. 298 (1949), reprinted in *Oeuvres complètes. La Marque des lettres* (Paris: Cercle du Livre Précieux, 1966), with other essays on the same subject: "La Rhétorique renaît de ses cendres," "La Demoiselle aux miroirs," etc.

3. Pierre Guiraud, *La Stylistique* (Paris: P.U.F., 1963), p. 24.

4. According to E. Magne, *La Rhétorique au XIXe siècle* (Paris: 1838), cited by Charles Perelman and L. Olbrechts-Tyteca, in *Rhétorique et philosophie: Pour une nouvelle théorie de l'argumentation en philosophie* (Paris: P.U.F., 1952), p. 10.

5. Roland Barthes, "Rhétorique de l'image," *Communications,* vol. 4 (1964), translated by Stephen Heath in Roland Barthes, *Image-Music-Text* (Glasgow: Fontana, 1977), pp. 32-51; and idem, "L'Analyse rhétorique," in *Littérature et société* (Brussels: Editions de l'Institut de Sociologie de l'Université Libre de Bruxelles, 1967), pp. 31-48.

6. Gérard Genette, "La Rhétorique et l'espace du langage," *Tel Quel,* no. 11 (1964): 44-54; reprinted in *Figures I* (Paris: Editions du Seuil, 1966).

7. Tzvetan Todorov, *Littérature et signification* (Paris: Larousse, 1967); see also F. Edeline, "Poésie et langage XXIV, XXV," *Le Journal des poètes,* nos. 4 and 5 (1968).

8. A. Kibédi Varga, "La Rhétorique et la critique structuraliste," *Het Franse Boek,* January 1968, pp. 66-73. These few references are given as examples. The return to rhetoric has spread even into circles hardly open to concerns of the times, as is proven by the special issue "Points de vue sur la rhétorique," put out by the conservative journal *XVIIe siècle,* nos. 80-81 (1968).

9. Henri Lefebvre, *Le Langage et la société,* (Paris: N.R.F., 1966), p. 288. We think that it would be useful to trace these stylistic figures even into the H.L.M. [public housing projects]. We believe also that this is precisely the objective of a generalized rhetoric, but it must be built on solid bases.

10. Jacques Lacan, *Ecrits* (Paris: Editions du Seuil, 1966), p. 507. Lacan's diagnosis is cited and commented on by J. Lyotard in "Le Travail du rêve ne pense pas," *Revue d'esthétique* 1 (1968): 26-61.

11. Genette, *Figures I,* p. 214.

12. Charles Bally, *Traité de stylistique française,* 2d ed. (Paris: Klinksieck, [1922]), vol. 1, p. 187.

13. René Géorgin, *Les Secrets du style* (Paris: Editions sociales françaises, 1964), p. 133.

14. Charles Bruneau, "La Langue de Balzac," mimeographed (C.D.U., 1954).

15. Robert Goffin, in the *Bulletin de l'academie royale de langue et de littérature française de Belgique,* November 1953; cited in Arsène Soreil, *De Liré à Liry* (Paris and Namur: Westmael-Charlier, n.d.), p. 125.

16. Bruneau, "La Langue de Balzac."

17. H. Hatzfeld, cited by Guiraud in *La Stylistique,* p. 93.

18. Gérald Antoine, "Stylistique des formes et stylistique des thèmes, ou la stylistique face à

l'ancienne et à la nouvelle critique," in *Les Chemins actuels de la critique* (Paris: Plon, 1967), p. 294.

19. See Henri Mitterand, "La Stylistique," *Le Français dans le monde,* no. 42 (1966): 13–18.

20. B. Gibert, *La Rhétorique, ou les règles de l'éloquence* (Paris: C. L. Thiboust, 1730).

21. See R. P. Bernard Lamy, *La Rhétorique ou l'art de penser,* 4th ed. (Amsterdam: Paul Marrey, 1694).

22. *Habent sua fata libelli....* A century and a half after its appearance, the work of Fontanier was published in a collection titled "Science de l'homme": Pierre Fontanier, *Les Figures du discours* (Paris: Flammarion, 1968). We owe this edition, which also includes the book *Figures autres que les tropes,* to Gérard Genette, who wrote the authorized introduction.

23. According to Edgard de Bruyne, *Etudes d'esthétique médiévale* (Bruges: De Tempel, 1946), vol. 1, p. 117. The author sends us to Vergil the grammarian, whose definition of the trope he cites: "Leporia . . . non enim formidat majorum metas excedere sed nulla reprehensione confunditur."

24. A lacuna noted by Perelman and Olbrechts-Tyteca in their *Rhétorique et philosophie.*

25. Chaim Perelman and L. Olbrechts-Tyteca, *The New Rhetoric: A Treatise on Argumentation,* trans. John Wilkinson and Purcell Weaver (Notre Dame: University of Notre Dame Press, 1969), p. 4.

26. Domairon, *Rhétorique française composée pour l'instruction de la jeunesse* (Paris: Deterville, 1816), p. 57.

27. Among the factors of decadence, the normative claims of classical rhetoric must be indicated. This procedure was condemned from the very beginning by the modern spirit. It was understandably incompatible with Romanticism.

28. For a history of the term, see André Sempoux, "Notes sur l'histoire du mot 'style,'" *Revue belge de philologie et d'histoire* 54 (1976): 736–46.

29. Guiraud, *La Stylistique,* p. 23.

30. Mitterand, "La Stylistique." We note that a large sector of contemporary stylistics defends the legitimacy of a stylistics of intent (see especially J. Mourot, "Stylistique des intentions et stylistique des effets," *CAIEF,* no. 18 [1965–66]: 71–79). It is true that "stylistics, just like semiology, is something that reminds us of the 'sea serpent,' as J. Rozwadowski used to say about semantics. People talk about it and write about it and give speeches about it, but it remains invisible" (S. Rospond, "Nowotwory czy nowopotworyj ęzykowe," *Język Polski* 25 [1945]: 97–105).

31. Guiraud, *La Stylistique,* pp. 48–55.

32. According to Bally, *Traité de stylistique française,* vol. 1.

33. Jean Lameere, *L'Esthétique de Benedetto Croce* (Paris: Vrin, 1936), p. 126.

34. See ibid., esp. chap. 3; and M. Leroy, "Benedetto Croce et les études linguistiques," *Revue internationale de philosophie,* vol. 26 (1953).

35. Roland Barthes, "Qu'est-ce que la critique?" in *Essais critiques* (Paris: Seuil, 1964). The article is commented on by M. Dufrenne, *Esthétique et philosophie* (Paris: Klincksieck, 1967), p. 134.

36. Roman Jakobson, "Closing Statement: Linguistics and Poetics," in *Style in Language,* ed. Thomas A. Sebeok (Cambridge, Mass.: M.I.T. Press, 1960), p. 377.

37. Paul Delbouille, "Sur la definition du fait de style," *Cahiers d'analyse textuelle,* no. 2 (1960): 103. In 1921 the young Jakobson could still be content with an affirmation like "poetry is language in its aesthetic function" (*Novejšaja russkaja poèzija. Viktor Xlebnikov* [Prague, 1921]).

38. Bally, *Traité de stylistique française,* pp. 184, 197–98.

39. T. Todorov, "Les Poètes et le bon usage," *Revue d'esthétique* 18 (1965): 300–305.

40. M. Du Marsais, *Des Tropes ou des diferens sens dans lesquels on peut prendre un même mot dans une même langue* (Paris: Chez la Veuve de Jean-Batiste Brocas, 1730), pp. 2–3.

41. Pius Servien, *Principes d'esthétique: Problèmes d'art et langage des sciences* (Paris: Boivin, 1935), pp. 4–5.

42. Samuel R. Levin, *Linguistic Structures in Poetry* (The Hague: Mouton, 1962) (the author is especially interested in showing the importance of couplings). See also Nicolas Ruwet,

"L'Analyse structurale de la poésie: A propos d'un ouvrage récent," *Linguistics,* vol. 2 (December 1963); and Francis Edeline, "Poésie et langage XVI," *Le Journal des poètes,* no. 10 (1966).

43. Cited in Arsène Soreil, *Entretiens sur l'art d'écrire* (Paris and Brussels: Baude, 1946), p. 209.

44. A. Ombredane, "Les Usages du langage," in *Mélanges offerts à P. Janet* (Paris: Editions d'Artrey, 1939), pp. 37–50.

45. See Roman Jakobson, "A la recherche de l'essence du langage," *Diogène,* no. 51 (1965).

46. Etienne Gilson, *Matières et forme* (Paris: Vrin, 1964), p. 218: "Why these rules of verbal arithmetic? Are they not hindrances to speech? Yes, and this is precisely the *raison d'être* for versification. Verse is there to keep the poet from speaking."

47. According to the definition of art defended by Etienne Souriau, especially in *L'Instauration philosophique* (Paris: Alcan, 1939).

48. See Pierre Guiraud, *Le Français populaire* (Paris: P.U.F., 1952), p. 92: "It is certainly not a language of creative artists, but of artisans who copy the models."

49. According to the formula of André Malraux: "The artist creates less to express himself than he expresses himself to create" (in *Le Musée imaginaire de la sculpture mondiale* [Paris: N.R.F., 1952], p. 62).

50. According to Soreil, *Entretiens sur l'art d'écrire.*

51. Paul Valéry, "The Poet's Rights over Language," in *The Art of Poetry,* trans. Denise Folliot (Princeton: Princeton University Press, 1958), p. 172.

52. Gérald Antoine, "La Stylistique française, sa définition, ses buts, sa méthode," *Revue de l'enseignement supérieur,* no. 1 (1959): 57.

53. Paul Robert, ed., *Dictionnaire alphebétique et analogique de la langue française* (Paris: P.U.F., 1953–), s.v. "norme."

54. Todorov, "Les Poètes et le bon usage."

55. See Antoine Badeau de Somaize, *Le Dictionnaire des précieuses* (Paris: Jannet, 1856).

56. Saint-Pol Roux, "La Carafe d'eau pure," *Les Reposoirs,* vol. 3 (1889).

57. *Institutio* 1. 5. 38, cited in H. Lausberg, *Handbuch der literarischen Rhetorik* (Munich: Max Hueber, 1960), vol. 1, p. 250; we note that Lausberg has frequently upheld the continuity from ancient rhetoric to modern stylistics (see "Rezension," *Archiv für das Studium der neueren Sprachen* 108 [1957]: 335). In Quintilian, the four categories of transformation are called *adiectio, detractio, immutatio, transmutatio.* Lausberg's excellent treatise contains no doubt the most complete and sweeping synthesis of the classical heritage.

58. "Linguistique et poétique," in *Essais de linguistique générale* (Paris: Editions de Minuit, 1963). [First published in 1960 as "Closing Statement: Linguistics and Poetics," pp. 350–77. (See above, n. 36). *Trans.*]

59. Jakobson, "Closing Statement," p. 371: "The double-sensed message finds correspondence in a split addresser, in a split addressee...."

60. Henri Morier, *Dictionnaire de poétique et de rhétorique* (Paris: P.U.F., 1961).

61. Todorov, *Littérature et signification,* p. 115.

62. C. K. Ogden and I. A. Richards, *The Meaning of Meaning,* 8th ed. (New York: Harcourt, Brace and World, 1962), p. 11.

63. Todorov, *Littérature et signification,* p. 117.

64. On these attempts at nonsignifying poetry, see *Le Journal des poètes,* no. 3 (1969).

65. The question of knowing whether it is fitting to call such a study poetics rather than aesthetics has only a secondary importance. Todorov covers a large part of what is here called rhetoric in poetics, understood in the sense of the "science of the qualities of literature," and he lists under aesthetics the problem of effects and value ("Poétique," in *Qu'est-ce que la structuralisme?* [Paris: Editions du Seuil, 1968]). Eminent aestheticians—especially Etienne Souriau in *L'Avenir de l'esthétique* (Paris: Alcan, 1929)—have themselves defined their discipline by ousting the question of the beautiful. The side that we finally adopt is in conformity with the ordinary sense, which admits that a text is truly "poetic" only if its "rhetoric" is effective.

66. Jean Cohen, *Structure du langage poétique* (Paris: Flammarion, 1966), p. 225.

CHAPTER I

1. See on this subject E. Benveniste, *Problems in General Linguistics,* trans. M. Meek (Coral Gables: University of Miami Press, 1971), pp. 101–11.

2. A *hole* and not a *whole* [in French, "un chat et non un chas" (literally, "a cat and not a needle's eye"). *Trans.*]. See Pierre Guiraud, *Structures étymologiques du lexique français* (Paris: Larousse, 1967), pp. 121–22.

3. J. P. Boon, "Synonymie, antonymie et facteurs stylistiques," *Communications* 10 (1967): 167–68.

4. Claude Brémond, "Le Message narratif," *Communications* 4 (1964): 4–32.

5. See V. Propp, *The Morphology of the Folktale,* trans. Laurence Scott, 2d ed. (Austin: University of Texas Press, 1968), pp. 52, 125.

6. See, for example, Tzvetan Todorov, *Littérature et signification* (Paris: Larousse, 1967).

7. George E. Vander Beke, *French Word Book* (New York: Macmillan and Co., 1929).

8. See A.-J. Greimas, *Sémantique structurale* (Paris: Larousse, 1966), p. 69.

9. After Umberto Eco, *L'Oeuvre ouverte* (Paris: Editions du Seuil, 1965), p. 259.

10. A. Moles, *Théorie de l'information et perception esthétique* (Paris: Flammarion, 1958), p. 54.

11. On redundancy as a condition of style, see various remarks of Pierre Guiraud in "Langage et théorie de la communication," in *Le Langage* (Paris: N.R.F., 1968), p. 164.

12. Jean Cohen, *Structure du langage poétique* (Paris: Flammarion, 1966).

13. Vitold Bélévitch, *Langage humain et langage des machines* (Brussels: Office de Publicité, 1956), p. 115.

14. See Greimas, *Sémantique structurale.*

15. Our test consisted in offering to a linguistically competent group (students of literature) a descriptive text semantically isotopic. Of the 862 divisions in the text (letters plus spaces), 244 had been effaced randomly (about 28.3 percent). Each subject was invited to restore the defective portions of the text, indicating what "rationale" he used (phonetic, syntactic plus grammatical, or semantic). The correct surmise was obtained at least once for all positions, which confirmed that the rate of redundancy in written French exceeded 28 percent. Still, it seems to us that the rate of 55 percent for all redundancy is somewhat exaggerated. We shall return to this problem in a later work based on more elaborate tests.

16. "The kind of expectation we have as to the form of a particular occurrence depends on the degree of deep-seatedness of the occurrence matrix" (W. Koch, *Recurrence and a Three-Modal Approach to Poetry* [The Hague: Mouton and Co., 1966], p. 46).

17. In this chapter, *substance,* remember, is not taken in the sense employed by glossematics.

CHAPTER II

1. Francis Mikus, "En marge du sixième Congrès international des Linguistes," in *Homenaje à André Martinet: Estructuralismo e historia* (Canary Islands, 1957), vol. 1, pp. 161–62.

2. Leonard Bloomfield, *Language* (New York: Holt, Rinehart, and Winston, 1933), p. 173.

3. This is no doubt what Georges Galichet means, in rather imagistic terms: "Orthography is not, therefore, as some imagine it to be, a pure formality, a simple etiquette of language; in large measure it is a linguistic necessity" (in *Physiologie de la langue française,* 4th ed. [Paris: P.U.F., 1964], p. 32). Ferdinand de Saussure had already noted this fact: ". . . people forget that they learn to speak before they learn to write, and the natural sequence is reversed" (*Course in General Linguistics,* trans. Wade Baskin [New York: Philosophical Library, 1954], p. 25).

4. René Thimonnier, *Le Système graphique du français* (Paris: Plon, 1967), p. 71; cf. J.-M. Klinkenberg, "L'Orthographe française constitue-t-elle un système?" *Le Français moderne* 39 (1971): 236–56.

5. Louis Hjelmslev, *Prolegomena to a Theory of Language,* trans. Francis J. Whitfield, rev. ed. (Madison: University of Wisconsin Press, 1969), pp. 104–5. This point of view was taken up by Nicolas Ruwet in "La Linguistique générale aujourd'hui," *Archives européennes de sociologie* 5 (1964): 289.

6. The ancients had already noted that metaplasm could find its expression through writing and that, moreover, certain significant alterations could not be symbolized in this medium. But the conditions of Latin were quite different from what we now find. On the one hand, its more clearly phonetic spelling hardly allowed gratuitous graphemes; but on the other hand, certain elements not present in its graphics have phonological value: accent, length, etc.

7. Here the limits between metaplasms and metataxes are closed: metataxis does not alter the substance of the words whose order it upsets.

8. We are not considering here the table of compatibilities and incompatibilities of each operator with its operand.

9. We note that suppression is complete here. Since we are at the level of indivisibles, either the operation is complete or it has not taken place.

10. Here one must beware of lexicalizations of derived forms. *Cinema* is not the result of suppression of *cinematography*. Unusually, it is rather the latter term that is a metaplasm by addition. *Ciné* [in French at least] still remains the result of a suppression, but for how long?

11. The presence of punctuation is obviously unnecessary. Here is an example of omission taken from Joyce: "Want to keep your weathereye open. Those girls, those lovely. By the sad sea waves" (*Ulysses*). [The original cites an example from Claudel discussed by Henri Morier in *Dictionnaire de poétique et de rhétorique* (Paris: P.U.F., 1961), s.v. "blanchissement." *Trans.*]

12. Cited by Gaston Ferdière in *Mes mots maux-biles in Bizarre,* nos. 32–33, p. 138 (special issue devoted to Illiterate Literature or Literature According to the Letter). [The original offers as an example "the adjective *rajolivissant,* which was the rage in Toulouse society in the 1940s." *Trans.*]

13. Morier, *Dictionnaire de poétique et de rhétorique,* s.v. "rime."

14. Roman Jakobson, "Closing Statement: Linguistics and Poetics," in *Style in Language,* ed. Thomas A. Sebeok (Cambridge, Mass.: M.I.T. Press, 1960), p. 368.

15. Je me veux regadé en tes beaux yeux luysans:
    Car ce sont les misoirs des Amouseux enfâns,
    Après je modesay ta goge ma menonne.
    Soudain je laichesay ton joliet tetin,
    Puis je chatouillesay ton beau petit tounin
In this sonnet from *L'Amour passionneé de Noémie,* the childlike style (the last line reads: "For Love is made better in childy language") is primarily due to the suppression of *l* (*r* in the French) and its replacement by a bilabial.

16. We are here considering synonymy of terms that do not belong to the same morphological family (synonymy A, without a morphological base, which we oppose to synonymy B, or synonymy with a morphological base).

17. The first linguists who applied themselves to the analysis of semantics limited themselves by basing their work on privileged examples: Bernard Pottier's analysis of the lexeme *fauteuil* ("armchair"), for instance, cf. "Vers une sémantique moderne," *Travaux de linguistique et de littérature* 1 (1964): 107–38. In this type of analysis, in fact, one starts with the referent, with the extralinguistic reality, and not with the meaning, since each seme corresponds to a tangible, spatial characteristic. Under these conditions, it is posited that for each object designated there is a corresponding semic analysis, unique and reciprocal. But such is not the case at all in the examples we have cited. To define semes biunivocally is subject to caution.

18. "The most rigorously careful theoreticians neglect or exclude connotation" (Henri Lefebvre, *Le Langage et la société* [Paris: N.R.F., 1966], p. 20).

19. We discover here the superiority of distributional analysis to semic criteria. If *conceal* and *secrete* may be analyzed in the same way, nevertheless, they do not share the same distribution.

20. See the appendix to Pottier, "Vers une sémantique moderne."

21. We could call these stylistic marks "stylemes." These pairs seem to exist only in a literary language conceived of as architectural. In pure synchrony these opposites have as little real existence as the ultimate synonymic pairs: *civitatem* / *city, think* / *penser,* etc. For a

discussion of archaism, see Jean-Marie Klinkenberg, *Style et archaisme dans la Légende d'Ulenspiegel de Charles De Coster* (Brussels: Palais des Académies, 1973).

22. In the sense of "new usage."

23. We are considering here only pure archaisms or neologisms, that is, those that are obtained by complete suppression-addition. Other archaisms or neologisms can be obtained by suppression, addition, or simple suppression-addition (suffixation, morphological alternation, etc.).

24. Etienne Souriau, "On the aesthetic of invented words and language," in *Revue d'esthétique* 18 (1975): 19–48.

25. François van Laere, "*Finnegans Wake*, textuellement," *L'Arc* 36 (1968): 88–93.

26. Iona Opie and Peter Opie, *The Lore and Language of School-Children* (Oxford: Clarendon Press, 1959), p. 24.

27. In fact, such quasi-homonymic substitutions, while most often obtained by suppression-addition, can also be obtained by simple suppression or addition (as in the case of "When the moths got at the minister's clothes, his wife said, 'Let us spray'") and also by metathesis (*wayrail*). [The word play in the original—of Frédéric Dard, writing as San Antonio—is *émasculée contraception* ("emasculated contraception") for *immaculée conception* ("immaculate conception"). *Trans.*]

28. One of the most important of sequences of anagrams is to be found in Raymond Queneau's poem *Don Evane Marquy*.

29. The spoonerism is often called by the more honorable *antistrophe*, especially before the advent of the Reverend William A. Spooner (1844–1930). We know that Rabelais bestowed on it a title to respectability.

30. To which great names, however, have given their approval. Note, for example, Quintilian's lines: *Signa te signa, timere me tangis et angis! / Roma tibi subito motibus ibit amor*. On occasion the ancients practiced *versus anacyclicus* (or *cancrinus, recurrens, retrogradiens*). The anacyclic distichs of Planudus have remained famous.

31. In the cited examples, identical graphemes correspond to different sounds (*A*ble-Elb*a*, *w*as-sa*w*).

32. G. Peignot, *Amusements philologiques* (Paris: Renouart, 1808); and Alfred Liede, *Dichtung als Spiel: Studien zur Unsinnspoesie an den Grenzen der Sprache*, 2 vols. (Berlin: Walter De Gruyter, 1963). [For complete bibliographic references, see Barbara Kirshenblatt-Gimblett, ed., *Speech Play* (Philadelphia: University of Pennsylvania Press, 1976). *Trans.*]

33. Giacomo Devoto, "Introduction à la stylistique," in *Mélanges Marouzeau* (Paris: Les belles lettres, 1948), p. 151.

34. See the introduction.

35. Because it is obviously necessary to exclude suffixation, synonymy, etc.

36. Among the ancients, *metaplasmus* was already considered a barbarism (a fault in the phonic constitution of a word) tolerated as *ornatus* or for metrical reasons (see H. Lausberg, *Handbuch der literarischen Rhetorik* [Munich: Max Hueber, 1960], vol. 1, sec. 479). The same attitude is found in the sixteenth-century *L'art poétique françois* [or comparable English manuals: "it is somewhat more tollerable to help the rime by false orthographie, then to leave an unpleasant dissonance to the eare, by keeping trewe orthographie and loosing the rime..." (Puttenham) *Trans.*].

37. J. Marouzeau, *Lexique de la terminologie linguistique*, 3d ed. (Paris: Geuthner, 1951), s.v. "argot."

38. Alfredo Niceforo, *Génie d'argot* (Paris: Mercure de France, 1912), p. 144.

39. In a later volume we shall treat in detail metaboles of support and graphic substance, where the rhetorical concepts will be generalized by their application to semiological systems other than linguistic ones.

40. See Raymond Jean, "Qu'est-ce que lire," in *Linguistique et littérature* (Paris: La Nouvelle Critique, 1968), pp. 17–20.

41. Comic-strip authors understand this, for they know how to play with graphic onomatopoeia with a certain success. Film has also adopted these procedures. In *Potemkin*, for example, the titles try to indicate the loudness of the voices: "Brothers! BROTHERS! BROTHERS!"

42. In the "John Smith's *Secret Historie*" passage of John Barth's *The Sot-Weed Factor*,

part of the feeling of archaism comes from the use of the ampersand: "These & many other things I learn'd from this Wepenter. . . ."

43. The principle is to try to reflect the content of the poem by the graphics, as in Herbert's "Easter Wings," Mallarmé's "Un Coup de Dés," or John Hollander's "A State of Nature."

CHAPTER III

1. R. Lagane, "Problèmes de définition. Le sujet," *Langue française* 1 (1969): 58–62.

2. Roman Jakobson, "A la recherche de l'essence du langage," *Diogène,* no. 51 (1965): 22–38.

3. J. Kurylowicz, "Les Catégories grammaticales," *Diogène,* no. 51 (1965): 54–71.

4. In its general outline, this summary description is inspired, at least for French, by Jean Dubois, *Grammaire structurale du français: Le Verbe* (Paris: Larousse, 1967); see also idem, *Grammaire structurale du français: La Phrase et les transformations* (Paris: Larousse, 1969).

5. Thus, we consider symmetry a syntactic anomaly. We note here that Tzvetan Todorov, in *Littérature et signification* (Paris: Larousse, 1967), would rather see in it a figure, in the meaning he gives this word: "describable" expression, but carrying no infraction of a rule of language, neither "implicit nor explicit." Certainly symmetry does "draw attention to the message. . . ." This means, therefore, that there exists an implicit rule of "transparent" language: normal syntax proscribes manifest symmetries.

6. In *Structure du langage poétique* (Paris: Flammarion, 1966), p. 100.

7. Marcel Proust, *Remembrance of Things Past,* trans. H. Scott-Moncrief (London: Chatto and Windus, 1924–29), *The Captive, Part 1,* pp. 249–50; or *The Captive* (New York: Random House, 1932), vol. 2, p. 509.

8. Pierre Fontanier, *Les Figures du discours* (Paris: Flammarion, 1968), p. 216.

9. Henri Morier, *Dictionnaire de poétique et de rhétorique* (Paris: P.U.F., 1961), s.v. "syllèpse."

10. *The Captive,* vol. 2, p. 509.

CHAPTER IV

1. A.-J. Greimas, *Sémantique structurale* (Paris: Larousse, 1966), p. 6. We shall borrow some terms from this excellent work, all of whose teachings, however, we do not claim to have assimilated.

2. We are thinking, for example, of the work of Jean Follain, a sort of poetry of the anti-image. See F. Edeline, "L'Image et la Poésie (Poésie et langage XVII, XVIII)," *Le Journal des poètes* 37, nos. 1 and 2 (1967).

3. In recent years, this literature has been particularly rich in English-language philosophical and literary journals. See, for example, F. Edeline, "Poésie et langage XXVII," *Le Journal des poètes* 38 (1968), concerning three studies that appeared in the *British Journal of Aesthetics.*

4. This important distinction explains the difference between synonymical metaboles, ones that certain rhetoricians called simply metaboles, and tropes.

5. Tzvetan Todorov, *Littérature et signification* (Paris: Larousse, 1967), p. 95.

6. Du Marsais, *Des tropes ou des diferens sens dans lesquels on peut prendre un même mot dans une même langue* (Paris: Chez la Veuve de Jean-Baptiste Brocas, 1730), p. 14.

7. Greimas, *Sémantique structurale,* pp. 42–50.

8. We know that the term *catachresis* has had at least two different definitions, meaning either an extension of meaning or a metaphor that is excessive or worn out (see Du Marsais, *Des Tropes,* 1830 edition, p. 50). As Fontanier saw clearly, the purely instrumental trope is not a figure.

9. Jean Cohen, *Structure du langage poétique* (Paris: Flammarion, 1966), p. 116: "The different figures, therefore, are not, as classical rhetoricians thought, rhyme, inversion, metaphor, etc., but metaphor-rhyme, the inversion-metaphor, etc." Cohen, in fact, attributes a

synecdochal meaning to *metaphor*, as Jakobson had done for *metonymy*. In our convention, much less compromising, we can say that there are rhyme-metaboles, inversion-metaboles, and so on.

10. J. Piaget, *Traité de logique* (Paris: Armand Colin, 1949), pp. 145–46.

11. Yoshihiki Ikegami, "Semantic Changes in Poetic Words," *Linguistics,* no. 19 (1965): 64–79.

12. It is to be understood, therefore, that it is a question, respectively, of decomposition of a perceptual (or encyclopedic) type echoed in the relations between concepts and of decomposition of a conceptual (or logical) type. We are not unaware that this last type of decomposition can in its turn operate on the mode of the product just as on the mode of summation (as is the case with the endocentric series seen above). Only this last type of decomposition respects the condition of the logical product according to which $p.q \supset p;$ this is not true of our decomposition in mode II, which, therefore, is not subject to the rules of propositional logic, but rather to the rules of the encyclopedia.

13. Edgar Morin, *L'Homme et la mort dans l'histoire* (Paris: Correà, 1951), p. 85.

14. Jean Piaget, *Psychologie et épistémologie* (Paris: Gonthier, 1970), pp. 132–33.

15. Rigorously, of course, Cicero as an individual is not a species. See the article "Individu" in André Lalande, *Vocabulaire technique et critique de la philosophie,* 7th ed., rev. and augmented (Paris: P.U.F., 1956). But we do not understand "species" here in the meaning of the School.

16. Du Marsais, *Des Tropes,* pp. 93–94.

17. J. Dufresny, "Les Quatre âges," in *Entretiens sur l'art d'écrire,* ed. Arsène Soreil (Paris and Brussels: Baude, 1946), p. 46.

18. Cohen, *Structure du langage poétique,* p. 118. Such "marks of originality" ought to be considered as prosaic gears, able to be neutralized by poetic gears.

19. *Pensées,* no. 347 (Brunschwicg), Trotter translation, p. 97.

20. See the introduction above, n. 56.

21. Fontanier classifies figures of comparison in "figures de style," a distinct category for him of figures of thought. See also the excellent article by Jean Cohen, "La Comparaison poétique: essai de systématique," *Langages,* no. 12 (1968): 43–51.

22. Todorov, *Littérature et signification,* p. 112.

23. Marcel Pleynet, *Lautréamont par lui-même* (Paris: Le Seuil, 1967), p. 114.

24. Domairon, *Rhétorique française composée pour l'instruction de la jeunesse* (Paris: Deterville, 1816), p. 57.

25. P. Guiraud, *La Sémantique* (Paris: P.U.F., 1955).

26. Du Marsais, *Des Tropes,* 1830 edition, p. 87.

27. Yoshihiko Ikegami, "Structural Semantics," *Linguistics,* no. 33 (1967): 49–67.

28. L. Cellier, "D'une rhétorique profonde: Baudelaire et l'oxymoron," in *Cahiers internationaux de symbolisme,* no. 8 (1965): 3–14.

29. "Introduction," in Pierre Fontanier, *Les Figures du discours* (Paris: Flammarion, 1968), p. 14, n. 12.

CHAPTER V

1. Charles Baudelaire, "Le Chat," *Oeuvres complètes* (Paris: N.R.F., 1961), p. 48. [Translation by Roy Campbell, in *Flowers of Evil: A Selection,* ed. Marthiel Mathews and Jackson Mathews (New York: New Directions, 1955), pp. 49–53. *Trans.*]

2. Bertrand Russell, "Egocentric Particulars," chap. 7, in *An Inquiry into Truth and Meaning* (London: Allen and Unwin, 1940).

3. E. Benveniste, *Problems in General Linguistics,* trans. M. Meek (Coral Gables: University of Miami Press, 1971), p. 25.

4. Ibid.

5. Cited by Henri Morier in his *Dictionnaire de poétique et de rhétorique* (Paris: P.U.F., 1961), s.v. "antithèse."

6. Pierre Fontanier, *Les Figures du discours* (Paris: Flammarion, 1968). [For complete bibliographic information, see Genette's introduction in ibid. *Trans.*]

7. G. Genette, "Introduction," in ibid., p. 11.

8. Genette, *Figures I* (Paris: Editions du Seuil, 1966), p. 209.

9. Ibid., p. 214.

10. Ibid.

11. Benedetto Croce, *Estetica come scienze dell'espressione e linguistica generale* (Bari: Laterza, 1950), pp. 75 ff.

12. Paul Valéry, "Le Cimetière Marin," line 1, in *Oeuvres complètes,* ed. Jean Hytier (Paris: Gallimard, 1957), vol. 1, p. 147.

13. Paul Nougé, *Histoire de ne pas rire* (Brussels: "Les lèvres nues," 1956), p. 253.

14. Fontanier, *Les Figures du discours,* pp. 312 ff.; and Genette, *Figures I,* pp. 211 ff. It is true, as these authors claim, that catachresis is a "forced" trope. Its structure, nonetheless, is the same as that of a metaphor. Its degree zero is expressible only by periphrasis, but, then, how many metaphors are there just like this?

15. Genette, *Figures I,* p. 214.

16. M. Bréal, *Essai de sémantique,* 2d ed. (Paris: Hachette, 1924).

17. Raymond Queneau, *Exercises de style* (Paris: Gallimard, 1947).

18. Rudolf Carnap, "The Elimination of Metaphysics through Logical Analysis of Language," in *Logical Positivism,* ed. A. J. Ayer (Glencoe, Ill.: Free Press, 1959), p. 68.

19. Ryle, *The Concept of Mind* (Harmondsworth: Peregrine Books, 1963), p. 17.

20. C. M. Turbayne, *The Myth of Metaphor* (New Haven and London: Yale University Press, 1962), pp. 22 ff.

21. Ibid., p. 27.

22. André Breton, *Manifestes du surréalisme* (Paris: J. J. Pauvert, 1962), p. 27.

23. Ludwig Wittgenstein, *Philosophical Investigations,* trans. G.E.M. Anscombe (Oxford: Blackwell, 1953), p. 7.

24. Russell, *An Inquiry into Truth and Meaning,* pp. 197 ff. See also the famous controversy concerning the sentence by Noam Chomsky, "Colorless green ideas sleep furiously."

25. Max Black, *Models and Metaphors* (New York: Cornell University Press, 1962), pp. 25 ff.

26. Andrew Harrison, "Poetic Ambiguity," *Analysis* 13 (1962–63): 55.

27. Fontanier, *Les Figures du discours,* p. 401.

28. Ibid., p. 133.

29. Ibid., p. 123.

30. Benveniste, *Problems in General Linguistics,* p. 218.

31. A. Kibédi Varga, *Les Constantes du poème: A la recherche d'une poétique dialectique* (The Hague: Van Goor Zonen, 1963), p. 202.

32. Alcanter de Brahm, *L'Ostensoir des ironies* (N.p., 1898).

33. Tzvetan Todorov, *Littérature et signification* (Paris: Larousse, 1967), p. 111.

34. Jean Laplanche and J.-B. Pontalis, *The Language of Psycho-analysis,* trans. Donald Nicholson-Smith (New York: W. W. Norton, 1973), p. 263.

35. Jean Hyppolite, "Commentaire parlé sur la 'Verneinung' de Freud." in *La Psychanalyse* (Paris: P.U.F., 1956), p. 30, n. 1.

36. Laplanche and Pontalis, *The Language of Psycho-analysis,* p. 118.

37. Baudelaire, *Flowers of Evil,* p. 68.

CHAPTER VI

1. Paul Valéry, *Variétés III* (Paris: Gallimard, 1936), p. 42. The translation is from *The Art of Poetry,* trans. Denise Folliot (New York: Random House, 1961), p. 88.

2. M. Juilland, "Stylistique et linguistique autour de Charles Bruneau, L'époque réaliste, I," *Langage* 30 (1954): 323.

3. Elsa Dehennin, "La Stylistique littéraire en marche," *Revue belge de philologie et d'histoire* 42 (1964): 880.

4. *Structure du langage poétique* (Paris: Flammarion, 1966), p. 25.

5. Damaso Alonso, *Poesía española* (Madrid, 1952), p. 197.

6. Cohen, *Structure du langage poétique,* pp. 38-39.

7. See Anne Souriau, "La Notion de catégorie esthétique," *Revue d'esthétique* 19 (1966): 225-42.

8. Dehennin, "La Stylistique littéraire en marche," p. 902.

9. See Subodh Chandra Mukerjee, *Le Rasa* (Paris: Alcan, 1927).

10. Michael Riffaterre, "Vers la définition linguistique du style," *Word* 17 (1961): 323-24.

11. Ibid., pp. 318, 320-21.

12. Groupe μ, *Rhétorique de la poésie* (Brussels: Editions Complexe, 1977).

13. Stephen Ullmann, "Psychologie et stylistique," *Journal de psychologie,* April-June 1953, p. 133.

14. Roman Jakobson, "Closing Statement: Linguistics and Poetics," in *Style in Language,* ed. Thomas A. Sebeok (Cambridge, Mass.: M.I.T. Press, 1960), p. 356.

15. "Appendix," in *Littérature et signification* (Paris: Larousse, 1967), p. 116.

16. Roman Jakobson and Morris Halle, *Fundamentals of Language* (The Hague: Mouton, 1956), pp. 91-92.

17. Charles Bally, *Traité de stylistique française* 2d ed. (Paris: Klinksieck, [1922]), vol. 1, pp. 104-5 and *passim.*

18. Taken from the studies offered in Paul Imbs, ed., *Trésor de la langue française du XIXe et du XXe siècle (1789-1960),* 6 vols. (Paris: CNRS, 1971-).

19. Therefore, it is already at the level of the autonomous function that metaboles on the plane of ethos can disappear or, conversely, reappear. This takes account of Riffaterre's justified criticism of John Hollander: "Semantic deviation ... is interpreted as metaphoric or figurative usage, necessarily more 'original' than literal usage. Things are, however, not so simple, and many figures used are clichés, while many others in a saturated context serve only to give stylistic relief to a word used literally" ("Vers la définition linguistique du style," p. 334).

20. Ibid., summary, p. 1.

21. Ibid., p. 19, sec. 21*b*.

22. Ibid., p. 181, sec. 190.

23. See E. Coseriu, "Pour une sémantique diachronique structurale," *Travaux de linguistique et de littérature* 2 (1964): 139-86; and idem, "Structure lexicale et enseignement du vocabulaire" (Tübingen University, Romanisch seminar, 1969).

24. See the reprint in Louis Hjelmslev, "Pour une sémantique structurale," *Essais linguistiques* (Copenhagen: Naturmetodens, 1959), pp. 96-112.

25. In "Stylistique des intentions et stylistique des effets," *CAIEF* 18 (1965-66): 79.

26. Pierre Guiraud, *La Stylistique* (Paris: P.U.F., 1963), pp. 17-19.

27. Cf. Pierre Guiraud, "Les Tendances de la stylistique contemporaine," in *Style et littérature,* ed. P. Guiraud et al. (The Hague, 1962), pp. 11-23, in which this debt is indicated. Linguistics today has not gone any further in the examination of this aspect of the "theory of colors."

28. See Michael Riffaterre, "Stylistic Context," *Word* 16 (1960): 216; and idem, "Vers la définition linguistique du style," p. 335. Riffaterre has spoken of "words in themselves poetic" but asks us to note that this characteristic is secondary as soon as the word is put into a context. The remark could have been broadened to include all other cases of ecology.

29. Paul Imbs, "Analyse linguistique, analyse philologique, analyse stylistique," in *Programme du Centre de Philologie romane de Strasbourg (1957-1958)* (Strasbourg, 1957), p. 75.

30. Guiraud, *La Stylistique,* p. 20.

31. Rebecca Posner, "Linguistique et littérature" in *Marche romane* 13 (1963): 49.

32. Nicolas Ruwet, "Sur un vers de Charles Baudelaire," *Linguistics,* no. 17 (1975): 69-77.

33. It is fitting to add to the works already cited: "Criteria for Style Analysis," *Word* 16 (1960): 207-18; "Problèmes d'analyse du style littéraire," *Romance Philology* 14 (1961): 216-27; and "Comment décrire le style de Chateaubriand?" *Romanic Review* 53 (1962): 128-38. The most debatable point in these articles is the determination of an "Average Reader." [See *Semiotics of Poetry* (Bloomington: Indiana University Press, 1978). *Trans.*]

34. Riffaterre, "Stylistic Context," p. 212.

35. Imbs, "Analyse linguistique, analyse philologique, analyse stylistique," p. 76.

CHAPTER VII

1. E. Benveniste, *Problems in General Linguistics,* trans. M. Meek (Coral Gables: University of Miami Press, 1971), pp. 195–204.
2. Michel Butor, "L'Usage des pronoms personnels dans le roman," *Répertoire II* (Paris: Editions de Minuit, 1964), pp. 61–72.
3. Raymond Bellour, *Henri Michaux ou une mesure de l'être* (Paris: Gallimard, 1965), p. 85.
4. Jean-Pierre Richard, *Littérature et sensation* (Paris: Le Seuil, 1954), p. 37.
5. D. H. Lawrence, *Studies in Classic American Literature* (Garden City: Doubleday, 1951), p. 190.
6. See Wayne C. Booth, *The Rhetoric of Fiction* (Chicago: University of Chicago Press, 1961), p. 150, n. 3.
7. M.-A. Séchehaye, *Journal d'un schizophrène* (Paris: P.U.F., 1960), p. 66.
8. Benveniste, *Problems in General Linguistics,* pp. 199–201.
9. In *Grammaire structurale du français: Le Verbe* (Paris: Larousse, 1967), p. 14.

CHAPTER VIII

1. Roland Barthes, "Introduction to the Structural Analysis of Narratives," in *Image-Music-Text,* trans. Stephen Heath (Glasgow: Fontana, 1977), p. 84. [The translator employs "narrative" for *récit. Trans.*]
2. Louis Hjelmslev, *Prolegomena to a Theory of Language,* trans. Francis J. Whitfield, rev. ed. (Madison: University of Wisconsin Press, 1969), chap. 13.
3. In "La Linguistique générale aujourd'hui," *Archives européennes de sociologie* 5 (1964): 287.
4. Hjelmslev, *Prolegomena to a Theory of Language,* pp. 49 and 58.
5. Nicolas Ruwet, *Introduction à la grammaire générative* (Paris: Plon, 1967), p. 26.
6. This explanation is important because the terminology is so imprecise, as we see by reading the special issues titled "Analyse structurale du récit" in the journal *Communications* 8 (1966), which is still the best treatment of the question. [English-language readers will want to look at the discussions in Robert Scholes, *Structuralism in Literature* (New Haven: Yale University Press, 1974); Jonathan Culler, *Structuralist Poetics* (Ithaca: Cornell University Press, 1975); Terence Hawkes, *Structuralism and Semiotics* (Berkeley and Los Angeles: University of California Press, 1977); and Seymour Chatman, *Story and Discourse* (Ithaca and London: Cornell University Press, 1978). *Trans.*]
7. A.-J. Greimas, Preface, in L. Hjelmslev, *Le Langage* (Paris: Editions de Minuit, 1966), p. 14, [translated as *Language* by Francis J. Whitfield (Madison: University of Wisconsin Press, 1970). *Trans.*].
8. Dennis Tedlock, *Finding the Center* (New York: Dial Press, 1972).
9. Voltaire, *Candide,* trans. Robert M. Adams (New York: Norton, 1966), p. 5.
10. Gustave Flaubert, *Madame Bovary,* trans. Francis Steegmuller (New York: Random House, 1957), p. 19.
11. Jean Rousset, *Forme et signification* (Paris: José Corti, 1962), p. 57. The author is speaking of Marivaux, but within the frame of our analysis the perspective can be widened.
12. Erich Auerbach, *Mimesis,* trans. Willard Trask (Princeton: Princeton University Press, 1968), pp. 525–53.
13. Nathalie Sarraute, "Conversation et sous-conversation," *L'Ere du Soupçon* (Paris: Gallimard, 1956), pp. 79–124.
14. Cf. Michel Butor, *Répertoire III* (Paris: Editions de Minuit, 1968), pp. 185–215.
15. Someone could object that this is a plot in a frame that clarifies the narrative. But certain stories of Chekhov bring out the same procedure, especially "Fat Man and Thin Man." The

changes in vocabulary and tone indicate a secret motivation. Temporal and causal lines are also involved.

16. Auerbach, *Mimesis,* p. 114.

17. Jean-Jacques Mayoux, "L'Hérésie de James Joyce," *English Miscellany* (Rome), 1951, pp. 222–46.

18. In other cases, beginning and end coincide artificially. Such is the case in Raymond Guérin's *Parmi tant d'autres feux,* where the word *feux* ("fire") is metaphoric at the end, or in Raymond Roussel's works, where the last sentence repeats the first sentence with but one change.

19. Tzvetan Todorov, "Poétique," in *Qu'est-ce que le structuralisme?* (Paris: Editions du Seuil, 1968), p. 118.

20. Ibid., p. 121.

21. Barthes, "Introduction to the Structural Analysis of Narratives."

22. Claude Brémond, "La Logique des possibles narratifs," *Communications* 8 (1966): 60.

23. Victor Shklovsky, "La Construction de la nouvelle et du roman," in *Théorie de la littérature,* ed. T. Todorov (Paris: Seuil, 1966), pp. 170–96.

24. These different processes are illustrated by T. Todorov in his "Poétique."

25. On *verisimilitude,* consult *Communications* 11 (1968), especially the introduction by Todorov and the article by G. Genette, "Vraisemblable et motivation."

26. Paul Claudel, "Introduction à la peinture hollandaise," in *Oeuvres complètes* (Paris: Gallimard, 1960), p. 44.

27. Jean Ricardou, *Problèmes du nouveau roman* (Paris: Seuil, 1967), pp. 171–79.

28. "Introduction to the Structural Analysis of Narratives," pp. 104–5.

29. Albert Thibaudet, *Gustave Flaubert* (Paris: Gallimard, 1963), p. 110.

30. Flaubert, *Madame Bovary,* p. 389.

31. Rousset, *Forme et signification,* pp. 123–35.

32. Letter dated 27 May 1680, in Madame de Sévigné, *Correspondence,* ed. Roger Duchêne, 3 vols. (Paris: Gallimard, 1972), vol. 2, pp. 949–51.

33. Roland Barthes, "La Métaphore de l'oeil," *Critique* (Paris: Editions de Minuit, 1963), pp. 195–96.

34. Etienne Souriau, *Les Deux Cent Mille Situations dramatiques* (Paris: Flammarion, 1950); Greimas, *Sémantique structurale* (Paris: Larousse, 1966).

AFTERWORD

1. Robert Ginsberg, "A Study in Styling and Significance," *Acter internationaler Kongress für Aesthetik Darmstadt 1976* (N.p., n.d.), p. 31.

2. In 1976, Larousse issued a new edition, "revised and corrected," in the collection "Langue et langage." Difficulties of time did not allow the authors to do anymore than correct the majority of typographical errors and small faults that detracted from the previous editions. Translations that have appeared until now are: *Allgemeine Rhetorik* (Munich: Wilhelm Fink, 1974); *Retorica geral* (São Paulo: Editora Cultrix e Editora da Universidade, 1974); *Retoricǎ generalǎ* (Bucharest: Editura Univers, 1974); and *Retorica generale* (Milan: Bompiani, 1975).

3. Nicolas Ruwet, "Synécdoques et métonymies," *Poétique* 23 (1975): 371–88.

4. T. Todorov, *Littérature et signification* (Paris: Larousse, 1967); J. Durand, "Rhétorique et image publicitaire," *Communications* 15 (1970): 70–95; A. Henry, *Métonymie et métaphore* (Paris: Klinksieck, 1973); and J. Cohen, "Théorie de la figure," *Communications* 16 (1970): 3–25.

5. P. Kuentz, "L'Enjeu des rhétoriques," *Littérature* 18 (1975): 3–15.

6. On this tendency, see the recent handling by Chaim Perelman himself in *Encyclopaedia Britannica,* 15th ed., s.v. "rhetoric."

7. Roland Barthes was already writing in 1964 a "Rhetoric of the Image," in *Image-Music-Text.* trans. Stephen Heath (Glasgow: Fontana, 1977), pp. 32–51, where the comprehensiveness was without equivocation. The same remark fits Durand, "Rhétorique et image publicitaire"; and Dominique Noguez, "Petite rhétorique de poche," *L'Art de masse n'existe pas,* special number of *Revue d'esthétique* 3-4 (1974): 107–38.

8. P. Kuentz, "Rhétorique générale ou rhétorique théorique?" *Littérature* 4 (1971): 108–15.

9. See J.-M. Klinkenberg, "Vers un modèle théorique du langage poétique," *Degrés* 1 (1973): d1–d12.

10. See above, Introduction and chap. 6. See also Ph. Minguet, "Du rhétorique au poétique," in *Vers une esthétique sans entraves: Mélanges Mikel Dufrenne* (Paris: "10/18," 1975), pp. 329–44.

11. Dan Sperber, "Rudiments de rhétorique cognitive," *Poétique* 23 (1975): 389; and later, p. 390: "General rhetoric, and not simply linguistics, contains the fundamentals of a rhetoric of figures."

12. See also T. Todorov, "Synecdoques," *Communications* 16 (1970): 25–35; and Francis Edeline, "Contribution de la rhétorique à la sémantique générale," *VS* 3 (1972): 69–78. This point was completely misunderstood by Michel Le Guern, *Sémantique de la métaphore et de la métonymie* (Paris: Larousse, 1973), esp. p. 13; concerning this hastily compiled work, see G. Lavis, "Le Statut sémantique de la métaphore, de la métonymie, et du symbole," *Cahiers d'analyse textuelle* 16 (1974): 86–108.

13. See chapter IV, sec. 0.6.

14. Gérard Genette, "La Rhétorique restreinte," *Communications* 16 (1970), reprinted in *Figures III* (Paris: Editions du Seuil, 1972), pp. 21–40. In the article "Métonymie et méthodologie," *Revue des langues romanes* 40 (1976): 145–64, Michèle Goslar adopts a procedure like Ruwet's. First, she attempts to cast doubt on the status of synecdoche by showing the diversity (and the fragility) of the mechanisms evoked to explain it. Second, she pulls together synecdoche and metonymy. The fundamental difference between Ruwet's criticism and Goslar's is the place where they choose to exercise it. If the point of view of Ruwet is linguistic and technical, the remarks of Goslar are formulated in the name of a rather fluid psychologism. We have no reason here to concern ourselves at length with this article, but we shall make at least two observations. The first will show that even the rhetorician can be duped by his words. M. Goslar sees a *non sequitur* in the fact that in our system "the same trope" (synecdoche) is explained one time by one mechanism, another time by another one (generalization or particularization): "This diversity at the level of mechanisms marks a reversal when compared with classical rhetoric, which described the two figures (synecdoche and metonymy) by the same word: contiguity. We thus move from a mechanism with two modalities of realization to three mechanisms, that is, to three different tropes. This diversification is not a happy one, and the mind that perceives intuitively a common genre is put off" (p. 152). In addition to the fact that common sense is not a criterion (the world is flat, there is but one trope . . .), we note that this rhetorician has been fooled by the terminology fixed by the tradition. Tradition has never succeeded in furnishing a definition of synecdoche and has been content with enumerating the different species (container for contained, antecedent for result, and so on). And with reason: a unified-concept *synecdoche* does not exist. The historical debate (and the contemporary one) would have been quite different if the terminology had adopted four terms instead of a single one. In any case, we note that *GR* explains the *whole* group of tropes by two simple mechanisms, starting with which different combinations are possible. Second remark: in order to telescope synecdoche and metonymy, Goslar intends to prove that in the number of synecdoches claimed, there is a term encompassing the perceived degree (e.g., *sail*) and the conceived degree (*ship*) of the figure, which makes them metonymies. In a number of claimed metonymies we have trouble finding the encompassing term, which makes them synedoches (for example, what collection encompasses *sword* and *military profession* in "I have dropped the toga for the sword"?). But in the first reasoning, our correspondent totally confuses decompositions Π and Σ (the "shiphood" she calls on can be obtained only by decomposition Σ, while the figure here is of the type Π—we shall come back to this error). In the second, she confuses the terms "includer" and "included" (since the including term is not *military profession* but *military world*, which encloses instruments like *sword* as well as functions like *sword carrier*).

15. "In virtue of a *centrocentrism* apparently universal and irrepressible there is the tendency to permit hardening in the heart of the heart of rhetoric—or whatever remains of it—not the polar opposition metaphor / metonymy, where there could still circulate a bit of air and some *debris of the grand game,* now only metaphor, fixed in its royal uselessness. 'If poetry,' Jacques Sojcher has written, 'is a space that opens onto language, if by poetry words learn to speak again and

meaning takes on new signification, this is because between common language and the rediscovered word there is displacement of meaning or metaphor. In this perspective, metaphor is no longer *a* figure among many, but *the* figure, the trope of tropes.' We notice here the implicit recourse to proof by etymology according to which every 'displacement of meaning' is metaphor'' (Genette, ''La Rhétorique restreinte,'' p. 33). The last remark can be applied correctly to the work we are criticizing.

16. See Groupe μ, ''La Chafetière est sur la table: Eléments pour une rhétorique de l'image,'' *Communications et langages* 29 (1976): 37-49.

17. See Sperber, ''Rudiments de rhétorique cognitive.''

18. Ruwet, ''Synecdoques et métonymies,'' p. 387.

19. At this point a Romanist would have consulted Walter von Wartburg, *Französisches Etymologisches Wörterbuch*, 2d ed. (Tübingen: Mohr, 1948), II, 8896, which notes the word in the meaning of ''imbecile'' in Paris, Seine-et-Marne, Ille-et-Vilaine, Vendée, Doubs, Dauphiné, Lozère, Limousin, Béarn, Puy-de-Dôme. The ordinary person could have opened the *Petit Robert*, entry 5, which gives: ''*Fig.* and *pop.* (16th cent.). Imbecile.'' Again we note, without wishing to strengthen this isotopy in any exaggerated way, that Ruwet goes a bit too far in affirming that this term [i.e., *couillon*], which he claims to be Belgian, would have the same meaning as *con* for all Francophonic speakers. In his amusing essay on vulgarisms, Pierre Guiraud makes some nice remarks on ''Cons et couillons'' (a chapter title in his *Les Gros Mots* [Paris: P.U.F., 1975]). ''The semiological status of *couillon*,'' he says, is not based on a ''congenital impotency, passive and sickly like the *con*, but is a foolish person mixed up and credulous. . . .''

20. Guiraud, *Les Gros Mots*, p. 63.

21. Groupe μ, *Rhétorique de la poésie* (Brussels: Editions Complexe, 1977).

22. Ruwet, ''Synecdoques et métonymies,'' p. 379.

23. Certain critical fields that obviously are not negligible, such as that of metaplasms, do not figure in Ruwet's criticism; thus no argument has been offered concerning the *internal coherence* of our proposed system. All criticism has come from another direction, one not defined precisely, which is the reason for the somewhat vague reasoning.

24. Ruwet, ''Synecdoques et métonymies,'' p. 374.

25. Finally, let us say that the power of the figural effect is a function of the distance between the conceived and the perceived degrees, this distance itself being emphasized or obliterated by the context. Therefore, we caricature rhetorical theories by selecting cases where this distance is reduced or hardly sustained. We note in this regard that Ruwet is careful not to use the following example, whose construction makes the synecdochic effect flagrant: ''Radishes awaited him, and the cat, which mewed hoping for sardines, and Amelia, who was afraid of a too serious conflagration of the stew. The master of the house nibbles some vegetables, caresses the animal, and answers the human being, who is asking him about news of the day'' (R. Queneau). [Group μ used this example in chapter IV, sec. 1.1, on synecdoche, where we replaced it with an example from John Barth. The Barth example would not work here, however. *Trans.*] In this last case, the synecdochic effect is emphasized by the extent of the displacement on the general-particular axis (Amelia→woman→human being) as in ''When the mussels are served, Zazie throws herself on them. . . . The lamellibranchia that have resisted the process of cooking are forced out of their shells with merovingian ferocity'' (R. Queneau).

26. ''There was someone sufficiently misguided to draw up once, in the preface to an anthology, a table of some of the images to be found in the work of one of our greatest living poets; you could read there *the day after some worm dressed for a ball*, meaning ''butterfly''; *breast of crystal*, meaning ''carafe.'' What Saint-Pol-Roux wished to say, you can be certain that he said'' (in André Breton, *Point du jour* [Paris: Gallimard, 1970], p. 23).

27. Philippe Dubois, ''La Métaphore filée et le fonctionnement du texte,'' *Le Français moderne* 43 (1965): 202-13.

28. Ruwet, ''Synecdoques et métonymies,'' p. 372.

29. In a preface to the work by E. Bach, *An Introduction to Transformational Grammars*, 2d ed. (New York: Holt, Rinehart and Winston, 1973), Robert Schrick explains: ''The notion of language use, which Bach has already alluded to in his *An Introduction to Transformational Grammars*, ought by some to be considered as an integral part of competence; and finally, we are

today not far from proposing for semantics, now considered as the basis of the theory, the reintroduction of the 'encyclopedia' ('pragmatic' is understood) next to the 'dictionary' (Bach, 1973, pp. 14–15).'' Ruwet's position will perhaps explain why the single semanticist whom he has used is Fillmore (who has shown an allegiance in some ways to interpretative semantics as Ruwet describes it); perhaps it will explain also certain lacunae in his rhetorical information (our study of slang synecdoches [1970] is based on criteria such as the perceptive complexity of the rhetorical referent, procedures of explication of certain semantic features, and so on). There is a similar attitude in M. Goslar, who is certain ''that the referent . . . is exterior to linguistics, and more so to semantics'' [but to rhetoric?]; she declares that the distinction between modes of decomposition Π and Σ is unacceptable, since she says, following a particularly clairvoyant critic, it ''confuses two levels of analysis'' [see above, n. 14. Trans.]. To which we can answer that distinguishing is the opposite of confusing, especially when we are careful to explain that the two concepts are given, not as complementary, but as orthogonal, independent. But M. Goslar believes that we are dividing the lexicon into concrete terms, decomposable in mode Π, and abstract terms, justifiable exclusively by an analysis in Σ, which ''would be the same as denying any possibility of semic characterization by addition of semes of the signs of the second category.'' She suggests, consequently, that one may well wish to admit ''that it is a question in every case of concepts that can be handled by the two types of analysis.'' This is certainly the thesis we have always held.

30. Schematically: in decomposition of the type Π, there is a distribution of semes between the parts resulting from the operation (the ''navigability'' of the ship lies in the sail but disappears in the cabin). Neglecting this development leads Ruwet, in a discussion of examples like ''Ney charged at the head of a squadron of three hundred cuirasses,'' compared with ''Ney charged at the head of a squadron of three hundred cuirrassiers,'' to the following judgment: ''[The first] seems hardly natural. This is due, no doubt, to the fact that the lance is an offensive weapon and the cuirass a defensive one. In the context given—a charge—only an offensive weapon seems an appropriate 'synecdoche.' '' Again we let the ''hardly natural'' pass and note simply that the concept of ''essential semes'' takes care of this effect easily.

31. Groupe μ, ''Rhétoriques particulières,'' *Communications* 16 (1970): 70–124.

32. Does N. Ruwet not admit his uneasiness before this complexity when he writes: ''If the metaphor of the birch tree [for a young girl] can seem appropriate, this can be for reasons quite different from its flexibility (the analogy between the pale skin of some girls and the white bark of the birch; the delicateness of the leaves of birches, etc.); nor is there any reason to think that a single common 'seme' is underlying a metaphor—metaphors in general and especially successful ones evoke a whole bundle of associations and analogies, more or less strong or clear.'' The quarrel here is quite nasty: we have, in fact, said (*a*) that the intersection of two semic wholes united by metaphor were not necessarily a ''singleton''; (*b*) that a metaphor often makes a lateral seme of the two signifieds appear—and it owes this property to its synecdochic structure; and (*c*) that the metaphor has the effect of activating the search for analogies, which makes the intersective whole fluid—in the mathematical sense of the word. And truly we do not see that there is any gain in introducing vague phrases like ''evoke a whole bundle of associations and analogies'' into the discussion.

33. Paul Ricoeur, *La Métaphore vive* (Paris: Editions du Seuil, 1975), translated as *The Rule of Metaphor*, trans. Robert Czerny (Toronto and Buffalo: University of Toronto Press, 1977).

34. G. Genette, *Figures I* (Paris: Editions du Seuil, 1966); Jean Cohen, *Structure du langage poétique* (Paris: Flammarion, 1966); Michel Le Guern, *Sémantique de la métaphore et de la métonymie* (Paris: Larousse, 1973).

35. Appearances of the mark in the utterance have, however, been explained in our most recent works, where we have developed especially the idea of isotopy (Group μ, ''Lecture du poème et isotopies multiples,'' *Le Français moderne* 42 [1974]: 217–36; idem, ''Rhétorique médiatrice: Relations entre isotopies dans un distique de Paul-Jean Toulet,'' in *Du linguistique au textuel* [Assen, Amsterdam: Van Gorcum, 1974], pp. 4–19; idem, ''Isotopie et allotopie: Le fonctionnement rhétorique du texte,'' *VS* 19 [1976]: 41–68; and J.-M. Klinkenberg, ''Le Concept d'isotopie en sémantique et en sémiotique littéraire,'' *Le Français moderne* 41 [1973]: 285–90).

36. Ricoeur, *The Rule of Metaphor*, p. 172.

37. Todorov, *Littérature et signification*, p. 116.

38. Ricoeur, *The Rule of Metaphor,* p. 160.

39. See his two articles cited in notes 5 and 8 and also "Le Rhétorique ou la mise à l'écart," *Communications* 16 (1970): 143–57.

40. See also S. Marcus, *Poetica matematică* (Bucharest: Editura Academiei, 1970).

41. Kuentz, "L'Enjeu des rhétoriques," p. 8.

42. Kuentz, "Rhétorique générale ou rhétorique théorique?" p. 114.

Index of Authors